THE BRITISH ISLES

ROBERT CROFT
SARAH DIXON
SIMON BURTON
BECKY BURTON
MARK PENROSE
DAVID PENROSE
JENNY LEINERT
KIM DIXON

Learning English

ORANGE LINE NEW 2

Unterrichtswerk für Mittelschulen,
Regelschulen, Sekundarschulen, Gesamtschulen
und sechsjährige Grundschulen

von
Helmut Reisener und
Gudrun Steinbach
sowie
Stephanie Ashford, Werner Beile und Alice Beile-Bowes,
Claudia Finkbeiner, Rosemary Hellyer-Jones,
Marion Horner, Peter Lampater, Harriette Lanzer,
Peter Pasch, Rolf W. Roth, Gunter Volk, Klaus Stenzel,
Margaret Winck, Harold Wonham

Ernst Klett Schulbuchverlag Leipzig
Leipzig Stuttgart Düsseldorf

Learning English
Orange Line NEW 2
für Klasse 6 an Mittelschulen, Regelschulen, Sekundarschulen, Gesamtschulen und sechsjährigen Grundschulen

von
Dr. Helmut Reisener, Dipl.-Päd., Lüneburg und Dr. Gudrun Steinbach, Leipzig
sowie
Stephanie Ashford B.A., Villingen-Schwenningen; Prof. Dr. Werner Beile und Alice Beile-Bowes M.A., Wuppertal und Iserlohn; Dr. Claudia Finkbeiner, Heilbronn; Rosemary Hellyer-Jones M.A., Ehingen (Donau); Marion Horner M.A., Cambridge; Peter Lampater, Ehingen (Donau); Harriette Lanzer B.A., London; Prof. Dr. Peter Pasch, Tübingen; Alan Posener, Berlin; Rolf W. Roth M.A., Idar-Oberstein; Klaus Stenzel, Bopfingen; Gunter Volk, Villingen-Schwenningen; Margaret Winck B.A., Tübingen; Harold S. Wonham M.Litt., Stone

Beratende Mitarbeit
Marlis Brauckhoff, Stadtroda; Ramona König, Leipzig; Birgit Zens, Bugk; Marjorie Willey, Halle

Visuelle Gestaltung
Elsie Lennox, London (Zeichnungen);
Kirsten Walther, Bochum (Vokabularseiten)

Kassetten und CDs zu diesem Band

SB *Begleitkassette zum Schülerbuch* für zu Hause und für den Unterricht mit Unittexten, Liedern, Ausspracheübungen (Klettnummer 546828).
Die *Begleit-CD zum Schülerbuch* mit demselben Inhalt hat die Klettnummer 546883.

Lieferung durch jede Buchhandlung oder, wo dies auf Schwierigkeiten stößt, zuzüglich Portokosten per Nachnahme vom Verlag.

HV *Kassette zum Hörverstehen* für den Unterricht mit den Hörverstehenstexten aller Werkteile (Klettnummer 546829).
Die *CD zum Hörverstehen* für den Unterricht hat die Klettnummer 546884.

Lieferung direkt an Lehrerinnen und Lehrer, Schulstempel erforderlich.

Lernsoftware:
Passend zu diesem Band gibt es ein Vokabel- und ein Grammatiktrainingsprogramm. Die Programme bieten abwechslungsreiche Übungsformen, zahlreiche Abfragevarianten, Leistungs- und Lernzielkontrolle und ein Lexikon mit dem Wortschatz der gesamten Lehrbuchreihe.

2. Auflage

2 5 4 3 2 1 | 2001 00 99 98 97

Alle Drucke dieser Auflage können im Unterricht nebeneinander benutzt werden, sie sind untereinander unverändert. Die letzte Zahl bezeichnet das Jahr des Druckes.
Dieses Werk folgt der reformierten Rechtschreibung und Zeichensetzung.

Redaktion: Redaktionsdienst ETS, Stuart Amor, Stuttgart

Umschlaggestaltung: Christian Dekelver, Weinstadt
Umschlagfoto: John Birdsall, Nottingham
Satz: DTP-Verlag und Lihs, Satz und Repro, Ludwigsburg;
Bebop Sounds, Freiberg/Neckar (Noten)
Reproduktion: Repro Maurer GmbH + Co, Tübingen
Druck: Druckerei Appl, Wemding
ISBN: 3-12-546846-9

Gedruckt auf Papier aus chlorfrei gebleichtem Zellstoff, säurefrei.

Inhaltsverzeichnis

Hallo!
Ich begleite dich auch durch dieses Buch und gebe dir natürlich wieder Tips. Damit du dich leicht und schnell zurechtfindest, erkläre ich dir noch einmal kurz, wie das Buch aufgebaut ist.

Die neuen **Units** (Kapitel) behandeln interessante Themen. Am Ende jeder *Unit* kannst du auf einer *Let's check*-Seite wieder selbst überprüfen, was du in dieser *Unit* dazugelernt hast. Hinter jeder *Unit* kommt dann das Vokabular, also die neuen Wörter, die durch diese *Unit* dazugekommen sind. Natürlich gibt es hier eine Menge Lerntips. Neben den *Units* gibt es drei mal **Revision and fun**, also je zwei Seiten zum Wiederholen und dabei Spaß haben. Nach der 9. *Unit* kommt auf S. 156 noch ein **Project.** Du willst ja am Ende des Schuljahres sicherlich auch mal etwas anderes machen, oder?

Ab S. 166 beginnt die **Extra line** mit weiteren interessanten Geschichten und zwei kleinen Theaterstücken. Ab S. 179 findest du die **Grammar**-Seiten, also unsere ‚Regeln', bei denen ich natürlich auch wieder helfe. Ab S. 200 kommt dann die **Alphabetical word list**. Hier kannst du alles nachschlagen, was du aus einer früheren *Unit* oder aus Band 1 nicht mehr weißt. Und alle unregelmäßigen Verben stehen in einer Liste auf den Seiten 214/215.

Also, auf geht's!

Du solltest auch noch wissen, was die **Zeichen** vor den einzelnen Texten und den Übungen bedeuten:

SB	Begleitcassette zum Schülerbuch
HV	Cassette zum Hörverstehen
Your turn	Hier kannst du über dich, deine Familie oder Freunde sprechen.
	Partnerarbeit
	Gruppenarbeit
WORD POWER	Wortschatzübungen
	Wiederholungsübungen
	schwierigere (wahlfreie) Aufgaben
〈 〉	fakultativ (wahlfrei)

Units/Steps	*Kommunikative Schwerpunkte Arbeitstechniken (AT)*	*Strukturen (R = Revision/Wiederholung)*	*Seite*
Unit 1 Back to school			
A New timetables	jemanden begrüßen; Auskünfte über andere Personen geben	R: *simple present*	**7**
	AT: einen Stundenplan lesen und diskutieren; Vergleich zwischen englischen und deutschen Fächern; eigenen Stundenplan schreiben	*have* als Vollverb Fragen mit *which*	
Looking at the UK: School			**10**
B The school play	eine kommende Veranstaltung diskutieren; über die Freizeit sprechen; Meinungen zu Fächern äußern und begründen AT: eine Umfrage durchführen	R: Fragen und Kurzantworten mit *do/don't/can/can't*	**11**
Simon's new school	Fragen zum Thema Schule stellen und beantworten	R: Entscheidungsfragen und Fragen mit Fragewörtern	**12**
The new pupil	Fragen stellen und beantworten	Which one? – The blue one	**13**
C Activities	über Schulaktivitäten und Pläne sprechen; AT: einen Vorschlag machen und ablehnen		**14**
D A little play: Simon's new friend	ein kleines Theaterstück lesen, besprechen und evtl. aufführen		**16**
E Workshop 1 u. 2	etwas begründen	Wortschatzarbeit	**13/19**
F Let's check			**20**
Unit 2 Adventures in Nottingham			
A The adventure centre	Vorschläge machen und darauf reagieren	R: *simple present*	**25**
B Robin Hood	über Tätigkeiten in der Vergangenheit sprechen	*simple past: was, were* und *had* und regelmäßige Formen	**27**
A special day for Jenny	AT: erzählen, was an einem Tag passiert ist	*simple past:* unregelmäßige Formen	**28**
Looking at the UK: In and around Nottingham			**31**

Units/Steps	Kommunikative Schwerpunkte Arbeitstechniken (AT)	Strukturen (R = Revision/Wiederholung)	Seite
C Ideas	ein vergangenes Erlebnis erzählen AT: Text als Modell benutzen		**32**
D Robin Hood and the bag of gold	eine Geschichte spielen und nacherzählen AT: eine gelesene oder gehörte Geschichte nacherzählen		**33**
E Workshop 1 u. 2	einem Sachtext Informationen entnehmen	Wortschatzarbeit	**35/36**
F Let's check			**37**

Unit 3 Nottingham Goose Fair

A A busy weekend	über das vergangene Wochenende sprechen	R: Adjektive	**41**
B Bad news	erzählen, was geschehen und nicht geschehen ist; sich entschuldigen	*simple past:* negative Aussagen	**43**
Was it fun?	sich nach Erlebnissen erkundigen und darüber berichten	*simple past:* Kurzantworten und Fragen	**44**
Sarah's teddies	Sachen miteinander vergleichen	Steigerung von Adjektiven mit *-er* und *-est; not as ... as ...*	**45**
C All the fun of the fair	Vorschläge machen und darauf antworten		**47**
D Friends	das Verhalten einer Person diskutieren AT: Signalwörter erkennen und sammeln		**48**
E Workshop 1 u. 2	Vergleiche anstellen; eine Geschichte erzählen	Wortschatzarbeit	**50/51**
F Let's check			**52**
⟨Revision and fun 1⟩	Wiederholung bisher geübter Strukturen und Sprechabsichten		**53**

Unit 4 The junior school play

A The Canterville Ghost	die eigene Meinung ausdrücken; über Kleidung sprechen	R: *this, that, these*	**58**
B Tickets and prizes	sagen, was einem gut bzw. am besten gefällt	Steigerung von Adjektiven mit *more* und *most; more ... than*	**59**
Robert the ghost	sagen, was man in der Zukunft machen wird; Angst zum Ausdruck bringen; jemanden beraten und ermutigen	*will-future;* Sätze mit *when*	**60**
Looking at the UK: Theatre groups			**62**
C The raffle	Hoffnung ausdrücken	Grundzahlen 1 - 1000	**63**
D Well done!	Geschichte nach Modell nacherzählen AT: einen Text gliedern		**64**
E Workshop 1 u. 2	Horoskope; Texträtsel	Vergleiche anstellen	**66/67**
Let's check			**68**

Unit 5 In town

A In the shopping centre	über Läden sprechen; AT: Informationen aus einem Plan versprachlichen	Präpositionen	**72**
B Just looking	sich einen Kauf überlegen	*some* und *any*	**74**
Pieces of pizza	Bedingungen ausdrücken	*will-future* in Sätzen mit *if*	**76**
Looking at the UK: Shopping in Nottingham			**77**
C A guessing game	Wörter erraten	*some* und *any* und Zusammensetzungen	**78**
At the information desk	Auskunft geben über Wege und Lage	Präpositionen	**79**

Units/Steps	Kommunikative Schwerpunkte Arbeitstechniken (AT)	Strukturen (R = Revision/Wiederholung)	Seite
D TUFF	ein Gedicht besprechen	Adjektive	80
E Workshop 1 u. 2	Wegbeschreibung; Krimigeschichte	Wortschatzarbeit	81/82
F Let's check			83

Unit 6 At school and at home

Units/Steps	Kommunikative Schwerpunkte Arbeitstechniken (AT)	Strukturen	Seite
A About food	Kurzbriefe lesen und schreiben AT: eigene Textproduktion	Wortschatzarbeit	87
B Sunday morning	über gerade abgeschlossene Handlungen sprechen AT: Umgang mit einer Verbliste	*present perfect*: regelmäßige und unregelmäßige Formen	89
The guest from Dessau	sich nach Aktivitäten erkundigen	*present perfect*: Fragen und Kurzantworten	91
C Lunch with the Penroses	Essen und Getränke anbieten; um Essen und Getränke bitten	*Would you like...? / Can I have...?*	93
Looking at the UK: Nottingham 'takeaways'			95
D Saturday lunch	über Gefühle sprechen AT: Text anhand von Bildern nacherzählen		96
E Workshop 1 u. 2	Rezept umsetzen	Wortschatzarbeit	98/99
F Let's check			100

⟨Revision and fun 2⟩

⟨Revision and fun 2⟩	Wiederholung bisher geübter Strukturen und Sprechabsichten		101

Unit 7 Holidays

Units/Steps	Kommunikative Schwerpunkte Arbeitstechniken (AT)	Strukturen	Seite
A Holidays in Britain	über Urlaubsziele sprechen; Angaben zum Urlaub machen	R: *simple past*	106
Looking at the UK: Wales			108
Looking at the UK: Scotland			109
B Before the Easter holidays	einen Urlaub planen; über Hobbys sprechen	*I like/enjoy/hate/ ...-ing . .*	110
From Jenny's travel diary	Angaben zu neuen Ereignissen machen	Gebrauch: *simple past* und *present perfect*	111
Have you ever?	über vergangene Erlebnisse sprechen; AT: Global- und Detailhörverstehen	*present perfect* mit *ever* und *already*	112
C At Fort William	einen Ausflug planen; Bedingungen setzen	*What about ...-ing...*	113
D On Ben Nevis	AT: eine Geschichte zusammenfassen		115
E Workshop 1 u. 2	Empfehlungen/Weisungen befolgen	Wortschatzarbeit	116/117
F Let's check			118

Unit 8 A bad week!

Units/Steps	Kommunikative Schwerpunkte Arbeitstechniken (AT)	Strukturen	Seite
A The super skater	sich nach dem Befinden erkundigen AT: nach Hörinformation ein Bild anfertigen		122
Mr and Mrs Dracula are ill	über Krankheiten berichten		123
B The next morning ...	sagen, dass ein Vorhaben unnötig ist; eine Geschichte beurteilen	*needn't*	124
The doctor's visit	notwendige Vorhaben und Verbote erstellen AT: Grammatikbeispiele eintragen und selber finden	*must/mustn't*	125
Barry Newman – super skater	Gespräch mit dem Arzt im Krankenhaus Berichte über vergangene Tätigkeiten	*must/mustn't; can/can't* *past progressive*	126 127

Units/Steps	*Kommunikative Schwerpunkte Arbeitstechniken (AT)*	*Strukturen (R = Revision/Wiederholung)*	*Seite*
C At the doctor's	Gespräch mit einem Arzt führen		**128**
D Happy Helpers	AT: einem Bericht Informationen entnehmen		**130**
E Workshop 1 u. 2	über Krankheiten sprechen; ein krankes Tier pflegen	Wortschatzarbeit	**132/133**
F Let's check			**134**

Unit 9 The end of the school year

A The Haywood Fete	AT: *Note-taking* AT: Wörter definieren		**138**
A normal day – an unlucky day	einen Cartoon versprachlichen	Wortschatzarbeit	**139**
B Plans for Saturday	Pläne ausdrücken	*going to-future*	**140**
Uniforms	Verbot und Erlaubnis ausdrücken	*to be allowed to*	**142**
Looking at the UK: Helping charities			**143**
C The money from the fete	Vorschläge/Gegenvorschläge machen	*to have to*	**144**
D Lucky weather	Handlungen bewerten	R: Fragen mit Fragewort	**145**
E Workshop 1 u. 2	ein Gedicht: Geschwister	*going to-future*	**147/148**
F Let's check			**149**

⟨Revision and fun 3⟩

Wiederholung bisher geübter Strukturen und Sprechabsichten **150**

⟨Project: The story of jeans⟩

From Buttenheim to San Francisco **156**
Your fashion show **159**
Let's dance the Longway **161**
Let's play with words **163**

⟨Extra line⟩

1. Robin Hood and the Sheriff (nach Unit 2) **166**
2. A story from Ireland (nach Unit 3) **168**
3. The Canterville Ghost (nach Unit 4) **169**
4. The sound of the cricket and the sound of money (nach Unit 5) **170**
5. Have you ever seen a spaghetti bush? (nach Unit 6) **171**
6. The haggis (nach Unit 7) **172**
7. The shrinking plant (nach Unit 8) **173**
8. A Christmas story (at Christmas) **176**

Grammar

Grammar **179**
Grammar list **198**

Vocabulary

Alphabetical word list **213**
List of irregular verbs **214**
⟨In the classroom⟩ **216**

Back to school

Step A

New timetables

SB

ⓐ It is 7th September. The summer holidays are over. The boys and girls are back at Haywood School. It is their first day at school and they have got their new timetables. Robert and Jenny are talking about them.

Step A

1 Robert's questions

Here are Jenny's answers, but what are Robert's questions? Go back to the dialogue and find them.

1. It's short for Physical Education.
2. Er, *Sport* … just sports.
3. Drama isn't a subject.
4. They are the same.

2 My dream timetable

Monny has got a dream timetable with only two subjects.
Can you make a dream timetable, too?
Here are some ideas:

	MONDAY	TUESDAY	WEDNESDAY	THURSDAY
11.00	computer games	swimming	Mr Bean videos	…
12.00	football			

Which subject?

ⓑ *Robert:* What's the last lesson today?
Becky: Technology, I think.
Sarah: Er … but haven't we got Science now?
Robert: I don't know.
Sarah: Let's look at the timetable.
Becky: Er … last lesson. Yes, you see – Technology!
Sarah: But it's Friday today, Becky, not Thursday! We have Science last lesson on Fridays.
Becky: Oh, of course.
Robert: So which subject is it now – Science or Technology?
Sarah: Science! Come on!

3 Their new timetable

	Monday	Tuesday	Wednesday	Thursday	Friday
8.50	A S	S	E M	B L	Y
9.05	Science	Art	P.E.	English	Maths
10.05	Technology	Drama	German	German	P.E.
11.00	B	R	E	A	K
11.15	Technology	Geography	History	Science	Geography
12.10	L	U	N	C	H
1.25	Maths	English	Maths	Music	English
2.20	B	R	E	A	K
2.35	History	German	English	Technology	Science

4 Their subjects

a) *Answer the questions.*
1. What have they got after Assembly on Monday?
2. Which lesson is after lunch on Wednesday?
3. What's the last lesson on Friday?
4. Which is the lesson after morning break on Friday?

b) *Work with a partner and ask more questions about the timetable.*
You can ask: – When is Maths on Monday?
– When have they got PE lessons?
– How many … lessons have they got?

5 Listening practice: Lessons and days

Listen to the dialogues and look at the timetable.
Which days are they talking about?

6 ⟨A song: Wonderful world⟩

2. Don't know much about Geography,
Don't know much Trigonometry,
Don't know much about Algebra,
Don't know what a slide rule is for.
But I know that one and one is two,
And if this one could be with you –
What a wonderful world this would be.

4. Don't know much about History,
Don't know much Biology, …

Looking at the UK: School

At 8.50 on Monday the pupils go into assembly. They sing a song. Then one of the teachers reads out important notices, for example about football or badminton matches, and times and dates of meetings.

At 9.00 the teacher calls the register.

Pupils in the UK wear school uniform …
… well, not all of them.

At lunch break the pupils have lunch in the canteen.

The school play

It is the morning break at Haywood School. The pupils are going to the playground. Robert sees a notice for the school play on the notice board.

Robert: Hey, look! There's a meeting about the school play after school today.
Jenny: Oh yes? What's the play?
Robert: Er ... I don't know. It doesn't say.
Jenny: Well, I don't want to take a role in it.
Robert: That's OK. They need lots of people for other jobs, too.
Jenny: OK, then. What about you, David?
David: No thanks.
Robert: Do you want to come to the meeting, Sarah?
Sarah: Sorry, Robert. I haven't got time for the play. I want to be on the hockey team.

1 What do they do?

How many questions can you ask and answer?

Do Does	the pupils like plays Robert know the play Jenny want a role Robert's friends see the notice Sarah have time to go to the meeting	?	Yes, ... do/does. No, ... don't/doesn't. I don't know.

2 What do you do?

Ask and answer questions with a partner.

Do you	play ...? go swimming? read funny books? watch TV every day? go to the cinema? listen to pop music? ...	Yes, I do No, I don't.

3 What about your school?

Ask questions and answer them.

Example: 1. you/wear/uniform   Do you wear uniform? – No I don't.

2. you/go to school/on Saturdays
3. your teachers/wear/jeans
4. you and your friends/have/Science/on Mondays
5. you/get/a new timetable every year
6. you/have/lunch/at school
7. your school/do a school play
8. you like/your school
9. your school/start/at nine o'clock

Step B

Simon's new school

Mrs Burton: Well, Simon. Do you like your new school?
Simon: Yes, I do. It's great.
Mrs Burton: What about your teachers? Are they OK?
Simon: Yes, Mr Stevenson is very funny.
Mrs Burton: And what about your new friends?
Simon: Mike Newman is my friend. We go to the computer club together. The computers are great.
Mrs Burton: What about lunch? Do you have lunch in the canteen with Becky?
Simon: No, I don't. – Well, I have lunch in the canteen, but Becky has lunch after me. Year 7 have lunch first.

4 Right or wrong?

Say what is right and what is wrong. Put the wrong sentences right.

1. Simon likes his new school.
2. Simon's teachers are terrible.
3. Simon and Mike go to the computer club together.
4. The school computers are terrible.
5. Simon has lunch in the canteen.
6. Becky doesn't have lunch in the canteen.
7. Year 7 have lunch first.

5 Our lessons

Ask four people in your class and make a list of their answers. You can ask:
- Which subjects do you like?
- And which is your favourite subject?
- Why?

Because		
it's easy.	We/I	do interesting things.
it's interesting.		play games.
it's exciting.		read good books.
it's great fun.		like the teacher.
…		…

	Maths	English	Music	History	Geography
Bettina		✓	✓		✓

6 What about you?

Talk about your school.
Example: I like my school. My teachers …

Here are some ideas to help you:

My favourite subjects …

I hate …

My friends are …

?day is a good day for me because …

"So do I, Gary, so do I."

The new pupil

There is a new pupil in Jenny's class this year. His name is John and he comes from Chicago in America. He is at Haywood School for a year. He doesn't go to school by bike, he doesn't play football and he doesn't like his new uniform.

7 Questions about John

Jenny knows all the answers. Can you ask the questions?

1. Does he come from Nottingham?	– No, he doesn't. He comes from Chicago.
2. … he …?	– Of course he speaks English.
3. … in Sherwood now?	– Yes, he lives in Arndale Road.
4. …?	– Yes, he plays badminton.
5. …?	– No, he doesn't like his new uniform
6. …?	– No, he goes to school by bus.

8 Role play: What does John ask?

Can you ask John's questions and give Becky's answers? Look at the timetable on page 8. Act little dialogues.
Example:
John: When do we have lunch break?
Becky: At ten past twelve.

			have lunch break?
		we	have PE?
When	do	you	wear at school?
What	does	our class	do on Saturdays?
			…?

		have English every day?
Do	we	play … at school?
Does	our class	finish at 3 o'clock?
		…?

9 Which one do I need?

Becky is helping John. He is looking for the right things for his lessons.
Can you make dialogues?
Example: "I've got two Maths books. Which one do I need now?" – "You need the blue one."

Step C

Activities

1 Do you like the clubs? *Talk about the notices.*

I like …
I don't think a … club is very interesting.
… is a good game.
A … club is interesting.
I think … is difficult.
We haven't got a … club at our school.

2 Let's go together

Make little dialogues with a partner.

go to the table tennis club — watch TV
do my homework — go to my grandma's house
help my dad — have my piano lesson

3 Your activities

Talk about your activities. When do you do them? What do you like? What don't you like?

Example: "Every Friday I go to a computer club. It starts at … and finishes at … ."
"I like badminton and table tennis, but I don't like …"

4 For the notice board

There is a group of pupils from England at your school for a month. You want to invite them to play badminton with you and your friends on Saturday morning. *Write a notice for the notice board. (Look at the notice about badminton on the notice board.)*

5 Kim's game

Sarah and Becky are playing Kim's game in the classroom.

Sarah: Look at my desk for a minute.
Becky: OK.
Sarah: Now turn round. Can you remember everything?
Becky: Well, you've got two pencils on your desk.
Sarah: That's right.
Becky: And there are some books.
Sarah: How many?
Becky: Three.
Sarah: Right.
Becky: And there is your purse and some money.
Sarah: Yes, good!

Go on, please. Then play the game with a partner.

6 My English folder

I like … very much.
I really like …
I like …
I don't like …
I don't really like …
I hate …

subjects
breaks
people
activities
?

7 Time for a school joke

Son: I don't want to go to school today, Mum. The teachers don't like me and the children bully me.
Mother: But you must go, son!
Son: Why?
Mother: Because you're 45 years old and you're the headmaster!

Step D

A little play: Simon's new friend

First scene

Sarah: Becky. Is that Simon over there?
Becky: Oh yes. He must be with a new friend.
Robert: That doesn't look like a friend. That's Barry Newman's brother.
Becky: But Barry Newman is a terrible bully. What's Simon doing with his brother?

Second scene

Becky: Robert, I can't find Simon in the playground and I'm worried about him.
Robert: Oh, don't worry, Becky. Let's look for him.

Third scene

Becky: The lesson is over. Look, there's Simon.
Robert: Let's run after him.
Mr Stevenson: Becky Burton and Robert Croft! Come here, please! – Don't run in school!
Becky: And where is Simon now, Robert?
Robert: I can't see him, Becky. There are so many people here.
Becky: Well, let's go home.

Fourth scene

Robert: Hey Becky, look over there. Isn't that Simon with his 'new friend' again?
Becky: Yes. Let's hide behind a car and watch them.
Robert: What are they doing?
Becky: Simon is giving his 'new friend' some money! Let's stop him.

Fifth scene

Becky: You bully. Give my brother his money back!
Robert: Go away, Newman!
Simon: Hey! Stop it. Mike's not a bully. He's my friend.
Mike: We're both computer fans. We want to buy a computer magazine together because they cost so much.
Becky: Oh! Er … I'm so sorry, Mike. It's just … well, your brother …
Mike: I know. My brother is terrible, but I'm not.

1 The story

Five scenes – ten questions: can you answer them? Work in groups (one scene – one group).

- Who do Robert and Becky talk about?
- What does Becky think of Barry Newman?

- Who is Becky worried about?
- Why is she worried?

- Where do they see Simon?
- Why can't they run after him?

- Where do Becky and Robert hide?
- What does Simon give Mike?

- What do Simon and Mike want to buy?
- What does Mike say about his brother?

2 ⟨Ideas for the play⟩

Maybe your class wants to act this little story – for other classes, or for your parents in the evening. But only five pupils can play the roles. (Of course, there can be two or three groups of five.) There are lots of other jobs, too.

- You need posters for the play. What can you write on them? Work in groups.
- What about school uniform for the four children?
- What can Mr Stevenson wear?
- One boy or girl must tell the audience which scene comes next, where we are and what time it is. What can he or she say or write? Can you make a big clock to show the time?
- In the fourth scene Becky and Robert hide behind a car. How can you do that?
- Perhaps the parents don't know all the words. For example, they don't know what a bully is. You can give them the important words in English and German on a transparency and use the overhead projector before the play begins. You can draw funny pictures, too.
  For example:  ➔ worried ➔ besorgt
- What else must you think of?

Step E

Workshop 1

1 School words

Let's make a mind map with school words. Use your exercise book. You can work with a partner.

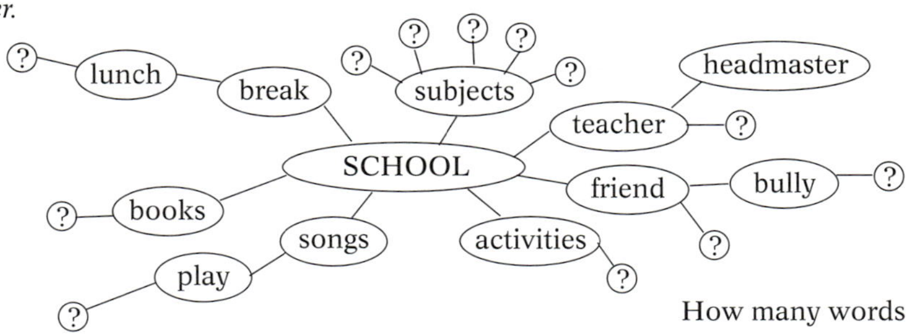

How many words have you got?

2 Three lists

Make three lists with these words. Read them out loud to find out where they must go.

[ʃ]	[dʒ]	[tʃ]
shop …	German …	lunch …

Geography teacher German
watch English special Technology
chair children orange
which sugar shop station subject lunch
wash fish

3 ⟨Do you remember them?⟩

a) *Let's write about Becky and her friends.*

Example: Becky has got a brother. His name is Simon. Her parents have got a bike shop.
The Burtons have got two dogs. Their names are Mini and Maxi.
And they have got a pond in their garden.

Now choose one of the other families and write down three or four sentences in your exercise book. (You can work together with a partner.)

b) *Do you remember the Richards family? What can you write about them?*

Workshop 2

Mrs Burton's purse

Mrs Burton is worried. She wants to go to the shops but she can't find her purse. She is looking for it in the kitchen. Suddenly Simon comes in.

Mrs B.: Simon, you must help me at once. I'm looking for my purse.
Simon: Oh no, not again!
Mrs B.: I'm sorry, but it's not in its place.
Simon: Try to remember … Is it in your bag?
Mrs B.: No. I always take it out when I come home. Well, let me see … No, it's not in my bag.
Simon: Sometimes you leave it on the table near the telephone.
Mrs B.: No, there's no purse on the table.

Simon: Wait a minute, Mum! Let's play a little game.
Mrs B.: Is that a joke? I can't play games. Be quick, Simon, I must find my purse.
Simon: I spy with my little eye …
Mrs B.: Oh Simon, stop it!
Simon: I spy with my little eye something beginning with P! Just turn round and go towards the shelf, the one with the fruit on it.
Mrs B.: Oh, there it is! Thank you, Simon. I'm probably wrong about you and your little games. Er … where's my shopping list?
Simon: Oh no, not again!

1 … because …

Can you say why?

1. Mrs Burton is worried …
2. The purse is not in the bag …
3. Simon's idea is the table near the telephone …
4. Simon suddenly says "I spy …"
5. Mrs Burton goes towards the shelf …
6. In the end she is worried again …

b
e
c
a
u
s
e

Here are some ideas to help you!

e) … can't find her purse
d) … Simon tells her
f) … sometimes leaves it there
a) … can't find her shopping list
b) … knows the place
c) … she always takes it out

2 WORD POWER

Find the right pairs. (Write them down.) Some are opposites, some are not, but they can go together. Example: to laugh – joke

French, to finish, always, It's boring., nobody, to hate, easy, to shout, anything, lesson, nice boy, to look for

somebody, difficult, to find, to like, something, sometimes, break, English, It's great fun., to speak, bully, to begin

Step F

Let's check

1 School subjects

What lessons have these pupils got now? Example: Number 1 has got Maths.

1 2 3 4 5 6

2 John from Chicago

You want to know more about John from Chicago. What questions can you ask him?

When Why What How Where	is are do does	school your teachers your parents your sister your favourite your father you get you wear	now like do begin subject here to school at school

Your turn 3 What about your school?

a) *Ask questions with* do, *and* does. *Then answer them with* does/doesn't *or* do/don't.
Example: Does your school finish at half past three? – No, it doesn't.

1. you wear/school uniform
2. your class/learn French
3. your teachers/use/videos in class
4. your parents/buy/your school books
5. your school week/begin/with Assembly
6. your English teacher/come from England
7. your headmaster/teach English
8. girls and boys/go to PE/together

b) *Write about your school. Is it like Simon's school?*
Our school is (the) … School. Our lessons start at … and finish at … We don't have lunch at school …

4 Whose is it?

Example: 1. It is Becky's bag.

1. Whose bag is it?
2. Whose PE things are they?
3. Whose pullover is it?
4. Whose pencils are they?
5. Whose lunch box is it?
6. Whose timetable is it?

5 WORD POWER

Find the opposites.

the last	to work	a bully	bad
pupils	teachers	to begin	little
to play	to like	big	new
to hate	easy	old	before
difficult	to find	good	to finish
to hide	the first	after	a nice boy

Vocabulary

Lautschrift

Wie die englischen Wörter ausgesprochen werden, lernst du im Unterricht. Die Lautschrift im Vokabular hilft dir, die Aussprache und Betonung eines Wortes nachzusehen. Sie benutzt einige normale Buchstaben und einige besondere Zeichen. Die Aussprache der einzelnen Zeichen kannst du dir anhand eines einfachen Wortes merken. Die Betonung eines Wortes wird durch einen Betonungsstrich **vor** der betonten Silbe gezeigt: [ˈ] zeigt die Hauptbetonung des Wortes, [ˌ] die Nebenbetonung. Der Bindebogen [‿] zeigt, dass zwei Wörter in der Aussprache miteinander verbunden werden.

Konsonanten/Mitlaute		**Vokale/Selbstlaute**			
[ŋ]	morni**ng**	[ɑː]	f**a**ther	[aɪ]	**I**, m**y**
[r]	**r**ed	[ʌ]	b**u**t, **u**nder	[aʊ]	n**ow**, h**ou**se
[s]	cla**ss**	[e]	p**e**n	[eə]	th**ere**, p**air**
[z]	i**s**	[ə]	**a** sist**er**	[eɪ]	n**a**me, th**ey**
[ʒ]	televi**si**on	[ɜː]	g**ir**l	[ɪə]	h**ere**, id**ea**
[dʒ]	**G**ermany, pa**ge**	[æ]	**a**pple	[ɔɪ]	b**oy**
[ʃ]	**sh**e	[ɪ]	**i**t	[əʊ]	**o**ld, hell**o**
[tʃ]	**ch**air, lun**ch**	[iː]	**ea**sy, sh**e**	[ʊə]	**you're**
[ð]	**th**e	[ɒ]	g**o**t, **o**n		
[θ]	**th**anks	[ɔː]	b**a**ll	Die anderen Zeichen werden	
[v]	**v**ideo, ha**v**e	[ʊ]	b**oo**k	wie im Deutschen	
[w]	**w**ord, **o**ne	[uː]	t**oo**, tw**o**	ausgesprochen [j, k, …].	

Unit 1 Back to school

Erinnerst du dich noch an meine Lerntips vom letzten Schuljahr? Auch für das vor dir liegende Schuljahr sind diese Tipps gut zu gebrauchen:
Also denk dran:

- Du lernst Wörter schneller und leichter, wenn du sie dir in kleinen Lernportionen von 10-15 Wörtern vornimmst. Du lernst deine Wörter sicher schon so, indem du die englische oder deutsche Spalte abdeckst. Dies ist auch weiterhin sinnvoll.
- Die Vokabellernkartei kann auch in diesem Jahr als „Vokabellernmaschine" genutzt werden. Im *Workbook* findest du einen Bastelbogen, mit dem du dir eine Vokabellernkartei basteln kannst. Ansonsten kannst du auch einen Schuhkarton nehmen.
- Ganz schwierige Wörter kannst du dir auf Lernplakate oder Zettel schreiben und zu Hause an die Wand hängen. So wirst du bei jedem Hinsehen daran erinnert.
- Man kann Wörter auch mit einem Partner üben und wiederholen. Man kann sie gegenseitig abfragen, oder man kann das „Rememberspiel" zusammen spielen. Es geht so: Schreib die englischen Wörter, die du lernen willst, auf kleine Zettel. Auf die Rückseite jedes Zettels schreibst du in einer anderen Farbe die deutsche Bedeutung. Breite die Karte mit der deutschen Bedeutung nach oben aus. Wenn du den englischen Begriff nennen kannst, darfst du die Karten einsammeln. Wenn du beim Überprüfen feststellst, dass deine Antwort nicht richtig war, musst du die Karte wieder hinlegen. – Das Spiel geht natürlich auch umgekehrt.
- **Und ganz wichtig**: Du behältst neu gelernte Wörter besser, wenn du sie dir mehrmals vornimmst und sie zusätzlich vor dem Einschlafen noch einmal ansiehst.

Step A **New timetables**

(a)	**timetable** ['taɪm,teɪbl]	Stundenplan	
	over ['əʊvə]	zu Ende	
	to **know** [nəʊ]	wissen	
	PE = Physical Education [,pi: 'i:/'fɪzɪkl ,edjʊ'keɪʃn]	Sportunterricht	
	short for ['ʃɔ:t‿fɔ:]	die Kurzform von	
	sports [spɔ:ts]	Sport	
	drama ['drɑ:mə]	Drama, Theater-	
	lesson ['lesn]	Stunde, Unterricht	
	subject ['sʌbdʒɪkt]	Fach	Technology or English? Which is your favourite *subject*?
	History ['hɪstərɪ]	Geschichte	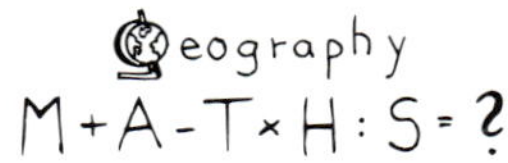
	Geography [dʒɪ'ɒgrəfɪ]	Erdkunde	
	Maths [mæθs]	Mathe(matik)	
	to **sound** ['saʊnd]	klingen	
	some [sʌm]	einige	
	°**word power** ['wɜ:d ,paʊə]	Wortschatz	
	°**isn't it** ['iznt‿it]	nicht wahr	
1	**dialogue** ['daɪəlɒg]	Dialog	
2	**dream** [dri:m]	Traum	
	only ['əʊnlɪ]	nur	
	Mr Bean [bi:n]	*engl. Komiker*	
	video ['vɪdɪəʊ]	Video	
(b)	**last** [lɑ:st]	letzte/r/s	
	Technology [tek'nɒlədʒɪ]	Technik; Informatik	 Achte auf die Aussprache!
	Science ['saɪens]	Naturwissenschaft; Wissenschaft	
	on Fridays [ɒn 'fraɪdeɪz]	freitags	
	so [səʊ]	*hier:* nun, also	
3	**Assembly** [ə'semblɪ]	Schulversammlung	
	break [breɪk]	Pause	I'm tired. Let's have a *break*.
	lunch [lʌntʃ]	Mittagessen	
	Art [ɑ:t]	Kunst	
4	**when** [wen]	wann, wenn	
⟨6⟩	world [wɜ:ld]	Welt	
	much [mʌtʃ]	viel	
	Biology [baɪ'ɒlədʒɪ]	Biologie	*Biology* is a Science subject.
	French [frentʃ]	Französisch	
	I took	(das) ich hatte/nahm	
	I do know that	ich weiß doch, dass	
	to love [lʌv]	lieben	
	would be [wʊd]	wäre	
	Trigonometry [trɪgə'nɒmətrɪ]	Trigonometrie	
	Algebra ['ældʒɪbrə]	Algebra	
	slide rule ['slaɪd ,ru:l]	Rechenschieber	
	could be [kʊd]	könnte sein	

Looking at the UK: School

pupil ['pju:pl]	Schüler/in	
into ['ɪntʊ]	in … hinein	
important [ɪm'pɔ:tənt]	wichtig	It's *important* to drive on the left in the UK!
notice ['nəʊtɪs]	Mitteilung	
°**badminton** ['bædmɪntən]	Badminton	
meeting ['mi:tɪŋ]	Treffen, Besprechung	Oh, is there a *meeting*? – Where is it?

	°**register** ['redʒɪstə]	Namensliste	
	°**canteen** [kæn'tiːn]	Kantine	

Step B **The school play**

	play [pleɪ]	Theaterstück	
	notice ['nəʊtɪs]	Aushang, Schild	Look, there's a *notice* about the school play.
	It doesn't say. [ɪt ˌdʌznt 'seɪ]	Das steht nicht darauf.	
	°**role** ['rəʊl]	Rolle	
	then [ðen]	dann, also	

Step B **Simon's new school**

	°**Stevenson** ['stiːvnsn]	*Familienname*	
	°**Mike** [maɪk]	*männl. Vorname*	
	°**Newman** ['njuːmən]	*Familienname*	
	first [fɜːst]	zuerst	
5	**interesting** ['ɪntrɪstɪŋ]	interessant	*interesting* ⟷ boring
	it's great fun ['greɪt fʌn]	es macht großen Spaß	
6	to **help** [help]	helfen	
	to **hate** [heɪt]	hassen, nicht ausstehen können	
	So do I. ['səʊ duː 'aɪ]	Ich auch.	
	°**Gary** ['gærɪ]	*männl. Vorname*	

Step B **The new pupil**

	°**Chicago** [ʃɪ'kɑːgəʊ]	*Großstadt in den USA*	
	°**America** [ə'merɪkə]	Amerika	People in *America* speak English, too.
9	**the blue one** [wʌn]	das Blaue	

Step C **Activities**

	°**activities** [æk'tɪvɪtɪz]	Aktivitäten	
	°**birdwatcher** ['bɜːdˌwɒtʃə]	Vogelbeobachter/in	
	°**bird** [bɜːd]	Vogel	
	°**club** [klʌb]	Klub, Verein	
	°**piano** [pi'ænəʊ]	Klavier	
	table tennis ['teɪbl ˌtenɪs]	Tischtennis	
	°**climbing** ['klaɪmɪŋ]	Bergsteigen, Klettern	Achte auf die Aussprache!
	°**detail** ['diːteɪl]	Detail, Einzelheit	
	to **try** [traɪ]	(aus)probieren, versuchen	
	fan [fæn]	Fan	
	lunchtime ['lʌntʃtaɪm]	Mittagspause	
	°**Annabel** ['ænəbel]	*weibl. Vorname*	
	sports centre ['spɔːts ˌsentə]	Sportanlage, Sportzentrum	
	°**Singh** [sɪŋ]	*Familienname*	
1	**difficult** ['dɪfɪkəlt]	schwierig	*difficult* ⟷ easy
2	**practice** ['præktɪs]	Übung, Training	
5	to **turn round** [ˌtɜːn 'raʊnd]	(sich) umdrehen	
	to **remember** [rɪ'membə]	merken, sich erinnern an	

	everything ['evrɪθɪŋ]	alles	
	purse [pɜːs]	Geldbeutel, Portmonee	
7	**joke** [dʒəʊk]	Witz	
	to **bully** ['bʊlɪ]	tyrannisieren, schikanieren	
	headmaster [ˌhed'mɑːstə]	Schulleiter	
	love [lʌv]	Liebe	
	homework ['həʊmwɜːk]	Hausaufgaben	

Monday ['mʌndeɪ]	Montag
Tuesday ['tjuːzdeɪ]	Dienstag
Wednesday ['wenzdeɪ]	Mittwoch
Thursday ['θɜːzdeɪ]	Donnerstag
Friday ['fraɪdeɪ]	Freitag
Saturday ['sætədeɪ]	Samstag
Sunday ['sʌndeɪ]	Sonntag

Step D **A little play: Simon's new friend**

	scene [siːn]	Szene	
	to **look like** ['lʊk laɪk]	aussehen (wie)	
	°**Barry** ['bærɪ]	*männl. Vorname*	
	bully ['bʊlɪ]	Tyrann, Schläger	
	°**worried** ['wʌrɪd]	besorgt	
	to **worry** ['wʌrɪ]	sich Sorgen machen	
	to **look for** ['lʊk fɔː]	suchen	
	to **run** [rʌn]	rennen, laufen	
	so [səʊ]	so	
	to **hide** [haɪd]	(sich) verstecken	
	away [ə'weɪ]	weg	
	Stop it! ['stɒp‿ɪt]	Hör/Hört auf!	*to stop* ⟷ to start
	to **cost** [kɒst]	kosten	
1	**story** ['stɔːrɪ]	Geschichte	
	corridor ['kɒrɪdɔː]	Korridor, Gang	
⟨2⟩	audience *(pl)* ['ɔːdɪəns]	Zuschauer	
	next [nekst]	nächste/r/s	
	transparency [træns'pærənsɪ]	Folie	
	to use [juːz]	benutzen	
	overhead projector ['əʊvəˌhed prə'dʒektə]	Tageslichtprojektor	

Step E **Workshop 1**

1	**mind map** ['maɪnd mæp]	Gedankennetzwerk

Step E **Workshop 2**

	suddenly ['sʌdnlɪ]	plötzlich	
	at once [ˌət 'wʌns]	sofort	
	place [pleɪs]	Platz, Ort	
	to **take out** [teɪk 'aʊt]	herausholen, -nehmen	
	to **leave** [liːv]	lassen, verlassen	
	quick [kwɪk]	schnell	
	to **spy** [spaɪ]	spionieren	
	I spy with my little eye ...	*engl. Kinderspiel*	
	towards [tə'wɔːdz]	auf ... zu	
	probably ['prɒbəblɪ]	wahrscheinlich	The weather is nice today. Robert is *probably* playing football.
	to **be wrong about** [biː 'rɒŋ ə'baʊt]	Unrecht haben mit	The teacher is *wrong about* Barry. He isn't a bully.
2	°**opposite** ['ɒpəzɪt]	Gegenteil, -satz	
	to **begin** [bɪ'gɪn]	beginnen	

Step F **Let's check**

4	**whose** [huːz]	wessen

Adventures in Nottingham

Step A

The adventure centre

ⓐ John, David and Mark are at Jenny's new house. Mr Leinert has got an idea for the weekend:

Mr Leinert: I want to take Jenny to 'The Tales of Robin Hood' next Saturday.
Mark: Can I come, too?
Mr Leinert: Of course! You can all come.
Jenny: 'The Tales of Robin Hood' – What's that? Is it a play or a film?
Mr Leinert: No, it's an adventure centre. Look, here's the leaflet.
John: Oh, look! Everything is like in Robin Hood's time. You meet Robin Hood and his outlaws in Sherwood Forest. And look – you can shoot with bows and arrows, too!
David: And you meet the Sheriff of Nottingham. You know, Jenny – Robin Hood's enemy. – Oh, and look at this! The Sheriff's men catch you and take you to the castle.
Mark: I don't want to come!

Mr Leinert: It's OK, Mark. It's all in the adventure. Robin Hood's men hear about it and save you.

1 'The Tales of Robin Hood'

Mark wants to go to the adventure centre. What happens there? *Find the verb for each sentence.*

1. You
2. and
3. You
4. The Sheriff's men
5. They
6. But Robin Hood
7. The outlaws

hear – shoot – catch – take – go – save – meet

to Sherwood forest ...
Robin Hood and his outlaws.
with bows and arrows.
you in the forest.
you to the castle.
about it.
you.

2 Nottingham in Robin Hood's time

Look at this picture. Take your time and be careful. Seven things are wrong!
Can you find them? And can you say why they are wrong?
Example: The bus stop is wrong. There were no buses in Robin Hood's time.
Go on: The ? is wrong. There were no ? in Robin Hood's time.

ⓑ Tourists or thieves?

Do you remember the statue of Robin Hood in *Orange Line New* 1? It shows him with his bow and arrow. But very often, early in the morning, the arrow is gone. Tourists come in the night and take it away as a souvenir. Are they thieves?
In Robin Hood's time the Sheriff's men took thieves prisoner. And sometimes the hangman, all in black, took a thief to the gallows.

3 Can you answer these questions?

What

does the statue in *Orange Line New* 1 show?
do the tourists very often do with the arrow?
can you say about thieves in Robin Hood's time?
do you know about the hangman?

Step B

Robin Hood

ⓐ *David:* It was great yesterday! And it really was an adventure! We had a great time, Dad.
Mark: Robin Hood was my favourite outlaw, Mum.
David: But the other outlaws were good, too.
Mrs Penrose: And what about the Sheriff?
Mark: He was terrible. I was a bit scared of him at first. But Robin was there, too, so it was OK.

to be

present tense		past tense
I am	**was**	I was
He is She is It is	**was**	He was She was It was
We are You are They are	**were**	We were You were They were

1 Simon and his new friend

Do you remember Simon and his new friend in Unit 1? Put in 'was', 'were' and 'had'.

1. It (be) the first week of school, and Simon (have) a new friend, Mike Newman. Becky (be) worried about Simon because Mike's brother (be) a terrible bully.
2. Becky and Simon (be) on their way home. Simon and his new friend (be) on the other side of the road. Simon (have) money in his hand. Becky (be) angry now: "Newman, you bully." First Simon and Mike (be) angry, and then Becky (be) really sorry.

to have

present tense	past tense
I have You have	**had**
He has She has It has	**had**
We have You have They have	**had**

ⓑ John's postcard to a friend in Chicago

She lives → She lived
They help → They helped
He wants → He wanted
He tries → He tried
She plays → She played

2 Can you remember?

Can you remember? Finish the sentences.
Example: Last autumn Robert …
Last autumn Robert arrived in Nottingham.

1. Last spring he and his mother …
2. Last year Jenny …
3. Last autumn Becky and Simon …
4. Last weekend Mr Leinert …
5. Last year Jenny's parents …

stayed at Springfield Farm.
arrived in Nottingham.
lived with the Penroses.
lived in Berlin.
started the pond in the garden.
invited Jenny's friends to 'The Tales of Robin Hood'.

ⓒ A special day for Jenny

The pupils in year 8 must write a story for Mr Stevenson in English this week. The story must be about a special day. "I know what I can write!" Jenny thinks.

My special day

Last spring I was still with the Penroses. One Saturday afternoon David, Mark and I were in the garden. It was very warm. My aunt and uncle came outside, and we all sat under the tree. David gave me his new comic, and I tried to read – but I was too excited. "Poor Jenny," said David. "Never mind – let's play ball until they come. Mark, can we have your new ball?"
Mark went to the garage and got his ball. Then I heard a noise – a car! At last! "They're here!" I shouted, and threw the ball to Mark. Yes, the car was in front of the house now – and my parents were inside! They saw me right away, of course, and got out of the car and gave me a big hug. I was so happy! Then I took them into the garden – and we all had tea together.

Jenny Leinert

is < was / were
come – came
give – gave
sit – sat
hear – heard
throw – threw
say – said
go – went
get - got
take - took
see – saw
have - had

3 Sound track: A weekend with friends

[t]	[d]	[ɪd]
1	2	3

a) *Listen to the text first.* b) *Now make a list of the verbs.*
c) *Listen again and put the numbers of the verbs in the right places.*
We **worked**[1] in the garden last Saturday. But our friends **phoned**[2] us at 1 o'clock. They **wanted**[3] to visit us. We **invited**[4] them to stay at our house for the weekend. Our friends **arrived**[5] at 3 o'clock. There were six people now and we **needed**[6] two extra chairs for tea in the garden. After tea we **played**[7] games together. Our friends **stayed**[8] until Sunday afternoon. We **watched**[9] a funny film on Saturday evening and we **laughed**[10] a lot.

4 New house – old things

The van from Germany comes early in the morning. Jenny and David are excited. They get up very early. After breakfast they go to the Leinerts' new house. The men take Jenny's things upstairs to her new room. Jenny sits down on her bed. Her mother comes in with two boxes. Jenny says, "Oh no, not those old pictures and posters!" And she pushes them away. But David has an idea: "Maybe Mark wants some of these things!" Now David is at his house with the two boxes and tells Mark about them.

Next day David tells the story.

The van from Germany	came	...
Jenny and I	were	...
We	got up	...
After breakfast we	went	...
The men	took	...
Jenny	sat down	...
Her mother	came in	...
Jenny	said	...
And she	pushed	...
But I	had	...

5 What Mr Leinert told his wife

In the evening Mr Leinert told his wife about the adventure centre. Put in the right form of the verbs.
"The children **1** it. Little Mark **2** a bit scared of the Sheriff's men because they **3** him prisoner. They **4** all happy when the outlaws **5** and **6** them, at last. David **7** to shoot with a bow and an arrow, but that **8** not easy. – Then suddenly Jenny **9** gone. I **10** for her and she **11** in the souvenir shop. She **12** to buy a T-shirt with Robin Hood on it. Then we all **13** into the snack bar. They **14** all hungry and so I **15** them a snack and a drink."

1 like **2** is
3 take **4** are
5 come **6** save
7 tries **8** is **9** is
10 look **11** is
12 wants **13** go
14 are **15** get

6 Listening practice: Jenny's parents

Listen to the dialogue. Then finish the sentences.
Example: The Leinerts got to England yesterday morning.

1. The ferry arrived at …
2. They stayed at …
3. On the way to Nottingham they stopped at …, but …
4. Yesterday Jenny was very busy in …
5. For tea today there's … . It's Mark's …

7 ⟨A song: This old man⟩

1. This old man, he played one,
He played nick nack on my drum,
Nick nack, paddy whack,
give a dog a bone.
This old man came rolling home.

2. This old man, he played two,
He played nick nack on my shoe,
Nick nack, paddy whack …

3. This old man, he played three,
He played nick nack on my tree,
Nick nack, paddy whack …

4. This old man, he played four,
He played nick nack on my door,
Nick nack, paddy whack …

5. This old man, he played five,
He played nick nack on my hive,
Nick nack, paddy whack …

6. This old man, he played six,
He played nick nack on my sticks,
Nick nack, paddy whack …

7. This old man, he played seven,
He played nick nack down in Devon,
Nick nack, paddy whack …

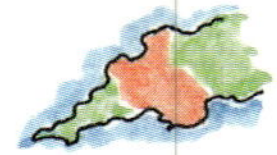

8. This old man, he played eight,
He played nick nack on my gate,
Nick nack, paddy whack …

9. This old man, he played nine,
He played nick nack on my line,
Nick nack, paddy whack …

10. This old man, he played ten,
He played nick nack on my hen,
Nick nack, paddy whack …

8 My English folder

There are so many verbs in Unit 2: regular verbs with -ed and irregular verbs. Can you put them in a list like this?

regular verbs with *-ed*	**irregular verbs**
arrive – arrived	hear – heard
shout –	give –

9 When …?

a) *How old were they?*
Example: Robert came to Nottingham when he was twelve. *Go on.*

Robert	come to Nottingham	12
Mark	start nursery school	3
Jenny	arrive in England	11
David	have his first guitar lesson	10
Becky	get Maxi for her birthday	8
Kim	start her Saturday job	16

b) *And you?*
Example: I got my first bike when I was six. *Go on.*

get your first bike / …

join the … club

have your first … lesson

get your cat/dog/bird/…

start school

Looking at the UK: In and around Nottingham

Every year there is a big fair in Nottingham – Goose Fair. It goes on for three days and is always in the first week of October. In Robin Hood's time, the fair was in the market square. But now it is outside the city centre. ▶

▲

This big old tree in Sherwood Forest is called the Major Oak. Robin Hood and his men sat under it and talked about their adventures. Well, that is what people say. Some of the oaks in Sherwood Forest are over 800 years old.

There are a lot of exciting old tunnels and caves in the rock under Nottingham Castle. The name of this cave is Mortimer's Hole

▼

My English folder

Write about your town. You can use these ideas. Can you find photos, too, or draw pictures?

- Is there a fair sometimes? When is it?
- Is there a forest near your town? Do you sometimes go there? What can you do there? Can you watch birds or animals?
- Is there an old castle in or near your town? Or an adventure centre?

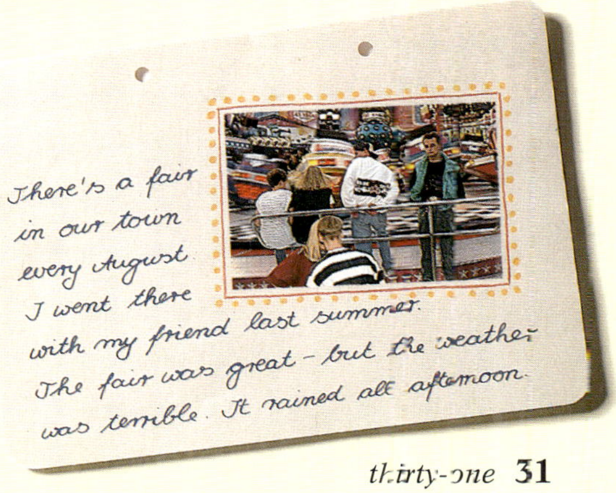

Step C

Ideas

1 Wanted!

In Robin Hood's time there were no newspapers. A town crier read out the important news to the people in the squares and streets. – Well, the Sheriff of Nottingham wanted to take Robin Hood prisoner. He hated Robin. So he used words like:

a) *Can you write four or five sentences for the town crier?*
b) *Take the town crier's role and read out your text to the people in the street.*

... is an outlaw
... is crazy
... shoots people
... hides in the forest
... is lazy
... wears dirty green clothes
... is a thief
... is terrible
... takes money from the poor people

2 A crazy dream

Dreams can be crazy. You can make crazy dreams, too. Use these ideas. Maybe you can think of other ideas, too.

1. It was late/early in the ...
2. The weather was ...
3. I was in/at a/an ...
4. My ... was/were with me.
5. Suddenly a/an ... came up to us.
6. He/She gave us a/an ...
7. I thought, this is ...
8. But then ...

1. Say **when** it was. (in the morning, at night, ...?)
2. Say something about **the weather**. (good, terrible, ...?)
3. Say **where** you were. (at school, in a shop, in Sherwood Forest, ...?)
4. Say **who** was with you. (your friends, dog, ...)
5. Say **who** came up to you. (a monster, Robin Hood, a fireman, ...?)
6. Say what he/she/it **gave** you. (a frog, ...?)
7. Say what **you thought**. (It was crazy, funny, ...)
8. Say **what happened then**.

3 Role play: Ideas for the weekend

Make dialogues with a partner.

What can we do at the weekend?
Have you got any ideas for the weekend?

Adventure Centre

park

Oh yes, let's do that.
Oh no, that's boring.

What can we do then?

What can we do there?

We can play with the dogs.

Well, we can watch a video at home.

We can meet Robin Hood.

Good idea!
That's not very exciting.

Step D

Robin Hood and the bag of gold

One day Little John, a very big man, came to Robin. He was worried.

Little John: Bad news, Robin! My brother Peter is in prison. The Sheriff wants to send him to the gallows.

Robin Hood: What? What happened?

Little John: Well, Peter stole a sheep from the Sheriff's farm. His family had nothing to eat.

Robin Hood: We must save him! But how? It's not easy to get into the prison. – Wait! I've got an idea! – The Sheriff always needs money. We've got 500 gold pieces! Let's write him a letter.

The next day the Sheriff got a letter.

Of course the Sheriff wanted the money. On Wednesday evening he rode to the forest. There were 20 men with him. They all had helmets on. – They rode into the forest. They came to the old oak and waited. Suddenly there were 21 men with helmets on. But no one noticed.

Robin and his men were in the trees.

Robin Hood: Good evening, Sheriff. We're watching you. Let Peter go now, please.

Sheriff: Where's the gold?

Robin Hood: It's under the tree on your left. But wait! Let Peter go first.

Sheriff: All right, but no tricks!

Peter ran into the forest. The Sheriff went to the tree. He saw the bag of gold pieces. It was very heavy. – Too heavy for him. One of the men with helmets came up to him. He was very big. "Let me carry the bag for you, sir."

"Oh, all right. But be careful! Let's go!"

They rode away. Suddenly the big man with the bag turned left into the forest. The other men and the Sheriff rode straight on.

The big man, Little John, took off his helmet and started to laugh. Five minutes later Robin Hood was with him: "Well done, Little John! You've got your brother, and we've got our gold back."

1 Can you say why?

1. Peter stole a sheep.
2. John was worried.
3. Robin wrote a letter to the Sheriff.
4. The Sheriff came to the forest.

Why?
Because

he wanted to save Peter.
he wanted the gold.
his family had nothing to eat.
the Sheriff wanted to send him to the gallows.

Example: Why did Peter steal a sheep?
Because ...

2 At the old oak

Find the answers in the bag.

1. How many men were with the Sheriff when he rode to the forest?
2. Where did Robin and his men wait?
3. How many men did the Sheriff have when he was near the oak?
4. Did the Sheriff let Peter go?
5. Did the Sheriff carry the bag of gold pieces?
6. Who carried it for him?

3 Let's play a game: LETTERS and LADDERS

Frogs can feel the weather. When the weather is good, the frog climbs up the ladder and sits at the top. You can use this for a game.

1. Think of a word, but don't write it down. Just draw little lines: One letter – one line, like this: __ __ __ G
(F) (R) (O) (G)

2. Now other pupils in class ask questions.

First pupil:	Is there a B in your word?
You:	No, there isn't a B! (Now the frog sits on No. 1 on the ladder. You make a X there.)
Second pupil:	Have you got an E in your word?
You:	Sorry, no E. (Frog on No. 2.)
Third pupil:	Is there a G?
You:	Yes, there's a G in it. (Write down the G. Frog still on No. 2.)

Go on.

Step E

Workshop 1

1 WORD POWER

My English folder: mouth verbs

a) *Can you make a list with these verbs?*
Start like this:

Verb	Past Tense
tell	told
...	...

b) *Choose four or five verbs and make sentences with them. Your teacher can help you.*
c) *Now draw a 'hand' and a 'foot' and write the 'hand' and 'foot' verbs.*

hand — ? ? ? ? ? ?

? write ? wash run do ? play walk ? draw ? make stand

foot — ? ? ? ? ? ?

2 Just for fun

"Somewhere with no irregular verbs."

3 A rhyme

A sailor went to sea, sea, sea
To see what he could see, see, see.
But all that he could see, see, see
Was miles of deep blue sea, sea, sea.

You can clap to this rhyme with a partner, too.

Workshop 2

Who was Robin Hood?

ⓐ Robert Hod

We find the name Robert Hod in an old book from 1225. The Sheriff at that time wanted to take this man prisoner, but Robert Hod always got away.

There are a lot of very old stories and songs about Robin Hood. But are they only stories? Or was there really a Robin Hood? History books do not really tell us anything about him. Nobody knows the details. One thing is certain: the hero in all the stories was an outlaw. There were a lot of outlaws in England in those days. Many of them lived in the forests. It was easy to hide there because the forests were big at that time. But sometimes they came to town, for example on market days, when there were big crowds in the streets and squares. And in those days there were no police. Big towns had a Sheriff. The Sheriff's men tried to catch the outlaws – but it wasn't an easy job.

ⓑ Life around 1200

Life around 1200 was very different: there were no newspapers, no calendars, no schools, no potatoes (no fish and chips!), and there was no water in the houses. Families usually had a lot of children, but many children died young. Life was not easy for children in Robin Hood's time. Nearly everybody was poor, and children started work as soon as they were old enough.

1 Right or wrong?

Some of the sentences are wrong. Can you correct them?

1. History books tell us a lot about the hero Robin Hood.
2. Nobody knows the details about Robin Hood.
3. Many outlaws lived in the forests because it was not easy to find them there.
4. The police tried to catch the outlaws.
5. The poor people ate fish and chips.
6. A lot of children died at school.
7. Most people were poor .

Let's Check

1 What can you say?

Make six sentences. Example: Last night I **helped at home**.

Yesterday On Sunday Last week Last …	I we	help at home ✓ have a late breakfast watch a good film on TV listen to the radio phone my friend …

2 Dialogues

Example: 1. *Becky:* Let's *go* to 'The Tales of Robin Hood'!
Jenny: (no/there last weekend) Oh no, I **went** there last weekend.

2. Mrs Leinert: Let's *take* a photo of the new house!
   Mr Leinert: (no/two yesterday)
3. Robert: 'Robin Hood' is on at the cinema. I want to *see* it. Let's go together.
   David: (no/with Jenny last week)
4. Becky: What can we *give* Mum for her birthday? A new CD maybe?
   Simon: (no/one last year)
5. Mrs Burton Can you go to the shops and *get* a packet of dog biscuits?
   Becky: It's OK, Mum. (Simon/two packets yesterday)

3 The Burtons

1

2

a) *Finish the sentences about picture 1.*
(*rain*) Last Sunday it …
(*stay*) So they …
(*play*) Becky and Simon …
(*watch*) Their parents …
(*sleep*) And Maxi the dog …

b) *Write a little text about picture 2. You can choose the words. Start:*
Yesterday …

4 WORD POWER

a) *Do you know the words?*

1. Not a friend!
2. Saturday and Sunday.
3. There are a lot of trees in it.
4. You make chips from them.
5. Your father's or mother's father.
6. It's in your purse.

NPARGDA STREFO
TEATOPSO NOYME
NEKEWED YEMEN

b) *Make a sentence with each word.*

Unit 2 Adventures in Nottingham

Vokabeltraining – kleine Tricks mit großer Wirkung

1. Plane fürs Vokabellernen mindestens dreimal 5–10 Minuten Zeit ein.
2. Lege vorher alles bereit, was du zum Lernen brauchst.
3. Arbeite zu Hause an einem Platz, an dem dich niemand stört und störe dich auch selbst nicht beim Wörterlernen, indem du z. B. nur noch die Hausaufgabe für ein anderes Fach heraussuchen oder Bleistifte spitzen musst. Arbeite konzentriert 5–10 Minuten an den Vokabeln. Du kannst dir auch einen Wecker stellen, der nach 10 Minuten läutet.
4. Wenn der Wecker klingelt, hast du (und dein Gehirn) eine kleine Pause verdient. Jetzt kannst du dir beispielsweise etwas zu trinken holen oder Bleistifte spitzen oder …
5. Als nächste Lernaufgabe solltest du danach etwas ganz anderes als Englisch machen. Aber vergiss nicht, dir die englischen Wörter später nochmals vorzunehmen.

Step A **The adventure centre**

ⓐ	**adventure** [əd'ventʃə]	Abenteuer	
	to **take s.o. to** ['teɪk]	jdn. mitnehmen	
	tale [teɪl]	Geschichte, Sage	A *tale* is a story.
	°**Robin Hood** ['rɒbɪn 'hʊd]	*der Held einer englischen Sage*	
	°**The Tales of Robin Hood** [ðə 'teɪlz‿əv 'rɒbɪn 'hʊd]	*ein Museum, wo die Geschichte von Robin Hood erzählt wird*	
	film [fɪlm]	Film	
	leaflet ['li:flɪt]	Prospekt, Informationsblatt	
	you [ju:]	man	
	outlaw ['aʊtlɔ:]	Gesetzlose/r, Vogelfreie/r, Bandit/in	 Robin Hood is an *outlaw*.
	°**Sherwood Forest** ['ʃɜ:wʊd 'fɒrɪst]	*Wald nördlich von Nottingham*	
	forest ['fɒrɪst]	Wald	
	to **shoot** [ʃu:t]	schießen	
	bow [bəʊ]	Bogen	
	arrow ['ærəʊ]	Pfeil	
	sheriff ['ʃerɪf]	Sheriff	
	enemy ['enəmɪ]	Feind	
	to **catch** [kætʃ]	fangen	
	to **hear** [hɪə]	hören	
1	**each** [i:tʃ]	jede(r)	
ⓑ	**thief, thieves** [θi:f, θi:vz]	Dieb/in, Diebe	
	night [naɪt]	Nacht	
	as [æz]	als	
	souvenir [ˌsu:və'nɪə]	Andenken, Souvenir	
	hangman ['hæŋmən]	Henker	
	gallows ['gæləʊz]	Galgen	

Step B **Robin Hood**

ⓐ	to **be, was** [wɒz]	war	
	to **be scared of** ['skeəd‿əv]	Angst haben vor	*Are you scared of* snakes?
	to **be, were** [wɜː]	warst, wart, waren	
	to **have, had** [hæd]	hatte	
1	**angry** ['æŋgrɪ]	verärgert, wütend	
ⓑ	**Dear** … [dɪə]	Liebe(r) …	
	All the best ['ɔːl ðə 'best]	Alles Gute	
2	**autumn** ['ɔːtəm]	Herbst	
ⓒ	**special** ['speʃl]	besondere/r/s	
	excited [ɪk'saɪtɪd]	aufgeregt	You're going to England. Are you *excited*?
	poor [pʊə]	arm	
	Never mind! ['nevə 'maɪnd]	Macht nichts!	
	until [ən'tɪl]	bis	
	noise [nɔɪz]	Geräusch	
	at last [ət‿'lɑːst]	Endlich!	
	to **shout** [ʃaʊt]	rufen, schreien	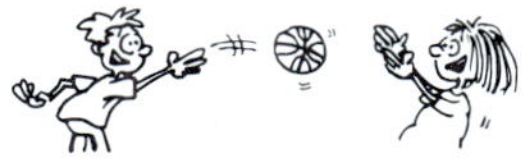 The boy *throws* the ball and the girl catches.
	to **throw, threw** [θrəʊ, θruː]	warf	
	hug [hʌg]	Umarmung	You can't give a fish a *hug*.
	°**irregular** [ɪ'regjʊlə]	unregelmäßig	
	°**verb** [vɜːb]	Verb	
3	**extra** ['ekstrə]	zusätzlich	
4	**van** [væn]	Liefer-, Möbelwagen	
5	**snack bar** ['snækbɑː]	Imbissstube	
	snack [snæk]	Imbiss	
	drink [drɪŋk]	Getränk	
6	**ferry** ['ferɪ]	Fähre	
⟨7⟩	bone [bəʊn]	Knochen	
	came rolling home ['rəʊlɪŋ]	kam nach Hause	
8	**regular** ['regjʊlə]	regelmäßig	
9	**nursery school** ['nɜːsərɪ ˌskuːl]	Kindergarten	
	to **join** [dʒɔɪn]	Mitglied werden	

Looking at the UK: In and around Nottingham

fair [feə]	Volksfest, Jahrmarkt	The 'Oktoberfest' is a famous German *fair*.
°**Goose Fair** ['guːs 'feə]	*Name eines Jahrmarktes in Nottingham*	
goose, geese *(pl)* [guːs, giːs]	Gans, Gänse	
°**Major Oak** [ˌmeɪdʒə 'əʊk]	*Name einer alten Eiche in Sherwood Forest*	
°**oak** [əʊk]	Eiche	*Oaks* are often very, very old.
to **sit** [sɪt]	sitzen	
tunnel ['tʌnl]	Tunnel	
cave [keɪv]	Höhle	There are a lot of *caves* under Nottingham Castle.
rock [rɒk]	Felsen, Stein	
°**Mortimer's Hole** ['mɔːtɪməz 'həʊl]	*Name eine Höhle*	

Step C **Ideas**

1	to **want, wanted** ['wɒntɪd]	wollen, wünschen
	newspaper ['nju:sˌpeɪpə]	Zeitung
	town crier ['taʊn 'kraɪə]	Ausrufer/in
2	**monster** ['mɒnstə]	Ungeheuer
	fireman ['faɪəmən]	Feuerwehrmann

Step D **Robin Hood and the bag of gold**

	gold [gəʊld]	Gold
	news [nju:z]	Nachricht(en)
	prison [prɪzn]	Gefängnis
	to **steal, stole** [sti:l, stəʊl]	stehlen
	nothing ['nʌθʊŋ]	nichts
	gold pieces ['gəʊld 'pi:sɪs]	Goldstücke
	to **ride, rode** [raɪd, rəʊd]	reiten
	helmet ['helmɪt]	Helm
	to **wait, waited** [weɪt]	warten
	to **notice, noticed** ['nəʊtɪs]	merken, sehen
	heavy ['hevɪ]	schwer
	too [tu:]	zu
	all right [ˌɔ:l'raɪt]	in Ordnung
	to **take off** ['teɪk‿ɒf]	abnehmen
3	**weather** ['weðə]	Wetter

Step E **Workshop 1**

	mouth [maʊθ]	Mund
	°**sentence** ['sentəns]	Satz
	hand [hænd]	Hand
	foot [fʊt]	Fuß

Step E **Workshop 2**

	°**Hod** [hɒd]	*Familienname*
	prisoner ['prɪznə]	Gefangene/r
	to **get away** [ˌget‿ə'weɪ]	entkommen
	hero ['hɪərəʊ]	Held/in
	from day to day [frəm 'deɪ‿tʊ‿'deɪ]	von Tag zu Tag
	water ['wɔ:tə]	Wasser
1	to **correct** [kə'rekt]	korrigieren, verbessern
	nearly ['nɪəlɪ]	beinahe, fast

in

in February
in the evening
in front of the house
in hospital

on

on holiday
on the radio/on TV
on the left/right
on 6th of June
on the telephone
on Monday

at

at the weekend
at once
at lunchtime
at the bottom of the hill
at the door
at 6 o'clock
at school
at the Burtons' house

Nottingham Goose Fair

Step A

A busy weekend

It is Monday morning at school. The friends are talking about their weekend.

ⓐ I went to the cinema on Saturday. The film was very exciting. But I ate two hot dogs and a lot of popcorn - and then I felt sick. But yesterday I learned my part for the school play.

ⓑ We had a big argument yesterday. Kim and I wanted to go to the American adventure centre. But Mum and Dad wanted to go for a walk. In the end we all went ice-skating together. It was fantastic!

ⓒ We visited Sherwood Farm Park. The young pigs were very nice, but *so* noisy! Mark wanted to take one home with us!

ⓓ We stayed at home and worked in our new house. But I had a good time. I painted my room blue. It looks really nice now.

ⓔ Simon went for a walk with the dogs on Saturday. So I went to town. I bought a cheap T-shirt and I saw a nice sweatshirt, too. But it was too expensive. I saw a poster for Goose Fair in town. It starts on Thursday!

1 Their weekend

a) *Who says what? How do you know? Start:*
ⓐ Robert says this. He is in the school play. ⓑ … says this. Kim is her … ⓒ … says this. Mark is … ⓓ … says this. The Leinerts are in their … ⓔ … says this. Simon …

b) *Now say what the friends did at the weekend. Make one or two sentences about them.*
Example: ⓐ Robert went to the cinema. But he ate too much and felt sick.

ⓑ Kim and … … to the adventure centre. But their mum and dad … . In the end they all …

ⓒ …

2 Listening practice: Ice-skating with the Dixons

Listen to Sarah. Find out who did what.
You can start: Mrs Dixon felt worried at first. – … fell over. – *Please go on.*

Sarah
Mrs Dixon
Mr Dixon
Kim
Mr Stevenson

– feel worried at first
– fall over
– meet a nice boy

– say hello to Sarah
– go to the snack bar
– have three sandwiches

3 WORD POWER

exciting	noisy	young	boring
fantastic	expensive	small	old
big	terrible	quiet	cheap

a) *Find six pairs of opposites.*
Start: exciting <-> boring
Please go on.

b) *Find good nouns for these adjectives and make sentences.*
Example: Computer games are exciting.
… are noisy.
Go on, please.

Your turn 4 What do you like?

Say what you like and don't like.

Example:
I like ice cream but I don't like popcorn.

Your turn 5 Say something about your weekend

I We	went were worked played visited stayed watched bought ate	in the to the at the a some at …	chocolate cake cinema city centre park beach farm home garden restaurant CD

Example:
We went to the cinema.
And I bought a CD.
…

Step B

Bad news

Listen, Kim. There was an accident in Mansfield Road with a lorry full of dodgem cars, but it wasn't too bad. The drivers were OK. They didn't need an ambulance. But they weren't very happy because the lorry didn't look too good after the accident.

1 The accident

What can you say about the accident?
Example: The accident was in Mansfield Road. *or:* The accident wasn't too bad.

The accident	was	in Mansfield Road	very happy
The drivers	wasn't	too bad	full of dodgem cars
The lorry	were	OK	
	weren't		

2 The police officer's questions

was/wasn't were/weren't didn't

Robert was in Mansfield Road when the accident happened. A police officer asked him some questions. What did Robert tell the police officer?

1. I … here when the accident happened. (be)
2. I … the lorry. (see)
3. I … an ambulance because the drivers … a doctor. (call, need)
4. The drivers … unhappy about their cars. (be)

3 Why not?

Make little dialogues.
Example: "Hey! You didn't come and see me yesterday." – "Sorry. I didn't have time."

Hey! You didn't …

- come and see me
- buy that magazine for me
- wait for me after school
- come to the Computer Club
- phone me
- give me my comic back

… yesterday. Why not?

Sorry, I didn't	
	think of it.
	have time.
	know your number.
	remember.
	…

4 School yesterday

Your turn

Say what you did or what you didn't do yesterday. Make sentences with these ideas.
have English/Science/ … – watch a video – work with computers – make a poster – stay in the classroom at break – go outside to the playground – play a game/football/… – have lunch at school – finish school early – go on a school trip
Example: We didn't have English yesterday. We watched a video in Geography.

Was it fun?

Becky and David are at Jenny's house.
Mrs Leinert is asking them about Goose Fair last year.

Mrs Leinert: Was Goose Fair good last year, David?
David: Yes, it was. It was great fun. I went on Saturday.
Mrs Leinert: Were you there all day?
David: No, I wasn't. I only went in the afternoon.
Mrs Leinert: What about you Becky? Did you go to the fair with David?
Becky: No, I didn't. I went with Sarah.
Mrs Leinert: Did you have a good time, too?
Becky: Yes, we did. We had a great time together.

Were you …? – Yes, I was./We were.
– No, I wasn't./We weren't.

Did you go …? – Yes, I did.
– No, I didn't.

5 More questions

Ask more questions about the fair last year.
You can start: "Were the dodgems fun?" – "Yes, …/No, …" *Please go on.*

Was Were	dodgems/fun	music/nice and noisy	weather/OK	people/friendly
	prizes/good	hot dogs/expensive	fair/open in the mornings	

?

6 What's your answer?

Yes, I did …
No, I didn't …

Example:
Did you go to the fair last year? – Yes, I did. It was fantastic. I had a great time.
– No, I didn't. We didn't have a fair in our town last year.

1. Did you have a good time last weekend?
2. Did you tidy your room on Saturday?
3. Did you watch TV yesterday evening?
4. Did you have an egg for breakfast this morning?
5. Did you come to school by bus?

7 Yesterday evening

a) *Ask four people in your class about yesterday evening. Ask them:*
"Did you watch TV yesterday evening? Did you …?"
and write down their answers.
b) *Now tell the others what is on your list.*

Sarah's teddies

Sarah has got three teddies. Of course she is too old for teddies – *she* says – but she doesn't want to give them away. So they live on a shelf in her room.
The white teddy is bigger than the others. He is newer, too. Sarah won him at Goose Fair last year.
The yellow teddy is not as big as the white teddy, but he has got a happier face – maybe because he has got the nicest clothes.
The brown teddy is the oldest and dirtiest of them all. He is as old as Sarah. He was her first teddy and he is still her favourite.

old – old**er** – (**the**) old**est**
big – big**ger** – (**the**) big**gest**
happy – happ**ier** – (**the**) happ**iest**

8 Are you sure?

Compare the things or the children with one another. Use the adjectives.
Example: The green ball is smaller than the blue ball.
The blue ball is the biggest.
The red ball is the smallest.

big – small

angry – happy

young – old

9 Older or not?

Find one of your friends or somebody in your family who is older/younger/smaller/bigger/quieter than you.
Example: My brother Tom is older than I am.

good – better – best
bad – worse – worst

10 Sarah, Becky, Jenny, Robert, David

What do you know about them? Please make questions and answers with a friend.
Example: "Who is the smallest of the friends?"
– "David is the smallest."

WHO
is the smallest/biggest of the friends/speaks the best German
lives in the smallest family/has got the biggest pet
has got the oldest sister/youngest brother
?

Jenny: Oh, look! Becky is as big as Sarah. But Mark is not as big. He is smaller.

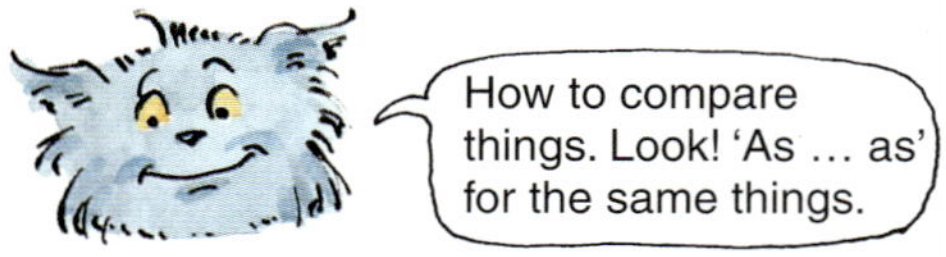

11 Can you compare?

Example: The red car is as small as the yellow car. The green car is not as small. It's bigger than the yellow and the red car.

12 Family pairs

Please compare the people (and dogs).
Start:
1. Kim is older than Sarah.
She is not as crazy as Sarah.
Sarah is … *Please go on.*

younger	bigger	smaller		than …
older	crazier	funnier		
better	quieter	sillier	worse	

not as	big	old	bad	as …
	funny	quiet		
	silly	good	…	

13 Jenny's notebook

Look at Jenny's notebook and find more sentences.

	how old?	how big?	quiet?
Robert	13	1.68 m	+
David	12	1.58 m	+
Sarah	12	1.60 m	-
Becky	13	1.60 m	-
Mark	5	1.32 m	-

Example: Robert is as old as Becky and David is as old as Sarah. David and Sarah are not as old as Robert and Becky. David and Sarah are younger than Robert and Becky. Robert and Becky are older than David and Sarah. Robert and Becky are the oldest and Mark is the youngest.

Step C

All the fun of the fair

1 Role play: Let's have a go!

What do you want to do at the fair?
Look at the photos and practise dialogues.

Come on: Let's have a go on the …
Do you want to have a ride on …?

Oh no! I don't want to die yet!
That's for little children.
I've got a better idea.
Let's …

Oh yes! That looks fun.
Maybe we can win a prize.
Let's be crazy!
…

2 Listening practice: Fair people

a) *Listen to the people. Can you find the right pictures? (Only three are right.)*
Start: The right picture for number one is picture …

b) *There is nothing on the cassette for two of the pictures from a). What can these people say? Write a little text for one of the pictures and act it in class.*

3 Sound track

a) *One word has got a different sound. Can you find it?*
[dʒ] German Jenny strange children dodgem subject
b) *Please say these sentences.*
Dodgems are stran**ge** cars! – Do you have fairs in **Ger**many, too, **J**enny?
c) *Can you think of more words with* [dʒ] *sounds and put them in sentences?*

Step D

Friends

Becky's problems started right away when she arrived at Goose Fair with Sarah and Jenny.
"Hey, look! The dodgems!" Sarah shouted.
The three girls ran to the dodgems. Sarah and Jenny jumped into one car together. But there was no seat for Becky. She drove a different car. – Crash! Sarah and Jenny hit Becky's car from behind.
Becky was unhappy. It wasn't so much fun without a friend.

After the dodgems, Jenny and Sarah wanted to have a go on the coconut shy. Sarah won a little teddy.
"Well done! Another for your shelf," Jenny said. "Come on, Becky. It's your turn now."
But when Becky threw the ball, she didn't hit the coconut. She hit the man behind the stall.
"You're dangerous! That was the craziest throw today," the man laughed. Jenny and Sarah laughed, too. But not Becky. She didn't like it when people laughed at her.

Then they saw The Spider near the coconut shy.
"Ooh, that looks exciting," Jenny said. But Becky felt scared of rides like that.
"Look, there's a nice children's roundabout," Sarah said. "That's better for you. You can wait for us there!"
She and Jenny ran off for their ride. Becky walked away. She was very unhappy. She thought of the fair last year, and the fun with Sarah. Of course, Jenny wasn't with them last year. Two was better than three …

1 Questions about the story

Please ask questions. Can you answer them, too?

Examples: Where did the friends go together? – They went to Goose Fair.
Why did Becky drive a different car? – Because there was no …
Please go on.

1. … did Jenny and Sarah want to do after the dodgems?
2. … did Sarah win?
3. … did Becky hit with a ball?
4. … did they see near the coconut shy?
5. … did Becky feel about rides like that?

2 The best ending

How can the story go on? What do you think? Which of these ideas makes the best ending? (Have you got other ideas?) Read your ending to the class.

a) Becky went home. She didn't want to see Sarah and Jenny any more. Next day she went to school and didn't talk to them.
b) After a minute Becky stopped and looked back. She thought that she was very silly and went back to wait for Sarah and Jenny.
c) Sarah and Jenny ran behind Becky. They were sorry and wanted to be friends again.
d) Sarah and Jenny were angry at Becky. Friends must understand jokes!

3 The three girls? *Can you use the words to talk about the three girls?*

silly
unhappy crazy bad
quiet boring good
funny noisy

4 Was Becky silly? *Think about how Becky felt in the story. Talk to a partner. (Maybe you have different ideas.)*

Was she silly	Yes, she was, because	No she wasn't, because
1. – at the dodgems?	– you can't always sit with a friend.	– everything is more fun with a friend.
2. – at the coconut shy?	– it isn't so bad when people laugh at you.	– it isn't nice when you can't do things.
3. – at The Spider?	– rides like that aren't dangerous.	– not everyone likes rides like The Spider.

5 ⟨A song: The Hokey Pokey⟩

Words/Music: Jimmy Kennedy

2. your left hand 3. your right foot 4. your left foot 5. your whole self

Workshop 1

1 WORD POWER

a) *Say what you did last weekend.*
b) *Say what your (mum/dad/brother/sister/friends …) did last weekend.*

last weekend:
- had …
- watched …
- did …
- went …
- cleaned …
- visited …
- stayed …
- played …
- wrote …
- made …
- read …
- worked …
- was/were …

2 Did you …?

Write down five interesting questions for your teacher about his/her last holiday.

Did you …?
Were you …?

Here are some words for you:
- go to the seaside/go to …
- go by car/go by …
- go swimming
- build sandcastles with your children
- play beach ball/play …
- walk in the park/walk in …
- … at the seaside or in a city?
- … in the cinema/…?

Yes, I did./No, I didn't.
Yes, I was./No, I wasn't.

b) *What do you think your teacher will answer? Write it down. Then ask your teacher and compare his/her answers with your answers.*

3 Can you compare?

Compare the things and people in the pictures.

Use: small, big, young, old, nice, happy, cheap

Example: The book in picture one is smaller than the book in picture two.
or: The book in picture two is bigger than the book in picture one.
or: The book in picture two is not as small as the book in picture one.
or: The book in picture one is not as big as the book in picture two.

Workshop 2

The ghost train

Mark visited Goose Fair with his mum. "Oh Mum, look! The ghost train! Oh please, Mum, let's have a go on the ghost train." His mother didn't look very happy. "Oh Mark! That's not for little children. Do you want to have a ride on a roundabout? After that we can buy some popcorn." "Mum, I'm not as old as David and Jenny but I'm big, too. And I'm not scared at all." said Mark. "Well, then let's go on it then." When they left the ghost train Mark was very quiet and his face was pale. That night he had a strange dream.

He was on the ghost train and he was a ghost in a ghost family, the Spooks. Mr and Mrs Spook were very tall and thin with long faces. They were in white clothes. Their children were Wilma, Gary and Victoria the vampires. They had black coats and very pale faces. Mark was scared of their long teeth. Their grandmother Gertrude was a witch. She looked terrible: a long red nose, green eyes, dirty hair and a broomstick in her hand. She had some pets around her: a small dragon, some rats and a cat. When she came up to him Mark was so afraid that he shouted "Help! Help!"

"Hey, Mark! What's the matter with you? Are you OK?" It was Jenny. Oh, good! He was at home in his bed. It was only a dream.

1 Mark's dream

Now you are Mark. Tell your friend about this strange dream. Your partner can ask questions. Start like this: I had a strange dream. I was …

ghost family, Spooks; very tall and thin, long faces; Wilma, Gary, Victoria the vampires; black coats, pale faces, scared of their long teeth; Gertrude the witch, red nose, green eyes, dirty hair, broomstick, pets; dragon, rats, cat came up to him; Help!

2 Your story

Here are some words for an exciting story.

dangerous
friends
to jump
be scared of
fantastic
hair
shout
holidays
What?
Who?
When?
Where?
Why?

3 On the ghost train

Now tell us about an exciting ride you had on a ghost train.

a) Say when it was
who was with you
what you saw
what you felt
what you liked and what you didn't like and why

b) *Imagine you don't like ghost trains. What can you tell a friend to keep him/her away?*

Step F

Let's check

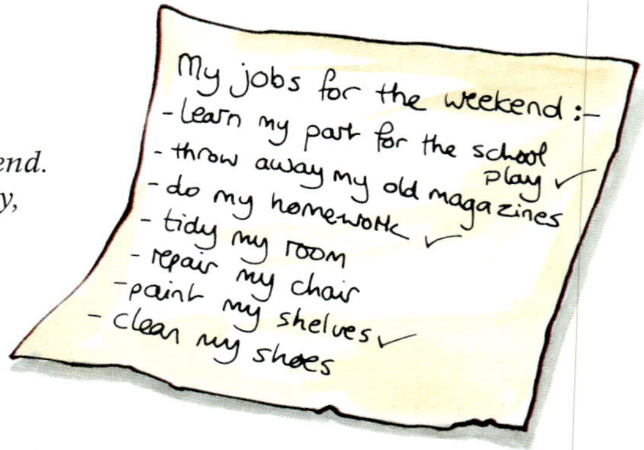

1 Robert's weekend

Robert wanted to do a lot of things last weekend. But of course he didn't feel so good on Sunday, so he didn't do everything.
He learned his part for the school play.
But he didn't …
He … *Go on.*

2 Questions about the unit

Make questions with **did**. *What are the answers?*
Start: 1. Did the Burtons go ice-skating? – No, they didn't. The Dixons went ice-skating.

1. the Burtons/go ice-skating
2. Jenny/paint her room blue
3. Mr Dixon/see the accident in Mansfield Road
4. a car/hit a bike
5. Mr and Mrs Leinert/visit Goose Fair last year
6. Sarah/win a teddy at the fair

3 Let's compare

What can you say about these pairs of things?
Example: Bikes are quieter than cars. *or:* Bikes aren't as quick as cars. *or:* …

cheap quick easy
quiet healthy
nice clever

4 What they think

What do these people say? Example: 1. *Sarah:* Tabby is the silliest cat in England.

– untidy place/the house
– friendly people/the school
– clever dogs/Nottingham
– silly cat/England ✔
– nice town/the UK
– good bike shop/Sherwood

2. *Becky:* Maxi and Mini …
3. *Simon:* Burtons' Bikes …
4. *Mrs Croft:* Robert! Your room …
5. *Jenny:* Nottingham …
6. *Mr Stevenson:* My pupils …

5 What can you ask?

What Why How Where	did you …?

What your friend tells you:
1. "I bought a nice T-shirt on Saturday."
2. "I made a really good cake yesterday."
3. "I won a prize in a competition last month."
4. "I felt unhappy at the weekend."
5. "I went to a very interesting place on Sunday."

What you ask:
- "Where/When did you buy it?"
- "How/Where did you …?"
- " …?"
- " …?"
- " …?"

⟨Revision and fun 1⟩

1 Time for some jokes

Teacher: Did your big brother help you with your homework, Freddy?
Freddy: No, he did all the work himself.

Q: What is the end of everything?
A: The letter G.

Teacher: Andy, say something beginning with 'I'.
Andy: I is …
Teacher: No, Andy, you must say 'I am'.
Andy: All right, I am the ninth letter of the alphabet.

"Doctor, doctor, I'm not feeling very well."
"What's the matter?"
"I work like a horse, eat like a bird and I'm just as tired as a dog."
"You don't need a doctor – you need a vet."

Girl: Did I tell you about the three eggs we had for school lunch?
Mother: No.
Girl: Too bad.

Teacher: Jimmy, spell 'mouse'.
Jimmy: M-O-U-S.
Teacher: But what comes at the end of it?
Jimmy: A tail.

Teacher: When do you like school best?
John: When it's the weekend.

Q: Where does Thursday come before Wednesday?
A: In the dictionary.

Tom: Sometimes I like teachers.
Bill: When?
Tom: When they're at home.

Q: What's the difference between a hill and a pill?
A: One is hard to get up, and the other is hard to get down.

SB 2 Sound track

[–]
Our German teacher knows a lot about the Sherwood outlaws. She can answer your questions. I'm sure. Ask her. She's over there.

[r]
Our English teacher is nice. She can answer all your English questions about the forest. I'm sure of it. Ask her about it. She's there at the window.

3 Everybody's story

In this game, everybody helps to tell a story. But each person can only say one word. Look at the example and go on.

⟨Revision and fun 1⟩

4 A memory map

This is a memory map of Robin Hood. Look at the words and then say something about Robin Hood, his friends, his enemies, his time, the town, Sherwood Forest, … .
Find seven more words and write them down in your exercise book.

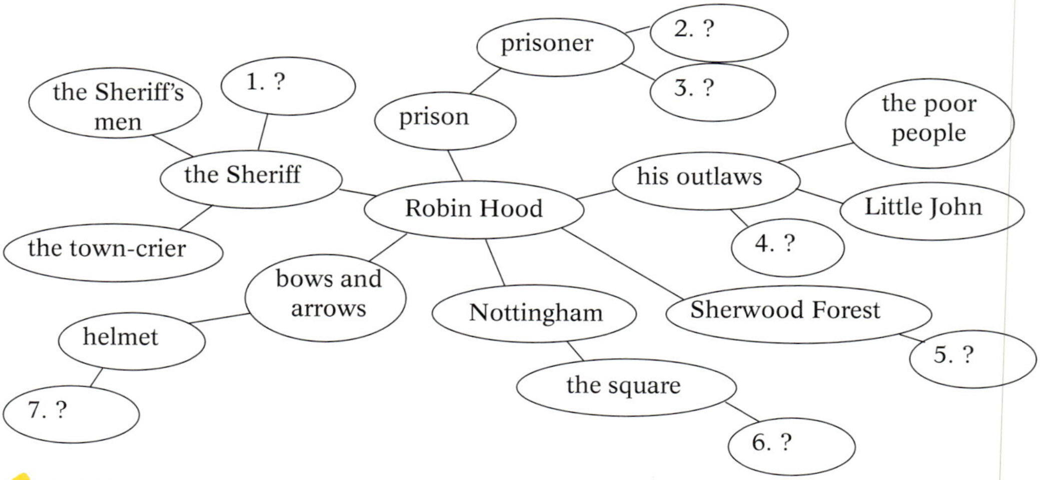

5 Mobiles

Let's make mobiles with adjectives like this.
Work with a partner or in groups of three.

6 Barry Newman

Put in the adjectives from list A, B or C.

This afternoon Simon is at Mike's house. Mike's brother Barry is there, too. He is a year (1) than Mike. He thinks he is (2) . And he thinks his things are much (3) than other people's.
"I've got a (4) bike," he tells Simon. "It was (4) bike in the shop. Nobody at Haywood has got a (4) bike than this!"
But Simon knows a lot about bikes. His parents have a (5) bike shop in Nottingham. A lot of the bikes in their shop are (4) than Barry's. But Simon doesn't say anything. Barry is (5) bully at Haywood. And he is much (6) than Simon, too.
When Barry goes out of the room, Mike says, "Don't listen to my brother. He's OK, really. He just wants to be (2) . So he says (7) things."

A	B	C
1. old	older	the oldest
2. great	greater	the greatest
3. good	better	the best
4. fast	faster	the fastest
5. big	bigger	the biggest
6. strong	stronger	the strongest
7. silly	sillier	the silliest

Unit 3 Nottingham Goose Fair

Vokabellernen mit Musik?

Viele Schülerinnen und Schüler brauchen zum Wörterlernen völlige Ruhe. Einige jedoch können sich besser konzentrieren, wenn im Hintergrund Musik läuft. Dies funktioniert aber nur, wenn die Musik einen ruhigen Rhythmus hat und nicht zu laut ist. Probiere aus, was für dich besser ist.
Eines aber geht **nicht** zusammen: Wörterlernen und Fernsehen. Dein Auge und dein Ohr sind dabei zu sehr abgelenkt.

Vokabellernen mit dem Cassettenrekorder?

Du kannst Wörter aber auch mit einem Cassettenrekorder üben:

- Nimm dir deine Lernportion von etwa 10–12 Wörtern vor und sprich die deutsche Bedeutung jedes Wortes auf die Cassette, lasse eine nicht zu kurze Sprechpause und sprich dann die englische Bedeutung des Wortes darauf.
- Beim Abhören sprichst du dann die englische Bedeutung in die Sprechpause.
- So kannst du nach und nach ein Lernpäckchen nach dem anderen aufnehmen. Ein „Walkman" ist dabei auch ganz praktisch. Du kannst damit die Wörter üben, wo du auch bist.

Step A **A busy weekend**

ⓐ	**hot dog** [ˈhɒt ˈdɒg]	Hotdog *(heißes Würstchen in einem Brötchen)*	
	popcorn [ˈpɒpkɔːn]	Popcorn	
	to **feel sick** [sɪk]	sich schlecht/krank fühlen	Well, I *feel sick* now.
	yesterday [ˈjestədeɪ]	gestern	Today is Monday, *yesterday* was Sunday.
	part [pɑːt]	Teil	
ⓑ	to **have an argument** [ˌhæv‿ən ˈɑːgjʊment]	einen Streit, eine Auseinandersetzung haben	 They *had an argument* yesterday.
	American [əˈmerɪkən]	amerikanisch, Amerikaner/in	
	ice-skating [ˈaɪsˌskeɪtɪŋ]	Schlittschuhlaufen	
	fantastic [fænˈtæstɪk]	phantastisch	
ⓒ	to **visit** [ˈvɪzɪt]	besuchen, besichtigen	 *young* ⟷ old 
	young [jʌŋ]	jung	
	pig [pɪg]	Schwein	
	noisy [ˈnɔɪzɪ]	laut, lärmend	My head hurts. Please don't be so *noisy*.
ⓓ	to **have a good time** [ˈgʊd ˈtaɪm]	sich gut amüsieren	
	to **paint** [peɪnt]	(be)malen; streichen	You can *paint* a picture with water colours.
	to **look nice** [lʊk ˈnaɪs]	nett/schön aussehen	
ⓔ	**cheap** [tʃiːp]	billig	
	sweatshirt [ˈswetʃɜːt]	Sweatshirt	
	expensive [ɪkˈspensɪv]	teuer	cheap ⟷ *expensive*
3	°**noun** [naʊn]	Substantiv, Nomen	
	°**adjective** [ˈædʒɪktɪv]	Adjektiv	

Step B **Bad news**

accident [ˈæksɪdənt]	Unfall	

	°**Mansfield Road** [ˈmænsfiːld ˌrəʊd]	*Straße in Nottingham*	
	lorry [ˈlɒrɪ]	Lastwagen	On the roads there are cars, vans, buses and *lorries*.
	full of [ˈfʊl‿əv]	voll mit	
	dodgem car [ˈdɒdʒəm ˌkɑː]	Autoscooter	
	ambulance [ˈæmbjʊləns]	Krankenwagen	
2	to **happen** [ˈhæpən]	passieren, geschehen	I had an accident yesterday. – What *happened*?
4	**early** [ˈɜːlɪ]	früh	
	trip [trɪp]	Ausflug	

Step B **Was it fun?**

5	**prize** [praɪz]	Preis	
6	to **tidy (up)** [ˈtaɪdɪ]	aufräumen	

Step B **Sarah's teddies**

	teddy [ˈtedɪ]	Teddybär	
	to **give away** [ˌɡɪv‿əˈweɪ]	verschenken	
	bigger than [ðæn]	… als	
	to **win, won** [wɪn, wʌn]	gewinnen	David *won* a prize in the school competition.
	dirty [ˈdɜːtɪ]	dreckig, schmutzig	
	still [stɪl]	noch	
8	to **compare** [kəmˈpeə]	vergleichen	
9	**somebody** [ˈsʌmbədɪ]	jemand	
10	**worst** [wɜːst]	schlechteste/r/s	
11	**(not) as … as** [əz … əz]	(nicht) so … wie	
13	**notebook** [ˈnəʊtbʊk]	Notizheft	

Step C **All the fun of the fair**

1	to **have a go** [ˌhæv‿əˈɡəʊ]	(es) probieren	Dodgem cars! Great! Let's *have a go* right away!
	to **have a ride** [ˈhæv‿əˈraɪd]	fahren	Do you want to *have a ride* on my new bike?
	That looks fun!	Das sieht spaßig aus.	
	°**Big Wheel** [ˈbɪɡ ˈwiːl]	Riesenrad	
	wheel [wiːl]	Rad	
	°**The Spider** [ðə ˈspaɪdə]	*Name eines Fahrgeschäfts* (die „Spinne“)	
	°**roundabout** [ˈraʊndəbaʊt]	Karussell	
	°**coconut shy** [ˈkəʊkənʌt ˈʃaɪ]	Wurfbude	
	°**coconut** [ˈkəʊkənʌt]	Kokosnuss	
	°**ghost train** [ˈɡəʊst ˈtreɪn]	Geisterbahn	
2	**cassette** [kəˈset]	Kassette	

Step D **Friends**

	to **jump** [dʒʌmp]	springen	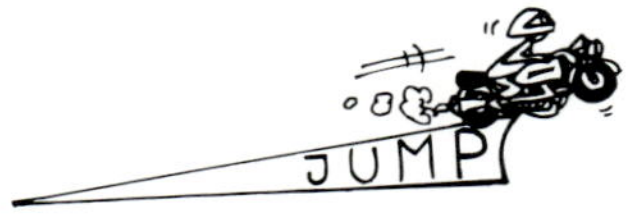
	seat [siːt]	Sitz	
	to **hit, hit** [hɪt, hɪt]	treffen, schlagen	
	Well done! [ˈwel ˈdʌn]	Gut gemacht!	
	stall [stɔːl]	Stand	

	dangerous ['deɪndʒərəs]	gefährlich	
	throw [θrəʊ]	Wurf	
	to **laugh at s.o.** ['lɑːf‿ət]	lachen über jmd.	
	to **run off, ran off** ['rʌn‿ɒf, ræn]	wegrennen	
2	**ending** ['endɪŋ]	Ausgang	
⟨5⟩	You put your right hand in [raɪt hænd]	Streckt eure rechte Hand nach vorne	
	right hand out	rechte Hand nach hinten	
	shake it all about ['ʃeɪk ɪt‿ɔːl ə'baʊt]	schüttelt sie fest aus	
	to turn around [ˌtɜːn‿ə'raʊnd]	herumdrehen	
	that's what it's all about [ˌɔːl‿ə'baʊt]	so wird's gemacht	
	left [left]	linke/r/s	Some people write with their *right hand*, some with their *left hand*.
	foot [fʊt]	Fuß	
	put your whole self in ['həʊl 'self]	macht einen Schritt vorwärts	
	whole self out	einen Schritt rückwärts	

Step E **Workshop 2**

pale [peɪl]	blass	
strange [streɪndʒ]	seltsam, merkwürdig	
°**Spook** [spuːk]	*Familienname*	
tall [tɔːl]	groß	
thin [θɪn]	dünn	fat ⟷ *thin*
°**Wilma** ['wɪlmə]	*weibl. Vorname*	
°**Victoria** [vɪk'tɔːrɪə]	*weibl. Vorname*	
vampire ['væmpaɪə]	Vampir	
coat [kəʊt]	Mantel	
teeth [tiːθ]	Zähne	
witch [wɪtʃ]	Hexe	
hair [heə]	Haar	
broomstick ['bruːmstɪk]	Besenstiel	
dragon ['drægən]	Drachen	
rat [ræt]	Ratte	
to come up to s.o. [kʌm‿'ʌp tʊ]	auf jdn. zukommen/-gehen	
Help! [help]	Hilfe!	
What's the matter with you? [ðə 'mætə]	Was ist mit dir los?	
to **imagine** [ɪ'mædʒɪn]	sich vorstellen	
to **keep s.o. away** [ˌkiːp‿ə'waɪ]	jmd. zurück halten	

⟨**Revision and fun 1**⟩

1	himself [hɪm'self]	(er) selbst	
	to spell [spel]	buchstabieren	"Can you *spell* the word *dictionary*?" – "Yes. D-I-C-T-I-O-N-A-R-Y."
	dictionary ['dɪkʃənrɪ]	Wörterbuch	
	difference ['dɪfrəns]	Unterschied	
	pill [pɪl]	Tablette	
	to get up [ˌget‿'ʌp]	heraufkommen	
	to get down [ˌget 'daʊn]	hinunterbekommen	
4	memory ['memərɪ]	Gedächtnis	
5	mobile ['məʊbaɪl]	Mobile	

Unit 4

The junior school play

Step A

The Canterville Ghost

ⓐ The junior school play is in three weeks. It is a ghost story!

Mr Otis .... John Underwood
Mrs Otis .... Sally Cooper
Virginia Otis, their daughter....... Shabina Ismaili
Washington Otis, their son .... Mark Blackwell

An American family comes to live in England. Their name is Otis. They buy Canterville Chase, an old English castle. There are frightening stories about a ghost in the castle. But the Americans aren't scared of ghosts. At first nothing happens. Then one night there is a strange noise in the castle. ... !!!

1 I like ghost stories

I like
I read a lot of
I often read

ghost stories.
comics.
funny books.
music/computer magazines.
books about horses/... .
...

Oh yes, they're

great.
fantastic.
interesting.

Oh no, they're

silly.
boring.
frightening.
terrible.

SB

ⓑ Jenny hasn't got a part in the play, but she is the prompter. She and Shabina Ismaili are looking for clothes for the play in the drama group cupboard.

Jenny: Look, Shabina. This long skirt is pretty. Maybe you can wear it as Virginia. A hundred years ago women wore really long skirts and dresses.

Shabina: Oh, lovely. – This short jacket is good, too.

Jenny: Yes, one of the boys can wear that. What have we got for the ghost?

Shabina: Let's look in this box here. There are a lot of useful things here. These white tights look good.

Jenny: Here's a long white shirt, too. But it's not very clean. Oh look, there's even a white beard.

Shabina: Yes, that's important for the ghost. Let me try it on. – Aaah! Do I look frightening?

Jenny: No, you look silly! Come on, try the skirt on now.

2 Out of the drama group cupboard

Talk about the clothes with a partner. What can you say about them?

Example: – The red jacket is good.
– Yes, but the black jacket looks newer.
I think the black jacket is the nicest.

long dirty pretty old new clean nice short small good big

Your turn

What other clothes do you know in English? Write them down. Then talk about your favourite clothes.

Example: jeans: I wear jeans almost every day. My black jeans are old, but they're nice.

Tickets and prizes

Robert: Hi, David. Have you got a ticket for our play yet?
David: Yes, I have.
Robert: Look, we're selling raffle tickets, too. They're only 20p. Every ticket has a number, and the lucky numbers win a prize.
David: What are the prizes, then? Oh, they look more interesting than the prizes last year.
Robert: Well, Becky likes the computer game. She thinks it's the most exciting prize of all!
David: But it isn't as exciting as the other things.
Robert: That's only because you haven't got a computer.

1 Look at the prizes!

Which prize is the most useful / interesting / exciting / expensive ?

Example: Well, I think the book is the most interesting prize. – I think so, too.
Well, I don't think so. I think the computer game is the most interesting prize.

2 More exciting?

... more / ... not as | exciting | than ... / as ...

What do you think?
Example: computer games – videos: exciting?
– I think computer games are **more exciting than** videos.
– Oh no! Computer games are**n't as exciting as** videos. Videos are **more exciting**!

1. tennis – football: interesting? 2. English – Biology: important? 3. a science book – a joke book: useful? 4. the Ghost Train – the Spider: frightening? 5. an adventure playground – boating lake: exciting?

3 The most interesting, the best ...

Example:
1. *Robert:* I like English. I think it's **the most interesting** subject at school. It's my **best** subject, too.
What can the others say? Use different adjectives when you can.

2. *Jenny:* I like Berlin very much. I think it's the ... city in Germany.
3. *David:* Robert says Mrs Mason is the ... teacher at our school. But I think Mrs Dane is the ...
4. *Becky:* I try to take Maxi and Mini out every evening. For them, that's the ... time of the day!
5. *Sarah:* I like German. But it isn't the ... subject at school.
6. *Simon:* The computer club is the ... club at Haywood School.
7. *Kim:* 'Just Jeans' isn't the ... clothes shop in Nottingham, but I think it's the ... .

interesting **easy** **exciting** **nice** **good** **popular** **busy** **important** **fantastic**

Robert and the ghost

Robert has got a good part in the play – he is the ghost! He is very happy about this. But he is a bit nervous, too. A lot of people will be there.

Robert: Hey, Mum! Next week at this time I'll be on stage. I hope I'll be OK.

Mrs Croft: Of course you will.

Robert: Oh, I'll be so nervous. I'm sure I'll forget my words.

Mrs Croft: No, you won't. You know your part by heart.

Robert: But it's so difficult, Mum. I'm sure people will laugh when they see me as the ghost.

Mrs Croft: No, they won't, Robert. They'll all be scared. – Say something in your ghost voice again.

Robert (with a terrible laugh): I will be back on Friday the thirteenth … Ha - ha - ha!

I will laugh
he will laugh
they will laugh

I'll = I will
you'll = you will
I won't = I will not

4 The play

Put in 'will' or 'won't'.

1. The play … be on next week. 2. A lot of people … be there. 3. All Robert's and Jenny's friends … come, of course. 4. But Jenny's father … be there because he … be away that week. 5. There are no more tickets, so there … be an empty seat! 6. The people in the play … have lessons that afternoon, of course. They … be too busy! 7. Jenny is sure the play … be good. 8. But Robert thinks people … laugh in the wrong places. 9. Mrs Croft hopes Robert and his friends … feel too nervous.

5 Don't worry!

Say the opposite.

Examples: 1. Oh dear, I'll be so nervous! – No, you won't! I'm sure you won't be nervous.
2. People won't like the play! – Yes, they will! Of course they'll like the play.

3. I'll forget my words!
4. I won't look good in my costume!
5. People will laugh when I come on stage!
6. They won't understand the play!
7. People won't like the music!
8. The play will be terrible!

6 Sound track

a)

[w]

I **w**on't be **w**ith you on **W**ednesday.
Will you be a**w**ay?

[v]

I'**v**e got se**v**en **v**ideos.
The **v**et arri**v**ed **v**ery late in the e**v**ening.

[w] – [v]

We **w**alked down Lar**w**ood Gro**v**e.
Da**v**id **w**on't **w**ait!

b) *Listen to these words. Make two lists and put the number of the word in the list.*
Example:

[w]	[v]
1	

7 All about Jenny

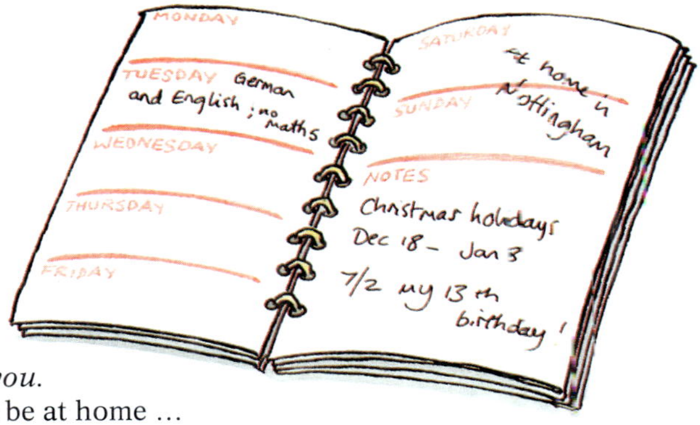

1. Jenny will have German and English tomorrow, but she won't have a Maths lesson.
2. She'll be at home next weekend.
3. Her next school holidays will start on 18th December. They'll finish on 8th January.
4. Jenny will be thirteen next February.

Your turn *Now give details like this about you.*
I'll be … next … I'll be/I won't be at home …

8 The weather tomorrow

	morning	afternoon	evening
In Nottingham	☀	🌧	❄
In London	☀	☀☀	🌧
In Berlin	❄	☀	❄❄

Talk about the weather with a partner.
Examples: What will it be like in Nottingham tomorrow?
– It'll be sunny in the morning.
– But it'll be wet in the afternoon.
– Will it be cold in Berlin tomorrow?
– Yes, it'll be cold there in the morning and very cold in the evening.

9 Kim

Kim sometimes has arguments with her parents.
She often thinks, "When I have children, things will be different …"
a) *Say what Kim thinks.*

When I have children, I'll … / I won't …

try to understand their problems
give them enough pocket money
get angry about little things
have arguments with them
buy nice things for them
listen to their music
send them to bed early
ask questions about school every day

b) *What do you think?*

10 Listening practice: The Canterville Ghost

Is that right?
1. Mrs Leinert knows the story of 'The Canterville Ghost'.
2. The ghost lives in the castle garden.
3. The American family is scared of ghosts.
4. The ghost walks down the corridor every night.
5. He plays tricks on the American children.
6. Jenny tells her mother about one of the tricks.

Looking at the UK: Theatre groups

Some schools do a play every year.

Children at churches and Sunday schools do a Christmas play.

Puppet theatre.

Children's theatre.

Your turn 1 What about you?

Find four interesting questions and answer them.

1. Do you like to watch plays? Where and when?
2. Are you in a drama group at school/at church/at a youth centre?
3. Who writes your plays? Who makes the clothes/gets the stage ready?
4. Who comes to watch your plays?
5. Can you talk about a school drama project?

Step C

The raffle

On the morning of the junior play Mrs Benson came into assembly with a big box There were over a thousand raffle tickets in it. She closed her eyes and picked the first ticket.

Becky: I hope one of my tickets will win. That computer game looks fantastic.
David: What numbers have you got?
Becky: Two hundred and sixteen, two hundred and twenty, and three hundred and forty-two.
David: Oh, I've got five tickets. Listen, the first number is coming up.

216 220 342

Mrs Benson: The first prize, the computer game, goes to number six hundred and sixty-six.
Becky: Hey, David. You've got that number.
David: What? Let me see. – Oh no, Becky, I haven't got six hundred and sixty-six. I've got nine hundred and ninety-nine. Look!

666 999

Unit 4

1 Numbers

a) *Look at the raffle tickets. Can you say the numbers?*

311 108 96 395 473 52 281

b) *Do you know the answers?*

1. How many days are there in a year?
2. How many hours are there in a day? And in a week?
3. The Crofts get ten pints of milk every week. How much milk will they drink in a year?
4. There are seats for 275 people in the Assembly Hall. But for the play they need 27 extra seats. How many people have got tickets for the play?

2 ⟨A song: 500 miles⟩ © von Hecy West, EBONY MUSIKVERLAG

2. Lord, I'm one, Lord, I'm two,
Lord, I'm three, Lord, I'm four,
Lord, I'm five hundred miles from my home. Five hundred miles, (four times)
You can hear the whistle blow a hundred miles.

3. Not a shirt on my back,
Not a penny to my name,
Lord, I can't go back home this-a-way.
This-a-way, (four times)
No, I can't go back home this-a-way.

Well done!

"Good evening, everybody. We hope you will all like our play 'The Canterville Ghost'. I'm sorry to say that Shabina Ismaili can't be with us this evening. She has got flu. So Jenny Leinert will play the part of Virginia."

In the first scene Jenny didn't have many words. Soon she felt fine on stage with the others. It was the Americans' first evening at Canterville Chase. The family sat around the table and Mrs Umney, the housekeeper, gave them tea.

Jenny thought about the sound effects. "I hope Robert won't forget to play the cassette at the right time!"

The first sound effect was lightning followed by thunder. Then Mrs Umney said, "Terrible things happen in this house!"

Now it was time for the thunder. "Come on, Robert!" Jenny thought.

But nothing happened. Then it came – the sound of pop music. Really loud!

"Oh no!" thought Jenny. "He's got the wrong side of the cassette!" The music stopped. Now it was her turn to speak. "Listen to the thu-thunder!" she said. And, of course, everyone laughed. Robert felt terrible. "What an idiot I am!" he thought. "I hope I'll be OK on stage. I'll be on in a minute now. Oh dear!"

When Robert came on stage, everybody was very quiet. In his long white shirt and the white beard, he looked really good as the ghost. Nobody laughed. "That's the most important thing!" thought Robert.

It was the scene when Mr Otis and his two younger sons first see the ghost. The boys aren't scared of the ghost, and they throw pillows at him. "Silly old ghost!" the boys shouted – and threw their pillows. Everybody laughed. That was fine. But then one of the pillows hit Robert's face – and his beard came off! People laughed even more then."Hey, it isn't a ghost, Mum! It's Robert!" called a child. It was Mark. "Hello, Robert!"

But after that everything was OK. People laughed in the right places – and everybody clapped a lot at the end.

"Well done!" said Mrs Mason. "You were all fantastic, and everybody enjoyed the play."

1 Look at the text again

Look at the text again.

How many sections are there in the text?

Can you find a title for every section?

Say why is it a good title?

Start like this:

Section one is from line 1 to line 3.

You can call it 'Before the play' because Mrs Mason is talking to the people before the play starts.

…

Go on.

2 The story

Here is a short summary of the play:

When the Americans arrive at Canterville Chase, they meet the old housekeeper, Mrs Umney. She tells them terrible stories about the ghost, but they are not scared. One night they see the ghost. Mr Otis tries to talk to him. But the ghost does not answer and runs away. When the two youngest boys throw pillows at the ghost, he is very angry. He plans a lot of frightening things. But the children play more and more tricks on him. Only Virginia is sorry for the ghost. One day she sees him in one of the bedrooms. So she goes in and talks to him. He likes her because she tries to understand him. Then he tells her how unhappy he is. He wants to die like other people. Virginia helps him and he gives her a present when he says 'goodbye'. At the end, the ghost is dead – and everybody is happy.

Now tell the story in the past tense: "When the Americans arrived ..."

3 After the play

Read the sentences. Who will say this after the play? What do you think and why?

a) You were all fantastic and everybody enjoyed the play.

b) Oh Robert! Why did you put the wrong cassette on?

c) That was great! Your ghost voice was really frightening.

d) Hey ghost! Where's your beard?

Example: I think Mrs Mason says sentence a) because all the children were fantastic and people clapped a lot at the end.

4 Make a fortune teller

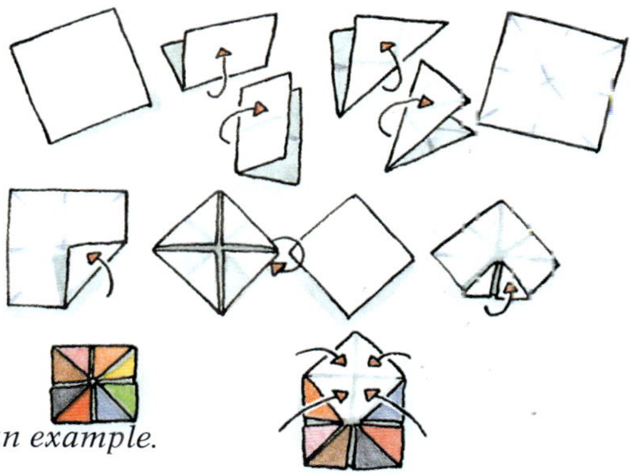

1. Take a square of paper and fold it.
2. Then fold the four corners to the middle.
3. Turn it over and fold the four corners to the middle again.
4. Colour it in eight different colours.
5. Then open one corner, and write four 'fortunes' in it.
6. Open the other three corners, and write 12 more 'fortunes' in them.
7. Then fold your fortune teller.

Now you can tell your friend's fortune. Here is an example.

You: Think of a number under ten.
Your friend: Three.
You: Right. One. Two. Three. Brown, black, yellow or green?

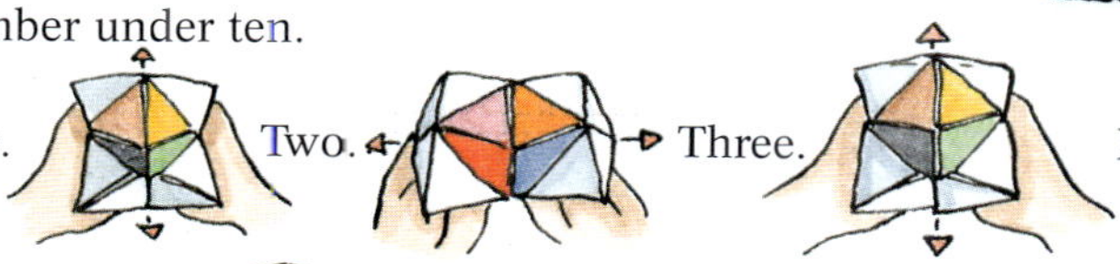

Your friend: Yellow.
You: Up or down?
Your friend: Up.

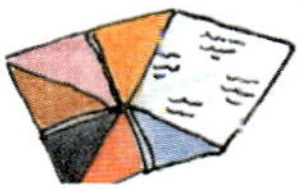

You: "You will win a prize in a competition."
Your friend: Oh, great!

Step E

Workshop 1

1 What's more ...?

a)

(frightening)

Example: The film at seven o'clock is frightening. The film at nine o'clock is more frightening. The film at eleven o'clock is most frightening.

b)

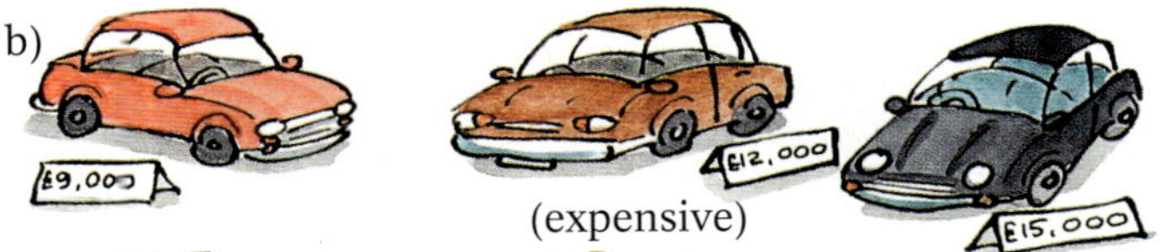

(expensive)

c)

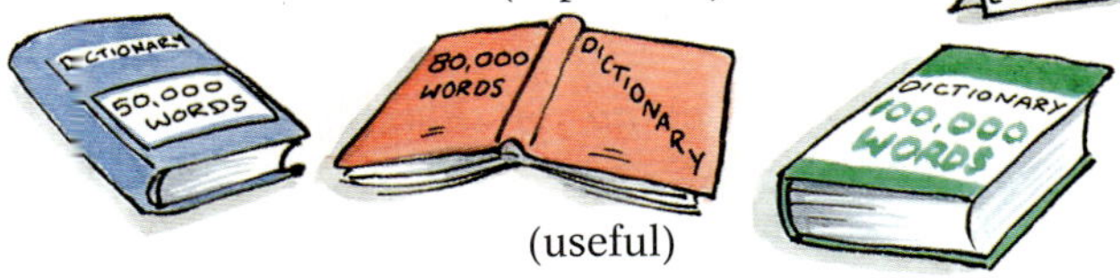

(useful)

2 Let's make a horoscope

These sentences are from horoscopes in English newspapers and magazines. You can use them to write new horoscopes for your friends. But read them through first.

You won't hear any bad news this week. There won't be too much homework. Your teachers will be very nice this week. This week there will be a big surprise for you. The weekend will be fantastic. There won't be any problems this week. Things won't be bad this week.	Careful! Somebody wants to play tricks on you. The streets will be dangerous. Be careful. Think before you talk to people. It will help you. Be clever and keep your money in your purse this week. Be careful! Somebody wants to bully you! A friend needs you. Why don't you talk to him or her? Bad news for you. But never mind. Everything will be OK.

1. Write sentences in the red box on a piece of red paper or with a red crayon.
2. Do the same with the 'green' sentences in green.
3. Now cut the paper so that you have seven green and seven red strips with the sentences on them.
4. Hold all the 14 strips upside down. Ask a friend to take three red and three green strips. That's his or her horoscope. Ask him or her to read it out to you.
5. Of course, you can write the horoscope down.
6. Maybe you have got some ideas for more red and green sentences?

Workshop 2

A riddle

Who is who and who does what?

There are five women in one town – Jane, Janet, Nora, Wendy and Liza. Next month it will be their thirtieth, fortieth, fiftieth, sixtieth and seventieth birthdays. All of them like different kinds of sports. Their family names are Black, Harris, Brown, Nosy and Cooper. Find out who is who. Here are some sentences to help you.

1. Only one woman has a first name and a family name starting with the same letter. She likes badminton. She's the oldest of the women.
2. Jane is not as old as Mrs Nosy. Janet, Wendy and Liza are younger than Jane and Nora. Janet is the oldest and Liza is the youngest of the three. They like football, hockey and cricket.
3. Janet's and Jane's family names are not Black or Brown. Liza's family name is not Black, Harris or Cooper, but Jane is not Mrs Harris. Jane, Wendy and Liza don't like hockey. Mrs Harris, Mrs Black and Mrs Brown don't like golf. So the youngest woman likes football.

Can you say who is who? Good luck!

	Jane	Janet	Nora	Wendy	Liza	30	40	50	60	70	badminton	football	…
Black													
Harris													
Brown													
Nosy													
Cooper													

1 Do you like sports?

1. What kind of sports do you know?
2. What's your favourite sport?
3. What about your brother/sister/friend …? What's his/her favourite sport?

2 Your riddle

Make a riddle about your family. Say the names, how old they are and what hobbies they've got. Now compare them.
Examples:

My brother's name is …

My sister is … old.

five years older than

three years younger than

the youngest/oldest

… likes …

Step

Let's check

Unit 4

1 The biggest, the most important …

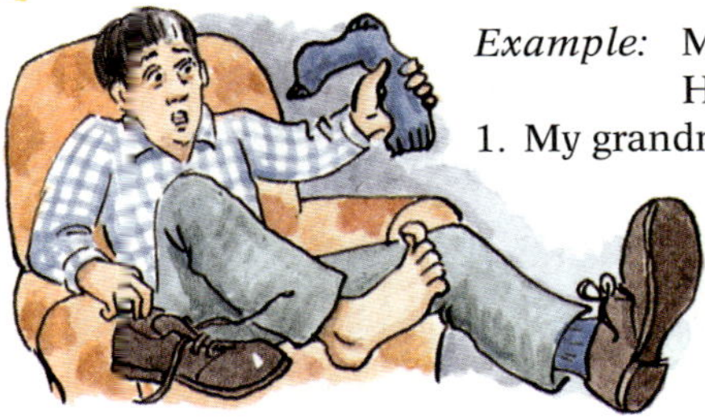

Example: My dad has got very big feet. (in the family)
He's got the biggest feet in the family.

1. My grandma has got a very important job. (at the Twinning Office)
2. I've got a nice room. (in the house)
3. My new story book is very exciting. (on my shelf)
4. My new shoes were very expensive! (in the shop)
5. My mum makes very good cakes. (in Nottingham)
6. My friend says Maths is a difficult subject. (at school)

2 Say it a different way

Example: *Becky:* Mini is cleverer than Maxi. – Maxi isn't as clever as Mini.

1. *Simon:* Comics aren't as interesting as computer magazines.
2. *Robert:* The Drama Club is more exciting than the Bird Club.
3. *Jenny:* The red dress isn't as pretty as the blue skirt.
4. *Mark:* The ghost wasn't as frightening as he Sheriff of Nottingham!
5. *Kim:* A book about science is more useful than a computer game.
6. *David:* Biology is easier than Maths.

3 I hope …

Make sentences with "I hope … will/won't …"
Example: *Robert:* I feel so nervous! (I – forget – words)
I hope I won't forget my words!

1. *Jenny:* Listen to the thunder! (it – rain)
2. *David:* I've got twelve raffle tickets now. (I – win – prize)
3. *Mark:* Here's Grandma! (she – play – game with me)
4. *Mrs Croft:* Shabina has got flu. (Robert – get it, too)
5. *Sarah:* This jacket is nice. (Mum – buy it for me)
6. *Simon:* I'm going to Mike's house. (his brother Barry – be at home)

4 Who is quicker?

Mrs Croft goes to London by car.
Mrs Dane goes by train.
Mrs Croft gets there in two hours and ten minutes.
Mrs Dane gets there in a hundred and fifteen minutes.

Who is quicker?

Unit 4 The junior school play

„Da steckt doch ein schon gelerntes Wort drin!"

Wörter behältst du besser, wenn du sie nicht einzeln lernst, sondern in möglichst vielen Zusammenhängen. Eine Möglichkeit dazu ist das Einhängen eines neu gelernten Wortes in seine Wortfamilie. Im Vokabular findest du dazu oft Hilfen (z. B. in dieser Unit *clean* → *to clean*). Bei einem neuen Wort solltest du dir immer die Frage stellen: Welches Wort kenne ich aus dieser Wortfamilie noch? Beispiele:

- In Unit 2 hast du die *past tense*-Form des Verbs *to meet* gelernt. Mit welchem Substantiv ist dieses Verb „verwandt"?
- Wie heißt das Adjektiv zum Substantiv *friend*?
- Man kann auch ein neues Wort in Verbindung mit seinem Gegenteil (z. B. *difficult* ⟷ *easy*), mit einer oder mehreren Zusammensetzungen (z. B. *shop – shop assistant – to go to the shops*) oder mit einem Wort mit gleicher Bedeutung (z. B. *at once* = *right away*) lernen.

Vocabulary

Step A **The Canterville Ghost**

ⓐ **junior** ['dʒuːnjə]	Unterstufen-, junger	
°**Canterville** ['kæntəvɪl]		
°**Otis** ['əʊtɪs]	*Familienname*	
°**Canterville Chase** ['kæntəvɪl 'tʃeɪs]	*Name eines engl. Schlosses*	
frightening ['fraɪtnɪŋ]	erschreckend, Furcht erregend	A strange noise in the night can be *frightening*.
°**Underwood** ['ʌndəwʊd]	*Familienname*	
°**Cooper** ['kuːpə]	*Familienname*	
°**Virginia** [və'dʒɪnjə]	*weibl. Vorname*	
daughter ['dɔːtə]	Tochter	Achte auf die Aussprache!
°**Shabina** [ʃə'biːnə]	*weibl. Vorname*	
°**Ismaili** [ɪzmɑː'iːlɪ]	*Familienname*	
°**Washington** ['wɒʃɪŋtən]	*männl. Vorname*	
son [sʌn]	Sohn	Becky is the Burtons' daughter, Simon is their *son*.
°**Blackwell** ['blækwəl]	*Familienname*	
strange [streɪndʒ]	seltsam, merkwürdig	
ⓑ **prompter** ['prɒmptə]	Souffleur, Souffleuse (*Stichwortgeber/in beim Theater*)	The *prompter* helps you in the play when you don't know your words.
cupboard ['kʌbəd]	Schrank	Where are the biscuits? – They're in the kitchen *cupboard*.
skirt [skɜːt]	Rock	At English schools girls usually wear *skirts*.
pretty ['prɪtɪ]	hübsch	
a hundred years ago [ə 'hʌndrəd jɪəz ə'gəʊ]	vor hundert Jahren	two weeks *ago*, ten days *ago*, *a hundred years ago*
ago [ə'gəʊ]	vor (*zeitlich*)	
dress [dres]	Kleid	
short [ʃɔːt]	kurz	
jacket ['dʒækɪt]	Jacke	

	useful ['ju:sfʊl]	nützlich	
	tights *(pl)* [taɪts]	Strumpfhose	
	shirt [ʃɜ:t]	Hemd	
	clean [kli:n]	sauber	
	even ['i:vn]	sogar	
	beard [bɪəd]	Bart	

Step B **Tickets and prizes**

	°**raffle** ['ræfl]	Verlosung, Tombola	
1	**most** [məʊst]	am meisten	What's the most *exciting* sport?
	I think so. [aɪ 'θɪŋk ˌsəʊ]	Ich denke schon.	
2	**Biology** [baɪ'ɒlədʒɪ]	Biologie	

Step B **Robert and the ghost**

	nervous ['nɜ:vəs]	aufgeregt, nervös	
	I'll = I will [aɪl, aɪ 'wɪl]	ich werde	
	stage [steɪdʒ]	Bühne	
	to **hope** [həʊp]	hoffen	
	to **forget, forgot** [fə'get, fə'gɒt]	vergessen	*to forget* ⟷ to remember
	they won't = they will not [ðeɪ 'wəʊnt, ðeɪ wɪl 'nɒt]	sie werden nicht	They *won't* come to the party. – Oh, I'm sure they will.
	voice [vɔɪs]	Stimme	
5	°**costume** ['kɒstju:m]	Kostüm	
7	**tomorrow** [tə'mɒrəʊ]	morgen	yesterday ← today → *tomorrow*
	°**detail** ['di:teɪl]	Einzelheit, Detail	

ten [ten]	zehn	**twenty** ['twentɪ]	zwanzig
eleven [ɪ'levn]	elf	**twenty-one** [ˌtwentɪ'wʌn]	einundzwanzig
twelve [twelv]	zwölf	**thirty** ['θɜ:tɪ]	dreißig
thirteen [ˌθɜ:'ti:n]	dreizehn	**forty** ['fɔ:tɪ]	vierzig
fourteen [ˌfɔ:'ti:n]	vierzehn	**fifty** ['fɪftɪ]	fünfzig
fifteen [ˌfɪf'ti:n]	fünfzehn	**sixty** ['sɪkstɪ]	sechzig
sixteen [ˌsiks'ti:n]	sechzehn	**seventy** ['sevntɪ]	siebzig
seventeen [ˌsevn'ti:n]	siebzehn	**eighty** ['eɪtɪ]	achtzig
eighteen [ˌeɪ'ti:n]	achtzehn	**ninety** ['naɪntɪ]	neunzig
nineteen [ˌnaɪn'ti:n]	neunzehn	**a hundred** [ə'hʌndrəd]	hundert

Looking at the UK: Theatre groups

	theatre ['θɪətə]	Theater
	°**puppet** ['pʌpɪt]	Marionette
	youth centre ['ju:θ ˌsentə]	Jugendzentrum
	to **get s.th ready** ['redɪ]	etw. fertig machen, vorbereiten
1	°**project** ['prɒdʒekt]	Projekt

Step C **The raffle**

°**Benson** ['bensn] *Familienname*

	a thousand ['θaʊznd]	(ein)tausend	There are more that *a thousand* pupils at Haywood School.
	to **pick** [pɪk]	nehmen, pflücken, auswählen	
1	**pint of** ['paɪnt‿əv]	*halber Liter*	= 0.5863 Liter
⟨2⟩	mile [maɪl]	Meile	= 1.609 Kilometer
	to miss [mɪs]	verpassen	
	to be gone [gɒn]	weg(gegangen) sein	
	whistle ['wɪsl]	Pfeife	
	to blow, blew [bləʊ, blu:]	blasen	

100	a/one hundred	**999**	nine hundred and ninety-nine
101	a/one hundred and one	**350**	three hundred and fifty
200	two hundred	**100**	a/one hundred

Step D **Well done!**

	everybody ['evrɪˌbɒdɪ]	alle, jede/r	
	to **be sorry** ['sɒrɪ]	bedauern	
	flu [flu:]	Grippe	
	to **feel fine** [faɪn]	sich gut fühlen	
	°**Umney** ['ʌmnɪ]	*Familienname*	
	°**housekeeper** ['haʊsˌki:pə]	Haushälter/in	
	°**sound effect** ['saʊnd ɪˌfekt]	Geräusch(effekt)	
	lightning ['laɪtnɪŋ]	Blitz	
	thunder ['θʌndə]	Donner	Before there's *thunder*, there's usually *lightning*.
	side [saɪd]	Seite	
	pillow ['pɪləʊ]	Kissen	You put your head on a *pillow* in bed.
	to **come off** [ɒf]	ab-, herunterrutschen	
	to **clap** [klæp]	klatschen	
1	°**section** ['sekʃn]	Abschnitt	
	title ['taɪtl]	Titel	The *title* of this book is Orange Line New.
2	°**summary** ['sʌmərɪ]	Zusammenfassung	
	°**dead** [ded]	tot	
4	°**fortune teller** ['fɔ:tʃu:n ˌtelə]	Wahrsager/in	
	square [skweə]	Quadrat, Platz	 A *square* has four corners.
	°to **fold** [fəʊld]	falten	
	middle ['mɪdl]	Mitte	
	°**fortune** ['fɔ:tʃu:n]	Weissagung	

Step E **Workshop 2**

°**Jane** [dʒeɪn]	*weibl. Vorname*	
°**Nora** ['nɔ:rə]	*weibl. Vorname*	
°**Wendy** ['wendɪ]	*weibl. Vorname*	
°**Liza** ['laɪzə]	*weibl. Vorname*	
kind of ['kaɪnd‿əv]	Art (von)	
first name ['fɜ:st ˌneɪm]	Vorname	
family name ['fæməlɪ ˌneɪm]	Familienname	
cricket ['krɪkɪt]	Kricket (*engl. Schlagballspiel*)	
Good luck! ['gʊd 'lʌk]	Viel Glück!	

In town

Step A **Something for everyone**

In the shopping centre

1 The shopping rap

A Where is the car park?
B It's over there!
A And where are the trolleys?
B In the corner somewhere!
A But where can we go now?
A I can't see the door!
B Where are the radios?
A On the lower floor.
B Do we need any butter?
A Yes, half a pound!
B Where is the popcorn?
A Just turn around!

A And coffee and tea,
B And a sandwich for me!
A OK, and some cheese,
B And an ice cream, please.
B What about biscuits?
B They look very nice!
A No, no, stop it!
A Just look at the price!
A And now to the check-out.
B Number seven is free!
A But where is my purse?
A + B … In the car! Dear me!

THE SHOPPING CENTRE *Something for everyone*

2 Let's look

1. What shops are there in the shopping centre?
2. What else can you find there?
3. What do you think you can buy or do there?

3 Listening practice: Where is it?

People often ask where things are in the shopping centre. There are people near the clock. That is on the lower floor at the bottom of the escalators. They want to find these places:

1. Sue's Tea Shop
2. Broadwood's Bank
3. The Taj Mahal Indian Restaurant
4. The Post Office
5. The Chocolate Box

Listen to the text and find out where the people want to go.
Look at the letters A,B,C,D,E on the plan. Which places are they?

Step B

Just looking

1 In the shop window

There are	some	sweatshirts trainers jeans shoes jackets …	in the window	–	Yes, but there aren't	any	socks T-shirts dresses tights anoraks …

2 Looking for T-shirts

Complete the dialogues with 'some' or 'any'?
Sarah and Becky are at the shopping centre.

Becky: Look, there's a new shop, 'Teens'.
Sarah: Oh, yes. It looks fantastic. They've got … super trainers over there in the corner.
Becky: Where? Oh, I see. Yes, they're great. But I can't see … T-shirts.
Sarah: Well, there aren't … in the window, but I'm sure there are … inside.
Now Sarah and Becky are inside the shop.
Sarah: Have they got … T-shirts here?
Becky: Yes, there are … super T-shirts here, but look how much they cost.
Sarah: That's my pocket money for a hundred years!
Shop assistant: Do you need … help?
Becky: Er – no thanks. We're just looking.

3 Do you know any good bookshops?

Make sentences with 'some' and 'any' and the words on the right.
Example: 1. I need a bigger dictionary. Do you know any good bookshops?

2. She's good at English. She never makes …		pets
3. Mike and Simon went to the newsagent's to buy		computer magazines
4. I can't make a sandwich because there isn't …	***some***	great prizes
5. Mike's not a bully. Bullies haven't got …	***any***	bread
6. The coconut shy is great. There are …		friends
7. I've got two cats and a dog. Have you got …		mistakes

4 Listening practice: Mr Leinert's day

Listen to the recording and take notes. Can you finish Mr Leinert's list for him?

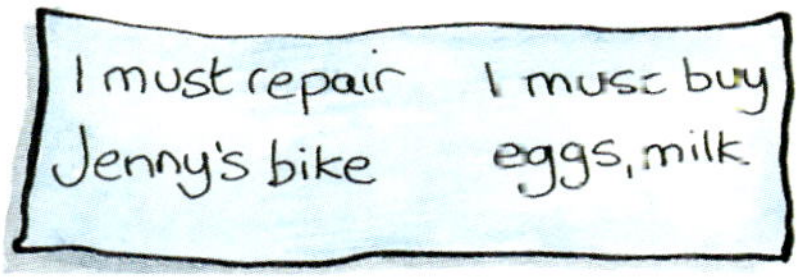

5 Looking at English

a) *'Some' and 'any' are a pair. Find other pairs in the posters. Make a list.*

some -	any -
something	anything

b)

Act little dialogues with a partner.

Are there … / Have you got …	a n y	boating lakes / old castles / snackbars / pizzas / forests / interesting animals / cheap houses	here?	Yes, / No, / Sorry,	there are / there aren't / we've got / we haven't got / you can get / you can't get	any / some	here.

c) *Write dialogues with the words.*
Example: Can you see anything? – Yes, I can see something near the door.

6 What would you like?

Ask the others:
What would you like for your birthday?
You can say:
I'd like …

7 Be careful!

What do they say?
Finish the sentences.

Example:
Be careful, Mark, or you'll fall over!

… you'll be late for school!
… you'll fall over!
… you'll feel sick.
… you'll get cold!
… I'll take them for a walk.
… I'll read it to you.

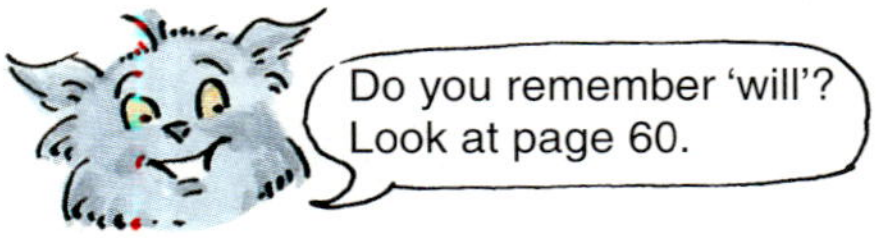

Be careful, Mark, or … .

It's OK, Mark … .

Come on, Kim, or … .

Don't worry, Becky, I … .

Wear your coat or … .

Don't eat too fast, or … .

Pieces of pizza

Last Sunday, Mark and David had lunch with Grandma Penrose at the shopping centre. Grandma Penrose bought a pizza for them. One pizza was big enough for two hungry boys – she thought!
"Can I cut the pizza, please, Grandma?" asked Mark. "If David cuts it, he'll take the biggest piece."
"Well, Mark," said David. "What if *you* cut it? If *you* cut it, *you'll* take the biggest piece."
"Stop it, you two," said Grandma. And then she had an idea.
"All right," she said. "I'll tell you what we'll do. If David cuts the pizza, then Mark will choose his piece of pizza first. And if Mark cuts the pizza, then David will choose first. If you don't like my idea, I'll cut the pizza."

If David cuts the pizza, he'll take the biggest piece.

8 What if …? *Make sentences.*

If David cuts the pizza, …	Mark will choose his piece first.
If Mark cuts the pizza, … ----→	she'll cut the pizza.
Grandma's idea: If Mark cuts the pizza, …	he'll take the biggest piece.
If David cuts the pizza, …	he'll take the biggest piece.
And if they don't like her idea, …	David will choose his piece first.

9 Plans for the weekend

Your turn

What will you do at the weekend?

If it's … 

I'll probably / I won't

read	go to	watch
play	visit	meet
see	tidy	make

Looking at the UK: Shopping in Nottingham

1. Do you like shopping?
   – Where do you go shopping and who goes with you?
   – Is there a large shopping centre where you live?
   – What is it called and what can you buy there?
   – Do you like it there?

2. Shopping centre or street market? Look at the pictures. What can you see in them?

Sneinton Market is a street market. It's open on Monday and Saturday mornings. There are lots of small stalls where you can buy many different things at very cheap prices.

The Victoria Centre was the first large shopping centre in Nottingham with a department store and smaller shops under one roof. The Victoria Market is in the centre, too. There you can buy fruit, vegetables, clothes and many other things.

Another big shopping centre is the Broad Marsh Centre. The shops and stores there are on two floors.

Step C

A guessing game

1 A game: Who, what or where?

Write on a piece of paper the name of a person, the name of a place or a word for a thing. Give the pieces of paper from your group to another group. They give you their words. Everyone in the group takes a piece of paper. You tell the others about your word, they try to guess who, where or what it is.

My word It	is	somebody somewhere something	
	isn't		anybody anywhere anything

Is it … ?
I think it's … .

in	the classroom. our school. a book. our town. …	on a CD. near … at home.
begins with a T (P…)		

Unit 5

2 ⟨A song: You'll never get to heaven⟩

1. Oh, you'll never get to heaven
in an old Ford car,
'Cause an old Ford car won't get that far.
Oh, you'll never get to heaven in an old Ford car,
'Cause an old Ford car won't
get that far,
I ain't gonna grieve my Lord no more.

Chorus
I ain't gonna grieve my Lord,
I ain't gonna grieve my Lord,
I ain't gonna grieve my Lord no more.

2. Oh, you'll never get to heaven
In a jumbo jet,
'Cause the Lord ain't got
No runways yet.

3. Oh, you'll never get to heaven
By Underground,
Because heaven isn't under
It's above the ground

4. Oh, if you get there
Before I do,
Just make a hole
And pull me through.

3 ⟨The Nothing-Doings⟩

Meet the lazy Nothing-Doings,
all they do is stand around,
when it's time for doing nothing,
Nothing-Doings can be found,
when it's time for doing something,
you won't find a single one,
for the Nothing-Doings vanish
when there's work that must be done.

nothing-doing ['nʌθɪŋ'du:ɪŋ] Nichtstuer – something ['sʌmθɪŋ] etwas – single ['sɪŋgl] einzig – to vanish ['vænɪʃ] verschwinden – work [wɜ:k] Arbeit – that must be done ['mʌs(t)‿bɪ 'dʌn] die erledigt werden muss

At the information desk

4 Excuse me please …

a) *Help the lady at the information desk and tell the customers where they can find the different places. Look at the table.* Where is the … ?

on	at	between	next to	opposite	–
the corner	the other end	the Post Office	the restaurant	the bank	upstairs
the ? floor	the bottom of	and the bank	the car park	the shop	downstairs
	the corner				over there

b) *You are in a large shopping centre in Great Britain. Ask for five places you would like to find. Then act it out with a friend.* Excuse me, please …

Where is the …?

Is there a …

Are there any …?

I'm looking for the/a …

Where are the .. ?

Example: Excuse me, please. Where is the bus station?
– It's on the upper floor above the supermarket.

5 Sound track

a) *Listen to the rhyme. Make two lists of the words with* [æ] *like 'sad' and* [e] *like 'wet'.*

Harry had a hat on his head.
Sally said she sat on the bed.
Barry fed a fat cat with bread.
Jenny's dad met a vet in red.

[æ]	[e]
sat	bed

b) *Listen again. Is there a 't' or a 'd' sound at the end of the words in your first list? Make four new lists. Read the words again, then say the rhyme.*

[æt]	[æd]	[æd]	[ed]
sat			bed

TUFF

I'm tough!
Mighty tough!
T-U DOUBLE F
See!
Good word 'tough' –
Strong! Rough!
Good enough
for me, see!

Don't need anyone,
not me, see!

Nobody loves me.
Love! Huh!
Who needs it!
L-U-V.
Silly word, love ...,
They say "I love you"
then they leave.
Empty words –
just deceive.

I get by,
Don't cry,
not me.
Got enough.

I'm tough.
See!

Plenty friends
on the street;
plenty places we can meet,
plenty food
for us to eat;
don't need shoes on our feet;
we're tough!
T-U-DOUBLE F! See!

Friends are mates,
there for me.
Special mates;
they care for me. See!

Is that love? ...
Could be ...

We'll see ...
we'll see ...
we'll see ...

1 Looking at the boy

– Say what the boy likes and what he doesn't like, what he needs and doesn't need.

2 Looking at the words

– Can you find the word 'tuff' in a dictionary?
– The boy spells the word 'tough' T-U-F-F. What does 'tough' mean?
– Go through the poem and find three words that rhyme with 'tough'.
– How does he spell 'love'?
– What does the boy mean by 'empty words'?
– Can you make a mind map with 'tough'?

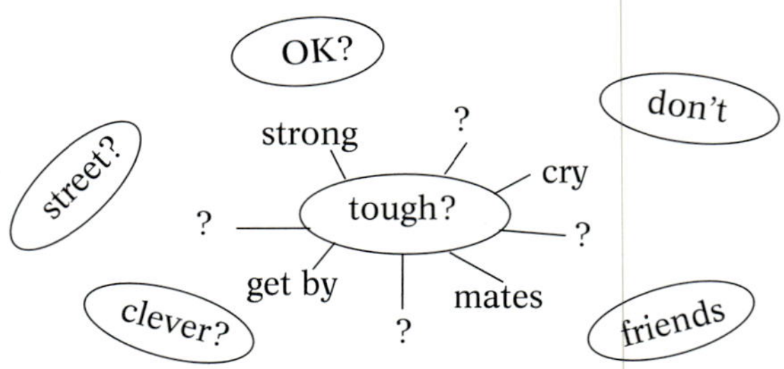

3 Looking at the sentences

– In most of the boy's sentences some words are missing. Can you find them?
– But the boy also uses 'full sentences'. Can you give two or three examples?

4 Looking at the boy again

– What can you say about the boy?

Is he nice? ... a bully? ... a friend?
... happy? ... friendly ... difficult?
... clever? ... crazy?

– How does he feel?
– Read the poem out loud and try to show with your voice how the boy feels.

5 A rap song

Make a rap song out of the poem. Find a rap beat.

Step E

Workshop 1

1 Some and any

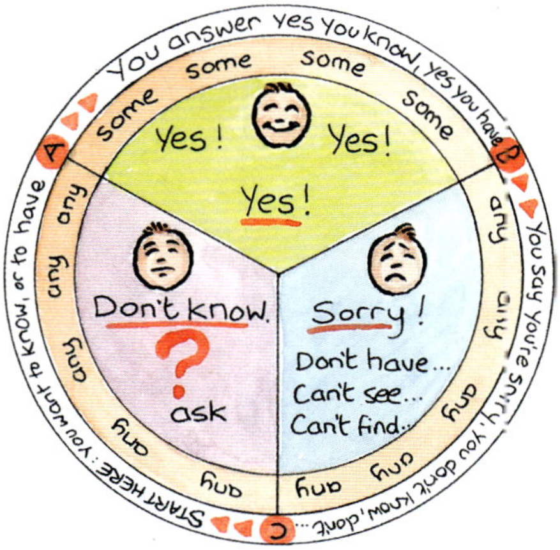

Make questions and answer dialogues with 'some' and 'any'.

Write two or three dialogues down in your exercise book. Then act one or two with a partner.

? famous people ? dictionaries? nice neighbours? picture postcards? ? ? leaflets about the town? Mr Bean videos? ? CD's with pop music? biros? ?

2 Posters

a) *Here is another poster from Monny's collection. Can you complete it? Use your exercise book.*

b) *Make another poster with 'no' words.*

3 WORD POWER

What can you do in a shopping centre? Start like this:
You can look at nice clothes.
You can eat … .

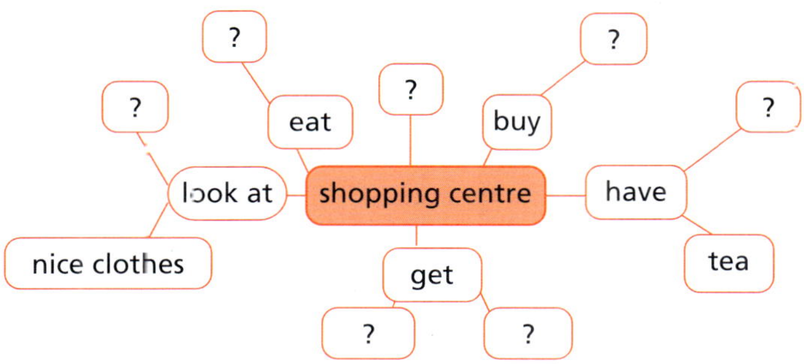

Unit 5

Workshop 2

1 Telling the way

a) *Fill in the missing words. Write them down in the right order (in your exercise book) like this:*

Dialogue 1	Dialogue 2
1= me 2= …	

b) *Check your two lists with a partner. (Has he or she got the same lists?)*
c) *Now act the dialogues with your partner.*

Dialogue 1

Man: Excuse **1**, please. Is there a post office **2** the shopping centre?
Girl: A post office? **3**, there's one over there, between Teens and **4** Centre Bank. Can **5** see it?
Man: Oh yes, I **6** it. Thank you very much.

Dialogue 2

Woman: Er, excuse **1**, please, I'm looking **2** a bank.
Boy: Well, there's **3** bank over there, next **4** the post office. And I think there's **5** upstairs, too. Hm, Broadwood's Bank, I think it is. You'll see **6** if you go **7** the escalator. It's opposite the top **8** the escalators next to the Market.
Woman: Thanks!
Boy: That's OK.

2 A true story

1. This is a true story. It happened in February 1986 near London. A young man, Mr David Morris, wanted to become rich but he didn't want to say a word. He wrote down this message on a piece of paper:

2. He went into a shop to try it out. It was a little jeans shop. He held up the message, but the young lady in the shop said: "I won't read that. Please go and play your tricks on someone else!" – Mr Morris left the shop.

3. The next shop was an Indian Restaurant. Again he held up his sheet of paper with the message on it. The man in the restaurant looked at it, then he smiled and shook his head and said, "I can't read English. Sorry!"

4. After that, Mr Morris tried it in the Chinese takeaway. But the manager there said that he did not have his glasses. He said he would look for them in the back room. From there he phoned the police. They were there in less than three minutes and took poor Mr Morris to the police station.

Step F

Let's Check

1 WORD POWER

Draw a small shopping centre. What shops do you want in it? What else does it need?

Escalators	Lift	Information	Bus Station
Toilets	Clock	Telephones	Car Park

2 A present for Jenny

What is the right word?

some **something** **somebody** **somewhere** **any** **anything** **anybody** **anywhere**

1. *Sarah:* Kim, it's Jenny's birthday soon. I can't think of … for her.
2. *Kim:* Well, I'm going to the Victoria shopping centre now. Maybe you can find a present for her there.
3. *Sarah:* That's a good idea. I'm sure I'll find … there. Can you see my purse …, Kim?
4. *Kim:* I think it's … near the telephone.
5. *Sarah:* Ah, here it is. Oh, there's nothing in it. Just 5p and … stamps.
6. *Kim:* Well, don't look at me, Sarah. I can't lend you … money. I want to buy the new 'Ghosts' CD today.
7. *Sarah:* But Kim. I've got that CD. … gave it to me for my birthday!
8. *Kim:* Oh yes! Can I listen to it now, Sarah?
9. *Sarah:* Yes, but later. If you listen to it now, I won't have … to go shopping with me

3 If …

Make sentences.
Example: 1. *Sarah:* If there's a table tennis club next year, I'll **join it.**

2. *Becky:* If I have time after school, …
3. *Robert:* If Mum is very busy, …
4. *Jenny:* If we have drama practice after school, …
5. *David:* If I don't have time today, …
6. *Simon:* If Mike lends me his new computer game, …
7. *Grandma Penrose:* If the weather is fine at the weekend, …
8. *Mark:* If David takes my crayons to school, …

do my guitar practice tomorrow.
make tea for her.
go for a walk with Maxi and Mini.
join it.
play it at the weekend.
take the children to the seaside.
not go swimming with Becky.
not give them to him again.

Unit 5 In town

Wörter lernen im Zusammenhang

Auch mit Wörternetzen kannst du neue Wörter besser behalten und wiederholen. Ein Wörternetz enthält viele andere Wörter, die mit dem Ausgangswort etwas zu tun haben. Das fertige Wörternetz kannst du dann in deinem *English folder* aufbewahren. Ähnliches kann man auch mit Wörtern machen, die in verschiedenen Zusammenhängen benutzt werden.

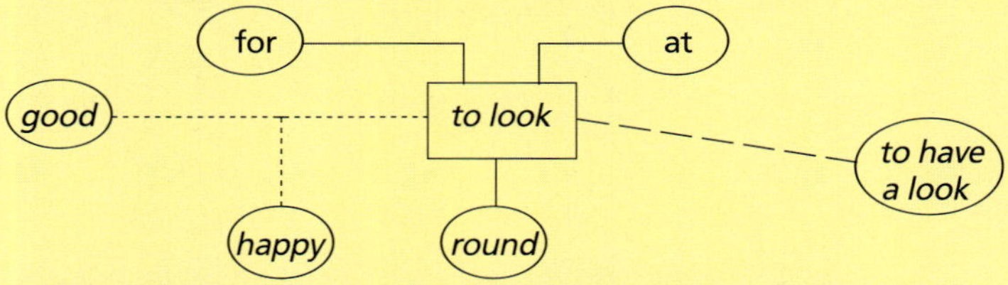

Du behältst Wörter gut, wenn du sie in Sätzen oder Wendungen lernst.

to forget → *I won't forget these words.*
→ *Don't forget the meeting this afternoon.*

morning → *In the morning ...*

ill → *You can't go swimming when you're ill.*

Versuche für möglichst viele Wörter selbst Sätze zu bilden, so lernst du sie am besten.

Step A **In the shopping centre**

escalator ['eskəleɪtə]	Rolltreppe	
lift [lɪft]	Fahrstuhl	How can I get upstairs? – Take the *lift* or the *escalator.*
clock [klɒk]	Uhr	Calendars show the date, *clocks* tell the time.
car park ['kɑːˌpɑːk]	Parkplatz, -haus	
information *(sg)* [ˌɪnfə'meɪʃn]	Information(en), Auskunft	
upper ['ʌpə]	der/die/das obere	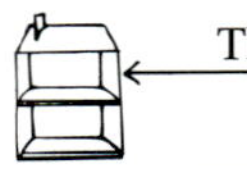 This is the *upper floor* of the house.
floor [flɔː]	Stockwerk/Etage	
newsagent's ['njuːzˌeɪdʒənts]	Laden für Zeitungen, Zeitschriften, Tabakwaren, Süßigkeiten, etc.	*At the newsagent's* ist eine Kurzform und bedeutet eigentlich *At the newsagent's shop.*
°**Jessop** ['dʒesəp]	*Familienname*	
department store [diː'pɑːtmənt 'stɔː]	Warenhaus	
store [stɔː]	Geschäft, Laden	
1 °**trolley** ['trɒlɪ]	Einkaufswagen	
corner ['kɔːnə]	Ecke	
somewhere ['sʌmweə]	irgendwo	
radio ['reɪdɪəʊ]	Radio	
lower ['ləʊə]	der/die/das untere	
around [ə'raʊnd]	um ... herum	
price [praɪs]	Preis	
check-out ['tʃek‿aʊt]	Kasse	
Dear me! [ˌdɪə 'miː]	Meine Gute!	

	sock [sɒk]	Socke	
	°**Teens** [ti:nz]	*Name eines Ladens*	
	°**Food Court** [ˈfu:d ˌkɔ:t]	*Name eines Restaurantbereiches*	
	food [fu:d]	Lebensmittel	*food*: eggs, apples, bread, cheese, …
	court [kɔ:t]	Hof	
	sandwich [ˈsænwɪdʒ]	belegtes Brot	 You make sandwiches with *bread* and *butter*.
	pizza [ˈpi:tsə]	Pizza	
3	°**Broadwood** [ˈbrɔ:dwʊd]	*Familienname*	
	°**The Taj Mahal Restaurant** [ðə ˌtɑ:dʒ məˈhɑ:l ˈrestərɒŋ]	*Name eines indischen Restaurants*	
	°**Indian** [ˈɪndjən]	indisch, Inder/in	 Achte darauf, dass *Indian* großgeschrieben wird.

Step B **Just looking**

	any [ˈenɪ]	irgendwelche	
	super [ˈsu:pə]	super	
1	**trainers** [ˈtreɪnəz]	Sportschuhe	
2	°to **complete** [kəmˈpli:t]	vervollständigen	
	window [ˈwɪndəʊ]	Fenster, Schaufenster	
	shop assistant [ˈʃɒp əˈsɪstənt]	Verkäufer/in	
3	°**bookshop** [ˈbʊkʃɒp]	Buchhandlung	
4	**someone** [ˈsʌmwʌn]	jemand	
	anyone [ˈenɪwʌn]	irgendeine/r	
	anybody [ˈenɪbɒdɪ]	irgendjemand	
	anywhere [ˈenɪweə]	irgendwo	
6	**Would you like** …? [ˌwʊd jʊ ˈlaɪk]	Hättest du/Hätten Sie gern …?	*Would you like* your tea with milk and sugar?
6	**doughnut** [ˈdəʊnʌt]	Krapfen, Berliner	
	I'd like … [aɪd ˈlaɪk]	Ich hätte gern …	
7	to **fall over** [ˌfɔ:l‿ˈəʊvə]	hinfallen	
	fast [fɑ:st]	schnell	

Step B **Pieces of pizza**

piece [pi:s]	Stück	Have another *piece* of pizza. – Yes, thank you.
to **cut, cut** [kʌt]	schneiden	
if [ɪf]	wenn, ob	
to **choose** [tʃu:z]	auswählen	He always *chooses* the biggest piece of cake.

Looking at the UK: Shopping in Nottingham

°**Sneinton Market** [ˈsni:ntn ˈmɑ:kɪt]	*Markt in Nottingham*
street [stri:t]	Straße
street market [ˈstri:t ˈmɑ:kɪt]	Straßenmarkt
roof [ru:f]	Dach
fruit [fru:t]	Obst
vegetable [ˈvedʒtəbl]	Gemüse
°**Broad Marsh Centre** [ˈbrɔ:d ˌmɑ:ʃ ˈsentə]	*Einkaufszentrum in Nottingham*

Step C **A guessing game**

1	**paper** ['peɪpə]	Papier	You can write on *paper* or draw pictures on it.
	to guess [ges]	(er)raten	
⟨2⟩	heaven ['hevn]	Himmel	
	Ford [fɔ:d]	*Automarke*	
	'cause [kɒz]	weil *(Kurzform)*	
	far [fɑ:]	weit	
	ain't (am not) [eɪnt]	werde nicht	
	gonna (= going to) ['gɒnə]	werde	
	to grieve [gri:v]	trauern	
	Lord [lɔ:d]	Herr	
	jumbo jet ['dʒʌmbəʊ ˌdʒet]	Jumbojet	
	runway ['rʌnweɪ]	Start- und Landebahn	
	Underground ['ʌndəgraʊnd]	Untergrundbahn	
	above [ə'bʌv]	über	The ball is *above* A.
	to pull [pʊl]	ziehen	

Step C **At the information desk**

	between [bɪ'twi:n]	zwischen	
4	**lady** ['leɪdɪ]	Dame	The ball is *between* A and B.

Step D **TUFF**

	tough [tʌf]	hart, knallhart	
	mighty ['maɪtɪ]	gewaltig	
	strong [strɒŋ]	stark	
	rough [rʌf]	hart, rau	
	empty ['emptɪ]	leer	
	to **deceive** [dɪ'si:v]	täuschen, betrügen	
	to **cry** [kraɪ]	weinen	
	plenty ['plentɪ]	eine Menge	
	mate [meɪt]	Kumpel	*Mates* are good friends.
2	to **mean** [mi:n]	bedeuten	

Step E **Workshop 1**

2	**collection** [kə'lekʃn]	Sammlung	

Step E **Workshop 2**

2	**true** [tru:]	wahr	
	°**Morris** ['mɒrɪs]	*Familienname*	
	to **become** [bɪ'kʌm]	werden	He got a new job: he *became* the *manager* of a *takeaway* restaurant.
	Chinese ['tʃaɪni:z]	chinesisch	
	takeaway ['teɪkəˌweɪ]	Essen zum Mitnehmen	
	manager ['mænɪdʒə]	Geschäftsführer	
	glasses ['glɑ:sɪz]	Brille	
	less [les]	weniger	

Step F **Let's check**

	to **lend** [lend]	(aus)leihen	

At school and at home

Step A

About food

The children in Jenny's class in Berlin are doing a project about food in different countries. They send Jenny a fax and ask her what people in Nottingham say about food. Well, Jenny is clever: she gives her friends and teachers some paper and asks them to write down what they think about food. After that Jenny collects the papers and sends a fax back to her class in Berlin. Here is what her friends and teacher have written down:

I think Chinese food is fantastic. Last year I got a Chinese recipe book for my birthday. – Now I often cook meals for my family.
Robert Croft

British food is the best! Roast beef with roast potatoes – that's my favourite meal. But I don't like cabbage. It tastes terrible!
Simon Burton

I love animals, so I don't eat meat or fish. I don't think it's right. Fruit and vegetables are also better for you.
Mike Newman

We grow carrots and beans in our garden. It's fun, and things from the garden taste much nicer. (And I think they're healthy too!)
Becky Burton

My wife always cooks healthy meals. Healthy food is OK. But sometimes I have crazy dreams: chicken soup … fish and chips … salami pizza … chocolate cake … a glass of wine … . Well, you know, it's only a dream!
J Stevenson (Teacher)

Hallo Leute,
und für Euch noch ein paar *'fly jokes'*. Ich habe sie bei den *lunch breaks* gehört und für euch aufgeschrieben!

Man: Waiter, there's a fly in my soup!
Waiter: Don't worry. It won't eat much!

Woman: Waiter, what's this fly doing on my ice cream?
Waiter: Maybe it likes winter sports.

Tschüs, Jenny

1 A 'food' word quiz

WORD POWER

Work in groups. Which group can finish the quiz first?

1. Think of four different vegetables.
2. What can you make with milk? Find three things.
3. What is the name for things like apples and bananas.
4. What do hens give us?
5. What is the name for the meat of a cow?
6. It's a meal, and you can drink it, too. What is it?
7. It's a famous Italian dish.
8. It tells you how to cook a meal?

2 Let's talk about food and meals

Talk to a partner. Ask and answer questions about food.
Example: Do you like fish? – No, I don't. I never eat fish.
or: Yes, fish and potato salad is my favourite meal.

Do you like bananas / …?

Do you cook meals for your family?

What do you usually have for breakfast / …?

…?

Do you eat meat / …?

…?

…?

What's in your lunch box today?

3 Words in English – words in German

a) *Look at the words in the basket. You know some 'food' words because they are like the German words. Start: I know 'banana'. It's like the German word 'Banane'.*
b) *Which food words aren't like the German words?*

4 WORD POWER

Put all the 'food and drink' words into groups. Make a list for your folder.

meat	fruit	vegetable	drinks	others
ham	kiwi	carrot	milk	butter

5 The ice cream rhyme

Listen to the recording.
Then say the ice cream rhyme.

I scream
You scream
We all scream
For ice cream!
Who screams for ice cream?
I scream for ice cream.
Why do you scream for ice cream?
Mmmmmmm
Ice cream is nice cream.
Don't you like it, too?

6 Sound track

These words with 'oo' go into four groups:
[u:] = food (8 words) [ʊ] = book (7 words)
[ɔ:] = floor (2 words) [ʊə] = (1 word).
Can you sort them out. Make four lists in your exercise book.

food book look too floor choose good cook foot shoot goose afternoon Sherwood door took poor soon school

7 The dinner rap

a) *Listen to the cassette and then say the 'dinner rap' (with a partner):*
A: Dinner's ready. Come and get it.
B: What's for dinner?
A: Something special.
B: Something special?
A: Chicken curry. Don't you like it?
B: Yes, I love it. What's for pudding?
A: Wait and see.

b) *You can make a new rap, too:*
– *Choose different words for box 1.*
(Example: fish and chips, beans and beef, chocolate cake, beans on toast, …
– Think of funny meals, too, but don't forget the rhythm!
– For box 2 you can say: 'No, I hate it!'

Step B

Sunday morning

(a) It is 12 o'clock. Mrs Penrose is working in the kitchen. David is helping her. He is peeling and cutting up the fruit for a fruit salad. And he is heating the soup. – And he is tasting everything, too.
Now it is quarter past twelve. Mr Penrose comes in.

Mr Penrose: How are things in the kitchen?
David: Fine. We've finished the big jobs. Lunch is almost ready. I'm just heating the soup.
Mrs Penrose: David has helped a lot. He has peeled and cut up all the fruit.
Mr Penrose: You make a good team, you two. – Mm. The fruit salad looks nice.
David: It *is* nice! I know – because I've tasted it!

Unit 6

1 Lunch is almost ready

Which sentences go together?
Start: 1. David has helped a lot. His mother says this.

1. David has helped a lot.
2. They have finished the big jobs.
3. David has peeled and cut up the fruit.
4. David has tasted the fruit salad.
5. David has heated the soup.

Lunch is almost ready.
It is ready for the fruit salad.
Now it is hot.
His mother says this.
It is very nice.

SB 2 Sound track

Do you remember the different sounds for -ed? Say these sentences:

a) [t]
I've worked all morning. But now I've stopped for lunch.

b) [d]
She has tried to save her pocket money. But she has only saved two pounds.

c) [ɪd]
David has heated the soup. He has tasted the fruit salad.

Now say these sentences. Do the -ed sounds go with a), b) or c)?

1. Mark has counted the knives.
2. We've cooked a nice meal today.
3. It's hot, so I've opened the window.
4. Thanks! You've helped a lot this morning.
5. David has peeled three apples.
6. Mark wanted to taste the fruit salad, too.

Ⓑ It is 12.30 now. Two guests have just come for lunch – Grandma Penrose and a young German, her bed-and-breakfast guest. Andreas Berger is from Dessau. He is looking for a job in Nottingham.

3 Jobs at home

a) *Say what the people are doing.*
Example 1. Jenny is peeling the potatoes.

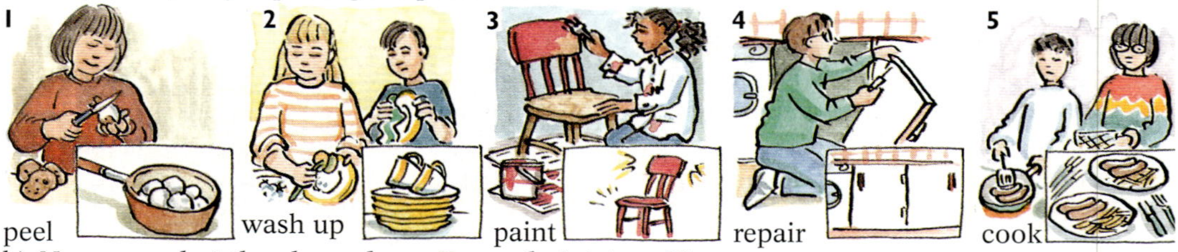

b) *Now say what they have done. Example (picture B):*
1. Jenny has peeled the potatoes. *Go on.*

4 Dialogues

Use the ideas and make little dialogues.
Example: "You look happy." – "Yes, I've just heard some good news."

You look	
scared	happy
excited	unhappy
angry	tired

Yes, I've just	
won a prize	hurt my leg
heard some good/bad news	had a big argument
run a long way	seen a monster
had a nice surprise	found some money under my bed

5 Listening practice: On the telephone

Read the questions, then listen to the recording. Find out what is wrong with these sentences. Please correct them.

It is 12 o'clock at the Dixons' house.
Kim hears the telephone.

1. Kim is talking to Jenny.
2. The Leinerts have invited Sarah to tea?
3. They never eat English food.
4. Mrs Leinert has cooked lunch today.
5. Sarah knows a lot about German food.
6. She'll be back after tea.

6 Cartoon fun

"Have you eaten?"
"Yes, often."

The guest from Dessau

The Penroses and their guests have had lunch. Now they are having coffee in the living-room.

Mark: Have you heard of Robin Hood, Andreas?
Andreas: Oh yes, I have, Mark. I've heard a lot of exciting stories about him.
David: And have you visited the 'Tales of Robin Hood' yet?
Andreas: The 'Tales of Robin Hood'? No, I haven't. You see, I've just arrived in Nottingham.
Mrs Penrose: You want to work here, Andreas. Is that right?
Andreas: Yes, for a year.
Mr Penrose: And have you found a job yet?
Andreas: Yes, I have. In a bookshop.
Grandma: But he hasn't started his job yet.
Andreas: No, I start next month. I hope I'll find a room somewhere.
Mrs Penrose: Don't worry, Andreas. We'll help you.

7 Have you done it yet?

a) *What have you done today? Answer the questions.*

1. Have you had breakfast yet?
2. Have you done your homework yet?
3. Have you watched TV yet?
4. Have you made your bed yet?
5. Have you seen your best friend yet?
6. Have you laughed yet?

b) *Make more questions like this for your class.*

have lunch yet? talk to your teacher yet? ... yet?
help anyone yet? hear about the accident yet?

8 Andreas

Make questions and answers about Andreas. Work with a partner.
Example: Has he come to England for a holiday? – No, he hasn't. He wants to work here.

Has he	come to England for a holiday just arrived in Nottingham heard of Robin Hood visited the 'Tales of Robin Hood' yet seen a film about Robin Hood started his job yet had lunch with the Penroses	?	– Yes, he has. – No, he hasn't. – I'm not sure.

9 Grandma's jobs

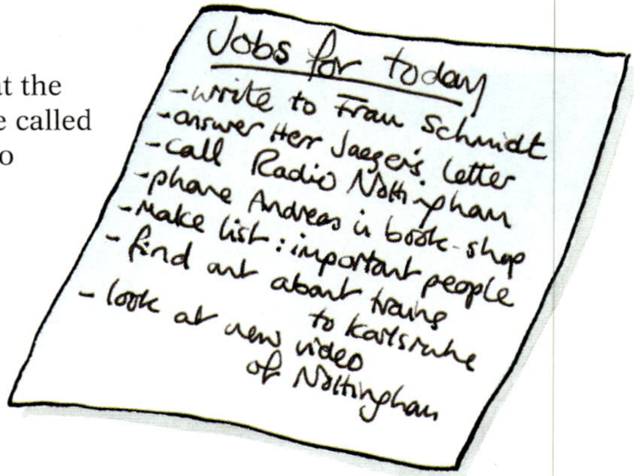

Grandma Penrose has got a lot of jobs to do at the twinning office today. But a lot of people have called her and now someone else is on the phone. So Grandma hasn't done anything yet!

She hasn't written to Frau Schmidt yet.
She hasn't … the letter from Herr Jaeger yet.
She hasn't … yet.
She … . *Go on.*

10 Have you done it yet?

A friend told you yesterday:

1. "I can't find my purse."
2. "I must write to my cousin."
3. "I want to try out my new computer game."
4. "I must talk to my teacher."
5. "Maybe I can repair that broken chair."
6. "I want to make a cake for my mum's birthday."

You have just met him today. You ask:

– "Have you found your purse yet?"
– "Have you … to your cousin yet?"
– "Have you … yet?"
– "Have you …?"
– "…?"
– "…?"

11 Looking at English

a) *Look through Step B and find examples of the present perfect.*
Write down on a piece of paper:
– a sentence with the signal word 'just'
– a question with the signal word 'yet'
– a sentence with 'not … yet'

b) *Now cut out the words and make a puzzle.*
Can your partner put the words back in the right order?

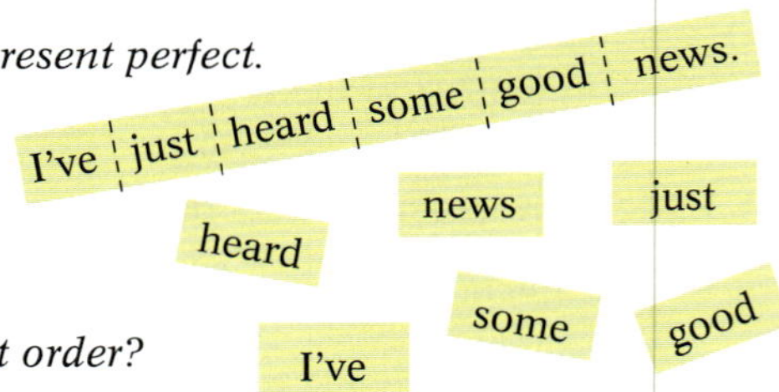

12 ⟨Some funny rhymes⟩

Humpty Dumpty sat on a wall,
Humpty Dumpty had a great fall;
All the King's horses and all the King's men
Couldn't put Humpty together again.

Humpty Dumpty sat on a wall,
Humpty Dumpty had a great fall;
All the King's horses and all the King's men
Had omelettes for breakfast.

Humpty Dumpty sat on a chair,
Eating ripe bananas.
Where do you think he put the skins?
Down his new pyjamas.

Step C

Lunch with the Penroses

1 At the table

Find the right pairs and read the dialogues with a friend.

A: Would you like a cup of tea? ---→ f)
B: Can I get you a glass of milk?
C: A glass of juice?
D: What about some fruit salad?
E: More soup, Andreas?
F: Can you pass me the sugar, please?
G: Another biscuit?

a) No, thank you. I don't like milk.
b) Of course. Here you are.
c) Yes, please. Fruit salad is great.
d) No, thank you. I can't eat anything else
e) Yes, please. The biscuits taste fantastic.
f) Yes, please. I'm very thirsty.
g) The sugar? Ah yes, it's over there. Here you are.

2 WORD POWER

Put the right words together to make new words. Example: chicken soup

roast	chicken	potato	orange	baked	beans	juice	salad	soup	potatoes

3 ⟨Let's play a game: Fruit salad⟩

a) Sit in a circle on your chairs. Now make 'fruit groups': some children are the 'apples', then there are the 'bananas', the 'kiwis' and the 'oranges'. Then take one chair away so that one boy or girl must stand in the middle. – Now you can start: The pupil in the middle shouts 'kiwis'! And all the 'kiwis' must run and find a different chair. They must be very quick. Of course, there is one boy or girl left over in the middle. Now he or she shouts 'bananas', and again … . But you can shout, 'fruit salad', too. Then <u>all</u> the children must run and sit on a different chair.

b) You can play this game with 'vegetables', too! (carrots, beans, potatoes, …)

c) Or you can play it with 'drinks'. (coffee, tea, coke, …)

d) You can choose 'animals', too. (alligators, hamsters, cows, …)

Unit 6

4 Listening practice: At the table

BREAKFAST? TEA? DINNER?

a) *What meals are the people in the dialogues having?*
Start: 1. They are having …

b) *Listen again. Find the words for these ideas. (Always try to be polite.)*

1. You don't want any carrots.
2. You want the milk.
3. You don't want anything else.
4. You like the coffee.

5 Role play: Would you like something to drink?

Practise with a partner.
Ask for different things to drink.

	something to drink	
Would you like	a cup of …	?
Can I get you	a glass of …	
What about	some …	
	…	

– Yes, please.	I'd like … .
	I'm very thirsty.
	…

– No, thanks.	I'm not thirsty.
	But can I have … , please.
	…

6 ⟨A song: There was an old lady who swallowed a fly⟩

1. There was an old lady who swallowed a fly.
   I don't know why she swallowed a fly.
   I think she'll die.

2. There was old lady who swallowed a spider
   that wriggled and wriggled and wriggled
   inside her.
   She swallowed the spider to catch the fly.
   But I don't know why she swallowed a fly.
   I think she'll die.

3. There was an old lady who swallowed a
   bird. But how absurd to swallow a bird!
   She swallowed the bird to catch the spider
   that wriggled and wriggled and wriggled
   inside her.
   She swallowed the spider to catch the fly.
   But I don't know why she swallowed a fly.
   I think she'll die.

4. There was old lady who swallowed a cat.
   Now fancy that to swallow a cat.
   She swallowed the cat to catch the bird.
   She swallowed the bird to catch the spider
   that wriggled …

5. There was old lady who swallowed a dog.
   My, what a hog to swallow a dog!
   She swallowed the dog to catch the cat.
   She swallowed the cat to catch the bird.
   She swallowed the bird to catch the spider
   that wriggled …

6. There was an old lady who swallowed a
   cow.
   I don't know how she swallowed a cow.
   She swallowed a cow to catch the dog.
   She swallowed the dog to catch the cat.
   She swallowed the cat to catch the bird.
   She swallowed the bird to catch the spider
   that wriggled …

7. There was an old lady who swallowed a
   horse. She died, of course.

Looking at the UK: Nottingham 'takeaways'

1 Food and takeaways

1. Look at photo A: What kind of food can you get there?
2. What kind of food can you get at the place in photo B?
3. Why do you call these places 'takeaways'?
4. Talk about the food.

I think … looks/tastes nice.

I don't like …

I like …

I'd like

…

Your turn 2 Your town

What about your town? Have you got any takeaways? What can you get there?

Step D

Saturday lunch

Sarah picked up her fork and looked at her plate.
"Mince and potatoes is boring," she said.
"Well, what's your idea of a good meal, then?" her father asked.
"Let's see," Sarah said "A nice curry with lots of vegetables."
"But vegetables take much more time, Sarah," her mother said, "and I've been very busy all morning."
"Well," said Sarah, "let me cook the lunch next Saturday."
"OK," said her mother. "That's a great idea."

Next Saturday morning Sarah showed her mother a shopping list.
"I've found a recipe for a curry, Mum. But I need some chicken and these other things. Can I have some money, please?"
Just then they heard the telephone. It was Jenny.
"Hi, Sarah. Do you want to come swimming with Becky and me?"
Sarah didn't want to say no. But this morning there was no time for fun with friends. "Sorry, I can't," Sarah said.

The shops in Mansfield Road were full, so Sarah arrived home late. She took the things out of her bag but she dropped some cream on the kitchen floor.
"Oh no!" she thought. But then she had an idea. "Tabby!" she called. "Look, cream! Good cat!"
And so Tabby made the floor nice and clean again and Sarah started to prepare the curry. First she cut the vegetables into pieces. It wasn't difficult really, but Sarah didn't often do jobs like that. She wasn't very quick. Tabby was quicker with the cream. When the vegetables were ready, Sarah looked at the recipe again. Time for the chicken now. She cut the chicken into smaller pieces. Tabby came and looked up at the table. "Mrrrow?" she said. "No, Tabby," Sarah said. "That's not for you! Go away!"
Sarah went to the cupboard to get a saucepan. When she looked back at the table, she saw Tabby with a piece of chicken in her mouth. – "You bad cat!" Sarah shouted. She opened the back door. Tabby ran out into the garden.
Kim put her head round the kitchen door. "Can I do anything?" she asked.
"No – er – thanks, Kim. Everything is fine."
But it was already twelve o'clock. Sarah worked hard in the hot kitchen. While she cooked, she thought of Jenny and Becky. They were luckier than she was!

The Dixons usually had lunch at one o'clock. That day they had it later – at quarter to two.
"Sorry it's so late," Sarah said when she brought her curry to the table. "But I've tasted it, and I think it's OK."
"You've cooked a fantastic lunch," her father told her. "You can be proud of this meal."
"This is the best meal of the week!" her mother said. "Do you want to make the lunch again next Saturday?"
Sarah laughed. "No thanks, Mum. Next week it's Dad's turn!"

1 Questions about the pictures

Answer the questions to tell the story.

PICTURE A: Why isn't Sarah happy with her lunch? – Who made the lunch? – What is Mr Dixon saying about next Saturday?
PICTURE B: What has Sarah got in her hand? – What does she want to cook? – Why is her mother giving her money?
PICTURE C: Where has Sarah been? – Why has she arrived home late? – What has happened to the cream? – What is Tabby doing?
PICTURE D: Where is Sarah working? – What time is it? – Why is Tabby outside? – What does Kim ask?
PICTURE E: What time is it now? – Why are Sarah's parents happy with her? – What does Sarah think about lunch next Saturday?

2 How does Sarah feel?

I think she feels...

tired, excited, worried, sorry, clever, proud, nervous, silly, angry, happy

Find a good word and say what you think.
How does Sarah feel:
1. when she says, "Let me cook lunch next Saturday"?
2. when Jenny phones?
3. when she drops the cream on the floor?
4. when Tabby cleans the floor for her?
5. when Tabby takes the piece of chicken?
6. when her sister asks her, "Can I do anything?"?
7. when she has made the curry?

3 More about food

-er, more ..., -est, most ...

What can they say? Find adjectives and put them in the right forms.
Example: 1. <u>Chicken curry</u> is more exciting than mince.

1. Sarah: Chicken curry is ... than mince.
2. Becky: This is the ... carrot in my garden!
3. Andreas: In Germany coffee is ... than tea.
4. Mrs Croft: An apple is ... than crisps, Robert.
5. Mrs Dixon: Kim! Breakfast is the ... meal of the day.
6. Mark: My piece of cake is ... than David's piece!
7. Simon: 'Woof' is the ... dog food at the supermarket.

cheap, small, popular, exciting, big, healthy, important

Workshop 1

1 Cups and glasses

Look at the pictures, and say what they are drinking.
1. Sarah is drinking a glass of … 2. Mr Dixon … a cup of … *Go on.*

2 Role play: What would you like?

Practise dialogues with a partner.
a) *Think of different things to drink.*

What would you like?

I'd like a … of …, please.

b) *Act little dialogues. Ask for things to eat. (Crazy things, too!) What does your partner say?*
Example: "Can I have some ice cream with my meat, please?"
"Oh no, that tastes terrible!"

Can I have some … with my …, please?

milk, carrots, ice cream, bread, fruit salad, roast beef, cheese, sugar, soup, cornflakes, tea, …

– Yes, of course. Here you are.
– What a crazy idea!
– Ugh! …
– Sorry, I haven't got any …

3 It's rhyme-time with past participles

Can you finish these rhymes? (You must say the words to find the rhymes.) Use your exercise book to write them all down.
You can check in the list of irregular verbs on page 207, but not No. 5, 6 and 7.

1
give – ?
drive – driven

2
spell – spelt
feel – ?

3
? – hidden
ride – ?

4
buy – bought
? – brought

5
wait – waited
? – hated

6
? – talked
walk – ?

7
? – looked
cook – ?

8
throw – ?
? – known

felt, talk, thrown, ridden, hate, given, cooked, hide, walked, look, know, bring

Workshop 2

Apple, blackberry and walnut crumble

This is a very simple recipe for a dessert for six people. You can prepare it in a short time.

Shopping list:
4-5 apples
frozen blackberries
half a pound of butter
a packet of sugar
a packet of rolled oats
a packet of flour
a packet of walnut pieces
a packet of brown sugar
cinnamon
lemon juice
frozen vanilla yoghurt

What you need in the kitchen:
a baking dish
a teaspoon
a cup

You can do it like this:

Put some butter in a baking dish. Take the apples and peel them and cut them into small pieces. Now put them in the baking dish.

Put the frozen blackberries over the apples and sprinkle them with sugar, lemon juice and some flour.

Mix half a cup of rolled oats, half a cup of flour and half a cup of walnut pieces with five teaspoons of butter, half a cup of brown sugar and a teaspoon of cinnamon.

Now sprinkle this mixture over the apples and blackberries. Bake it for 40 minutes. You can eat it with frozen vanilla yoghurt.

Your turn

1 A good meal?

a) *Name two meals which you like and two which you don't like.*
b) *Do you sometimes do the cooking for your family? Say which meal you can prepare. Make a shopping list for it.*
c) *Make a recipe for a meal which you would like to eat with your best friend. Write down:*
- *what you need*
- *how much you need*
- *what you do with the things*
- *what it tastes like*

You can draw a picture of it, too.

If you can't remember all the words, look at pages 103–105.

Let's check

1 WORD POWER

a) *Can you find the words? They are all new in this unit.*

1. It tells you how you can cook something.
2. You usually drink tea or coffee in this.
3. Carrots and cabbage are examples of this.
4. You feel like this when you've done something good.
5. You can use this when you want to put food in your mouth.

f••• v•••••••• c•• r••••• p••••

b) *Now can you explain these words?* CHICKEN GLASS FRUIT THIRSTY PLATE

2 David's room

Compare the two pictures. The second picture shows David's room 20 minutes later. What has he done?
Start: He has made his bed. He has … . *Go on.*

David's room at 9 o'clock

– and David's room 20 minutes later.

3 At school

Put in the right forms of the present perfect.

1. *(finish)* "Have you … the exercise yet?" – "No, I … . It isn't very easy."
2. *(start)* "Oh, has the lesson already …?" – "Yes, it … . You're late."
3. *(see)* "… you … my pen?" – "Yes, I … . Look – it's under your chair."
4. *(come)* "… Mr Stevenson … to school today?" – "No, he … . He isn't here today."
5. *(go)* "… Jenny and Becky … to the school shop?" – "Yes, they … . They want to buy some sweets."

4 Dialogues

Put questions and answers together, and make four little dialogues.
Start: "What would you like?" – "…"

What would you like? | Oh yes, please. | Can you pass the sugar, please?

Do you like this Yorkshire pudding? | Yes, here you are. | Yes, it tastes fantastic.

I'd like a cup of coffee, please. | Would you like some cheese?

⟨Revision and fun 2⟩

1 Mr Alligator

1. Mŕ Alligátor, máy we cróss the wáter?
   We've cóme to sée your daúghter
   Yés, you máy, yés, you máy,
   if you're wéaring sómething gréy.

   Mr Alligator, …

2. I don't mind what you do,
   if you're wearing something blue.

3. You may go and then come back,
   if you're wearing something black.

4. You may come, I think she said,
   if you're wearing something red.

5. Swim on down, swim on down,
   if you're wearing something brown.

6. That's all right, that's all right,
   if you're wearing something white.

7. It is quite OK, I think,
   if you're wearing something pink.

8. Yes, you may, my dear fellow,
   if you're wearing something yellow.

9. Yes, my friend, come join the scene,
   if you're wearing something green

2 Before the party

Becky and Simon want to have a party.

What they have already done:	What they haven't done yet:
1. ask their mum and dad about it ✔	tell their friends
2. write the invitations ✔	give them to their friends
3. buy things for a chocolate cake ✔	make the cake
4. get a book of party games ✔	write a list of the best games
5. find a good recipe for a fruit salad ✔	buy the fruit

Example: 1. They've asked their parents about it. But they haven't told their friends yet.

3 After the party

This is what the Burtons' kitchen looked like after the party …

But it looks better now!

clean
wash
close
throw away
tidy
wash up
put away

What have Becky and Simon done?
Example: They've washed up all the plates.

⟨Revision and fun 2⟩

4 Food sentences

Here are some English words for food.
Use the letters and write correct sentences.
Example: tomato – The old monster ate tomato omelettes.

cabbage salad potato beans carrot

5 Did you know that?

What is a fjord?
A Norwegian car.

How do you know that you've got elephants in the fridge?
Footprints in the butter.

Why do elephants paint their toenails red?
So they can hide in cherry trees.

6 Happy recipes

You can play this game in groups of three or four. First make the cards. You will need twenty-four. Draw the things for the six 'recipes' on the cards. Then turn them over (so you can't see the pictures).

CAKE	SOUP	FRUIT SALAD	CURRY	ROBERT'S SPECIAL	SANDWICHES
eggs	water	apples	chicken	sausages	bread and butter
butter	beef	bananas	curry	chips	ham
sugar	carrots	oranges	vegetables	beans	cheese
flour	salt	pears	cream	cabbage	tomatoes

Now deal the cards. (In a group of four, everybody gets six cards. With three people, everybody gets eight.) Look at your cards (but don't show them to the others). Have you got two or three 'things' for a recipe? Try to collect all four – like this:
Example: Daniel has got 'ham' and 'tomatoes'. So he wants to collect cards for 'sandwiches'.

Daniel: Alex! have you got any cheese, please?
Alex (looks at her cards): No, I haven't got any cheese. Sorry! – My turn now. Er … Felix, have you got any cream, please?
Felix: Yes, I've got some cream. *(He gives Alex the card.)* Here you are.
Alex: Thank you. And have you got any chicken, please?
Felix: Yes, I have. I've got some chicken. Here you are.
Alex: Thank you. Now I've got the 'curry' recipe! *(She puts the four cards on the table.)* – Er … Daniel, have you got any

Go on like this. The person with the most recipes wins the game. Remember: if someone asks you for a card and you've got it, you must give it to the person. If you haven't got it, it's your turn next. You must say 'please' and 'thank you'. If you forget 'please', you miss your turn. If you forget 'thank you', you must give the card back.

Unit 6 At school and at home

Lernen mit Eselsbrücken

Manches, was sich nur schwer behalten lässt, kann man sich – auch im Englischen – mit einer Eselsbrücke besser merken. Eselsbrücken helfen dir am besten, wenn du sie dir selbst ausdenkst. Du kannst sie aber dann auch mit Freunden austauschen.
Hier ein paar Beispiele:

- Wenn man nie so genau weiß, ob man *to choose* mit einem oder zwei „O" schreibt, sollte man daran denken, dass *to choose* „auswählen" heißt.
  Und beim Auswählen muss man sich ja auch zwischen zwei Sachen entscheiden, deshalb zwei „O".
- Man verwechselt die Fragewörter *where* and *who* nicht, wenn man daran denkt, dass in *where* die Antwort *here* schon drinsteckt.

Step A **About food**

	food [fu:d]	Essen, Nahrung	*food:* eggs, apples, bread, cheese, …
	fax [fæks]	Fax	
	to **send, sent** [send, sent]	schicken	
	to **write, wrote, written** [raɪt, rəʊt, ˈrɪtn]	schreiben	
	recipe [ˈresɪpɪ]	(Koch-)Rezept	Look! Here's a book with *recipes*.
	to **cook** [kʊk]	kochen	
	meal [mi:l]	Mahlzeit, Essen	– Great, let's *cook* a *meal*.
	chips [tʃɪps]	Pommes frites	
	roast beef [ˈrəʊst ˌbi:f]	Rinderbraten	
	cabbage [ˈkæbɪdʒ]	Kohl	I don't like *cabbage*. It's terrible.
	to **taste** [teɪst]	schmecken; probieren	Carrot cake *tastes* great.
	meat [mi:t]	Fleisch	
	to **grow, grew** [grəʊ, gru:]	(an)pflanzen, wachsen	
	carrot [ˈkærət]	Karotte, Möhre	Achte auf die Schreibung!
	bean [bi:n]	Bohne	
	chicken [ˈtʃɪkɪn]	Huhn	
	soup [su:p]	Suppe	
	°**salami** [səˈlɑ:mɪ]	Salami	
	glass [glɑ:s]	Glas	– Would you like a *glass* of water?
	°**wine** [waɪn]	Wein	
	waiter [ˈweɪtə]	Ober	
1	**hen** [hen]	Henne	
	cow [kaʊ]	Kuh	
	dish [dɪʃ]	Gericht	
3	**beef** [bi:f]	Rindfleisch	
	°**kiwi** [ˈki:wi:]	Kiwi	
4	**drink** [drɪŋk]	Getränk	
5	to **scream** [skri:m]	schreien	
7	**dinner** [ˈdɪnə]	Abendessen	
	°**toast** [təʊst]	Toast	
	rhythm [ˈrɪðəm]	Rhythmus	

Step B **Sunday morning**

ⓐ	°to **peel** [pi:l]	schälen	You *peel* oranges, potatoes and bananas.

Vocabulary

	°to **cut up** [ˈkʌt‿ʌp]	schneiden	
	°to **heat** [hiːt]	erhitzen, heiß machen	First you *heat* your meal, then you eat it.
	almost [ˈɔːlməʊst]	beinah	
ⓑ	**guest** [gest]	Gast, Besucher/in	

Step B **The guest from Dessau**

11	°**present perfect** [ˈpreznt ˈpɜːfɪkt]	Perfekt
	°**signal** [ˈsɪgnl]	Signal

Step C **Lunch with the Penroses**

	juice [dʒuːs]	Saft
	thirsty [ˈθɜːstɪ]	durstig
	cup [kʌp]	Tasse
2	to **bake** [beɪk]	backen
4	**polite** [pəˈlaɪt]	höflich
⟨6⟩	to swallow [ˈswɒləʊ]	(hinunter)schlucken
	fly [flaɪ]	Fliege
	to die [daɪ]	sterben
	spider [ˈspaɪdə]	Spinne
	to wriggle [ˈrɪgl]	sich schlängeln, zappeln
	absurd [əbˈsɜːd]	absurd
	fancy that [ˈfænsɪ ˈðæt]	so was
	what a hog [ˌwɒt‿ə ˈhɒg]	was für ein Schwein

January	[ˈdʒænjʊərɪ]	Januar
February	[ˈfebrʊərɪ]	Februar
March	[mɑːtʃ]	März
April	[ˈeɪprəl]	April
May	[meɪ]	Mai
June	[dʒuːn]	Juni
July	[dʒʊˈlaɪ]	Juli
August	[ˈɔːgəst]	August
September	[sepˈtembə]	September
October	[ɒkˈtəʊbə]	Oktober
November	[nəʊˈvembə]	November
December	[dɪˈsembə]	Dezember

Looking at the UK: Nottingham 'takeaways'

takeaway [ˈteɪkəˌweɪ]	Imbissstube, Schnellgaststätte mit Straßenverkauf

Step D **Saturday lunch**

	fork [fɔːk]	Gabel
	plate [pleɪt]	Teller
	°**mince** [mɪns]	Hackfleisch
	°**curry** [ˈkʌrɪ]	Curry *(indisches Gericht)*
	cream [kriːm]	Sahne
	to **prepare** [prɪˈpeə]	vorbereiten, zubereiten
	saucepan [ˈsɔːspən]	Topf
	already [ɔːlˈredɪ]	schon
	to **work hard** [hɑːd]	hart/schwer arbeiten
	while [waɪl]	während
	to **be proud of** [biː ˈpraʊd‿əv]	stolz sein auf
2	to **drop** [drɒp]	fallen(lassen)
3	**crisps** [krɪsps]	(Kartoffel-)Chips

Step E **Workshop 1**

2	°**cornflakes** [ˈkɔːnfleɪks]	Cornflakes

3	°**rhyme-time** ['raɪm ˌtaɪm]	Zeit für Reime	
	°**past participle** ['pɑːst 'pɑːtɪsɪpl]	Partizip Perfekt	
	to **drive, drove, driven** ['drɪvn]	fahren	*Have you driven* your father's new car?
	to **spell, spelt, spelt** [spelt]	buchstabieren	
	to **know, knew, known** [nəʊn]	wissen, kennen	
	to **throw, threw, thrown** [θrəʊn]	werfen	
	to **ride, rode, ridden** ['rɪdn]	reiten	

Step E **Workshop 2**

blackberry ['blækbərɪ]	Brombeere	*Blackberries* are a kind of fruit.
walnut ['wɔːlnʌt]	Walnuss	
crumble ['krʌmbl]	Streusel	
simple ['sɪmpl]	einfach	Apple *crumble* is *simple* to make.
dessert [dɪ'zɜːt]	Nachtisch	
to **freeze, froze, frozen** ['frəʊzn]	gefrieren, tiefkühlen	
rolled oats ['rəʊld 'əʊts]	Haferflocken	
flour ['flaʊə]	Mehl	
cinnamon ['sɪnəmən]	Zimt	
lemon ['lemən]	Zitrone	
vanilla [və'nɪlə]	Vanille	
yoghurt ['jɒgət]	Joghurt	*Yoghurt* is healthy and good for you
baking dish ['beɪkɪŋ 'dɪʃ]	Backform	
teaspoon ['tiːspuːn]	Teelöffel	
to **sprinkle** ['sprɪŋkl]	streuen	
mixture ['mɪkstʃə]	Mischung	

Step F **Let's check**

1	to **explain** [ɪks'pleɪn]	erklären
4	**Yorkshire pudding** ['jɔːkʃə 'pʊdɪŋ]	Yorkshire pudding *(engl. Gericht aus Mehl, Milch usw.)*

⟨Revision and fun 2⟩

1	may [meɪ]	dürfen
	to cross [krɒs]	überqueren
3	to clean [kliːn]	sauber machen
5	fjord [fjɔːd]	Fjord
	Norwegian [nɔː'wiːdʒən]	norwegisch; Norweger/in
	fridge [frɪdʒ]	Kühlschrank
	footprint ['fʊtprɪnt]	Fußabdruck
	toenail ['təʊneɪl]	Zehennagel
	cherry ['tʃerɪ]	Kirsche
6	beef [biːf]	Rindfleisch
	salt [sɔːlt]	Salz
	pear [peə]	Birne
	cream [kriːm]	Sahne
	chips [tʃɪps]	Pommes frites

Holidays

Step A

Holidays in Britain

Spend a weekend in **London** – one of the most exciting cities in the world. You'll love it, with its museums, theatres and shops.

*What about a holiday in a caravan or a hotel at the seaside? The **Isle of Wight** with its beautiful beaches is ideal for swimming and all water sports. And you can travel round the island in one day.*

ADVENTURE HOLIDAYS 12–16

Wales
Six full days with your own horse! You can ride for hours through the Welsh hills.

Scotland is great for an adventure holiday. Do you like mountain bikes? Volleyball? Hill walks? Climbing? You can do different things every day!

1 Can you find out?

a) Look at these leaflets for holidays.
Can you find the places on the map of the UK at the front of the book?
Say where the places are – and what you know about them.
Example: The Isle of Wight is in the south. It has got lovely beaches.

mountains sea hills city island

b) *Now say where you would like to go – and why.* *Example:* I'd like to go to London. I think big cities are exciting.

Your turn 2 Where did you go?

Talk about one of your holidays. Say where you went – and what you did there.

Last year Last spring/summer/autumn/winter Two/… years ago	I we	went to … stayed at/in … spent … days/weeks at/in … travelled round …	a the

caravan hotel beach forest castles farm mountains museums lake hills holiday flat

Example: Last summer we went to Rügen. We stayed in a holiday flat on the island. We went swimming every day. The beaches were beautiful.

3 Where is it?

a) *What's to the north (east, west, south) of your school? – Say two or three things.*
Example: The car park is to the …
(*Now think of:* canteen, playground, bike shed, bus stop, …)

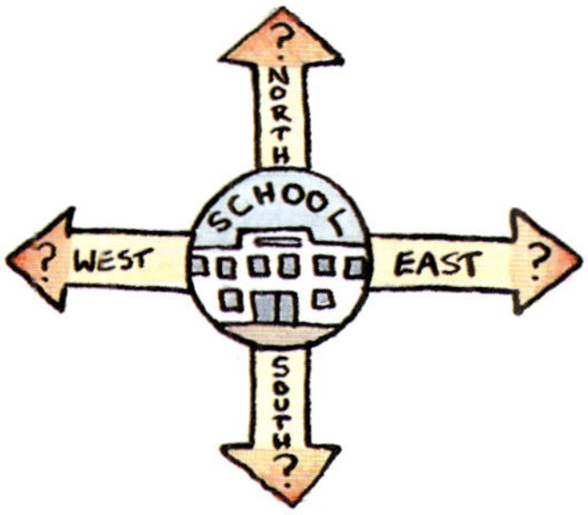

b) *What have you got to the west (east, north, south) of your village or town or city?*
Example: To the north we've got a/the …
or: To the east there is/are a/the …

4 WORD POWER

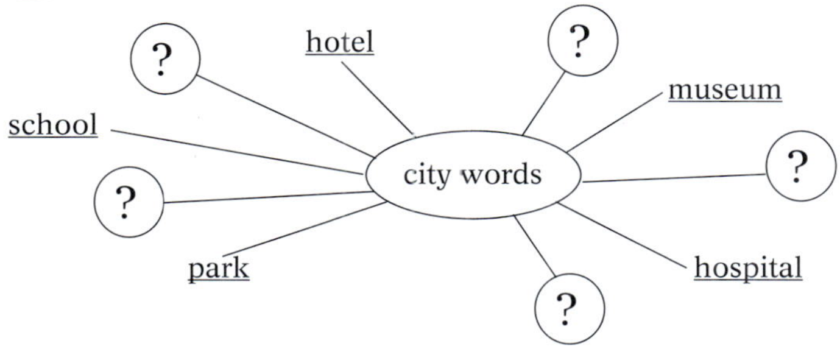

p•st •ff•c•
st•t••n
r•st••r•nt
c•r p•rk
th••tre
?

5 ⟨A song: Row, row, row your boat⟩

6 Sound track: Words with 'o'

Where do the words go? Which are the right families?

love
whose
worried
holidays
shop blue
hotel north
fork
only

Looking at the UK: Wales

What can you see on the map?
Find out what people can do in Wales.
These words will help you:

go sailing climb visit see surfing cycle go swimming go fishing go go pony-trekking

There is a lot of music and dancing and piping (with bagpipes). People wear their kilts.

I've got a farm in the south of Scotland. I've got more than a thousand sheep.
In summer it can be very warm and sunny in Scotland. But the weather can change quickly. Then it's wet and stormy, and the lochs and mountains can be dangerous.

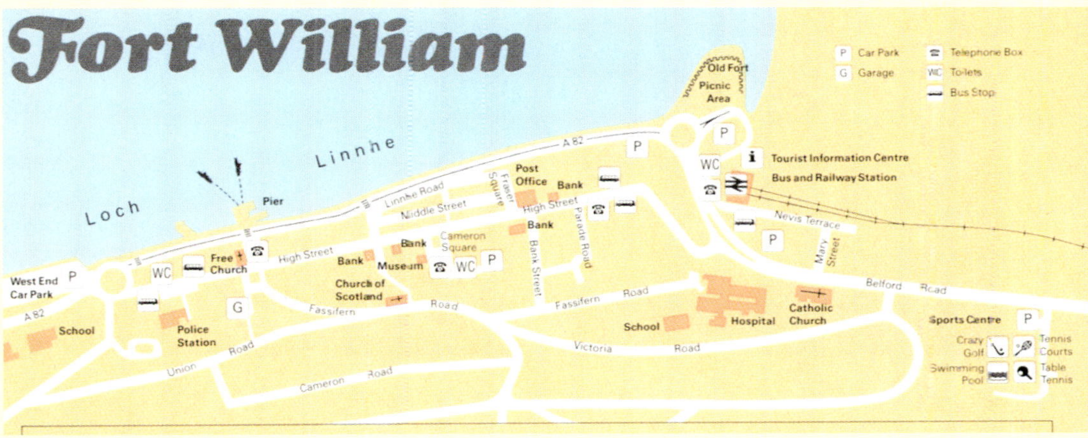

Look at all the information, and you'll find the answers to these questions.

1. You need some information.
   - Where's the Tourist Information Centre?
     – It's at the ... station.

2. You want to change some money.
   - Where are the banks?

3. You want to go swimming.
   - Where's the swimming pool?
   - Can you do anything else there?

Step B

Before the Easter holidays

The Leinerts want to go away for a week – and take David with them, too.

Jenny: Look, David. 'Cycling in the Lake District'. That's great!

David: I like cycling, too. But I hate cycling up hills!

Jenny: What do you like doing on holiday then?

David: Well, I like swimming, and I enjoy playing on the beach.

Jenny: So do I, David. But we can't do that in April!

Mrs Leinert: What about Scotland? Walking is nice at this time of the year. And you like looking at old castles, David.

David: Oh yes, great idea.

1 What do they say?

a)

Jenny:	Swimming Riding Cycling		fun!
David:	Cycling up hills Playing on the beach	is	great!
Mrs Leinert:	Looking at old castles Walking		terrible!
			no fun!

Example:
Jenny: Cycling is great.

b) *What do you know about them?*

Example: Jenny likes cycling.

Jenny	likes	swimming.
David	enjoys	… .
Mrs Leinert	hates	
Mr Leinert		

2 What do you like?

Example: I like cycling. But I hate cycling up hills!

I like …
I really enjoy …
But I don't like …
I hate …

swimming   acting   cooking   drawing   reading
cycling   running   walking   collecting …
watching TV   taking photos   going to the cinema   …

3 Looking at English

Write four sentences about your hobbies. Say what you like doing.

… is my hobby.   … is fun, too.
I love … .   I like …, too.

Football/Swimming is my hobby.
Playing football is my hobby.
I like watching football, too.

4 Who am I?

Collect information about the characters in your English book. Now you are one of the characters (or somebody in your class). But who? Can your friends find out?

Example: – Do you like acting?
You: No, I don't.
– Do you enjoy cooking?
You: Er, I'm not sure! But I don't think so.
– Do you like playing the guitar?
You: Yes, I do
– Then you must be David!
You: Yes, I am.

From Jenny's travel diary

April 3rd

Our first night in Scotland! We left Nottingham after breakfast, and drove up the M1. Dad drove in the morning (Mum read the map), and Mum drove in the afternoon (Dad read the map, and we went wrong twice!). We arrived here at five o'clock.
We have found a nice place for bed and breakfast with Mr and Mrs MacTavish.

Mrs MacTavish has given us a big Scottish tea. David and I can see Loch Lomond from our windows. Mum and Dad have taken the big room. But they can only see the garages from their windows.
The lake looks lovely. We haven't been out on it yet. But there's a boat for guests so we can go rowing tomorrow.

5 In Scotland

arrive — take/bags out of car — make/tea — write/travel diary — go/bed

a) It is the Leinerts' first day in Scotland. *Say what has just happened.*
Example: 1. Here you can see the Leinerts. They **have just arrived**.

b) Now it is the next day.
Finish the sentences. Use the simple past and say what happened on their first day.
Example: 1. It was five o'clock when **the Leinerts arrived**.
1. It was five o'clock when … .
2. Before they went in, Mr Leinert and David … .
3. First Mrs MacTavish showed them the rooms, then she … .
4. After tea Jenny … .
5. The Leinerts were tired in the evening, and at 9.30 … .

6 At home

Robert and his mother are at home in the Easter holidays.
Example: 1. *Mrs Croft:* (put your bike away) — *Robert:* (yes – two minutes ago)
Mrs Croft: **Have you** put your bike away? — *Robert:* Yes, **I have**, Mum. **I put it away** two minutes ago.

2. *Robert:* (see my new comic?) — *Mrs Croft:* (no – sorry)
3. *Mrs Croft:* (make your bed?) — *Robert:* (yes – after breakfast)
4. *Mrs Croft:* (eat the last apple?) — *Robert:* (yes – yesterday evening)
5. *Robert:* (wash my red pullover) — *Mrs Croft:* (no – sorry)
6. *Robert:* (buy a new film for the camera?) — *Mrs Croft:* (yes – last week)
7. *Mrs Croft:* (take those letters to the post?) — *Robert:* (no – sorry)
8. *Mrs Croft:* (do the washing-up?) — *Robert:* (yes – half an hour ago)

Have you ever?

Mrs MacTavish is talking to the Leinerts at breakfast time the next day.

7 What about you?

a)

Have you ever	travelled by plane? stayed at a hotel? ridden a horse? been to Britain?	– Yes, I have. I	travelled by plane to … stayed … rode … was …	last year/week/ … two years ago. …
		– No, I haven't./No, not yet.		

b) *Think of more questions. Then ask your friends.*

Here are some ideas:

swim in a lake · play beach ball · row a boat · eat porridge · …

8 David and Jenny

Find Jenny's answers.

1. Let's get some postcards.
2. Look at those two men in kilts over there!
3. I don't think I'll go in this museum.
4. I think I'll buy some chocolate.
5. Would you like the last cheese sandwich?
6. The new Robin Hood film is on at the cinema.

I've already seen them, David.

No, thanks. I've already had three.

But you've already eaten two bars today!

I know. But I've already seen it in Nottingham.

But David! Dad has already bought four tickets.

I don't need any. I've already written five.

9 Listening practice: Out on Loch Lomond

a) *Listen to the three scenes on the recording. Say where they are in the three scenes.*

b) *Now listen to the scenes again. Try to find out …*

(Scene 1) 1. … what the MacTavishes' boat is like. 2. … who gets in the boat first.
(Scene 2) 3. … who likes rowing. 4. … what David thinks is 'funny' when you're rowing.
(Scene 3) 5. … why David wants to go back. 6. … why it's better to stay on the island.

Unit 7

Step C

At Fort William

It is the Leinerts' third day in Scotland. Now they are staying at the MacTavishes' house near Fort William.

Mr Leinert: What about climbing Ben Nevis tomorrow? It's so near here.
Jenny: And it's the highest mountain in the UK. Great idea, Dad!
Mrs Leinert: Well, let's see what the weather is like tomorrow. It's no good being out all day in the rain!
David: It won't rain. We're having lovely weather!
Mrs Leinert: But you can never be sure in the mountains. I love hill-walking. But I can't stand getting wet and cold!
Mr Leinert: Well, we'll listen to the weather forecast. If it's good, we'll go.

1 What do they say?

Example: 1. Mr Leinert wants to climb Ben Nevis. (What about ...?)
Mr Leinert: What about climbing Ben Nevis?
2. Mrs Leinert wants to buy a good map of the mountains. (What about ...?)
3. Jenny thinks hill-walking is great. (I love ...)
4. Mrs Leinert doesn't want to walk in the rain all day. (It's no good ...)
5. She doesn't want to get wet. (I can't stand ...)
6. Mr Leinert wants to listen to the weather forecast. (What about ...?)

2 What about ...?

You are together with your friends and you don't know what to do. Suddenly you have an idea. Ask the others about it.

swim

have a cup of tea

eat an ice cream

cycle

play football

play the guitar

What can you say?
... is (no) fun.
... is great.
... is my hobby.
Oh, yes. I like/love ... .
I hate ... .
I don't like ... .
Good idea.
Let's ... .
... is terrible.
...

Example: What about swimming? – Oh, yes. Swimming is fun.
Have you got any more ideas? *Act them out with a friend.*

3 On the telephone

David is phoning home from Fort William. Can you finish the sentences?

David: Hello, Dad. It's David here.
Mr Penrose: Hello, David. Where are you now?
David: I'm phoning from ... .
Mr Penrose: Fort William! Oh, that's near Ben Nevis!
David: Yes, it's the highest ... . Tomorrow we want to ... .
Mr Penrose: That's great. But please be careful in the ... .
David: Don't worry. We always ... .
Mr Penrose: Good. Well, enjoy yourself, David, and say hello to ... .
David: Thanks, and love to ... .
Mr Penrose: Phone us again soon. Goodbye.
David: ...

4 Listening practice: The weather forecast

Listen to the weather forecast. What will the weather be like?

1. In the south and west?
2. In Scotland and the north of England?
3. In London and the east of England?

5 A walk in the countryside

What kind of things can you see in the countryside?
Perhaps you'd like to play this game. It's best to play it in groups.

Someone in the group can start: "I went for a walk, and I saw some sheep."
Then the next person says these words and adds another one:
"I went for a walk and I saw some sheep and a mountain.
Now it's the next person's turn.

How many words can you say before somebody makes a mistake? Which group can make the longest list of words?

cows pony lake farmer horses hills mouse dog trees

6 Monny's holidays

Monny has written a story about his holidays. Can you understand it? Read it out.

"I _____ (be)  with my . We _____ (go) there .
We _____ (live) . The weather _____ (be) .
 _________ (walk through)  and _______ (frighten) .
It was .

7 My English folder

Write about your nicest holiday. Draw a picture of where you stayed, or put in a photo.
Write:

- where you spent your holidays — in the mountains/at the seaside/at a lake/in a city
- how you got there — by car/by train/by boat/by plane …
- who went with you — my family/my friends/my …
- what you took with you and why — my bike/my swimming things … … because I like swimming/cycling …
- what you did there — go swimming or cycling/walk in the mountains/play …
- what the weather was like — fine/not so nice/sunny/cold …
- how you liked it there — fantastic/great/terrible …

Step D

On Ben Nevis

"Be careful out on the hills," said Mr MacTavish. The Leinerts were ready to leave the house now. "A lot of our guests climb Ben Nevis. But we always warn them. Don't go on if the weather changes."
"We'll be all right," said Mr Leinert.
"Yes, of course," said Mr MacTavish. "But there are bad accidents up there every year."
"Thanks, Mr MacTavish," said Mrs Leinert. "We'll be careful. Come on, everybody. Have we got everything?" It was sunny and warm when they got out of the car.
"Have you all got your anoraks?" asked Mr Leinert. "We'll need them later."
Walking was easy at first. The path wasn't steep yet. Jenny took some nice pictures with her camera.
After a time the path got steeper – and the stones on the path got bigger.
"I'm tired!" said David. "What about having our sandwiches now?"
So they sat down on some rocks. It wasn't so warm now, and they all had their anoraks on. When they went on 30 minutes later, it started to rain.
"This isn't much fun!" said Mrs Leinert.
"It'll stop in a minute," said Jenny. "Come on, Mum."
But it didn't stop. The weather got worse and worse. And everybody got colder and colder. The path was slippery. They were the only people on the path now. Mr Leinert stopped and looked at the dark clouds. "Let's go back," he said. "It's no good going on in this!"
He was right. Nobody wanted to go on now. It was really terrible now. "Why are weather forecasts always wrong?" said David.
They didn't see anyone else on the path when they went down.
"Forget the weather. We must hurry," said Mrs Leinert. "Come on."
"Hey, Dad, where are you going?" called Jenny. "The path doesn't go that way."
"I know, but this is a short cut. It's on our map here. – Look. If we go this way, we'll be back at the car sooner."
But Mr Leinert was wrong. An hour later they were still on the path.
But which path was it? And where was the car? It was almost seven o'clock.
And it was getting dark now. "We must stay where we are," said Mr Leinert. "Walking on in the dark is too dangerous." – "Will the MacTavishes phone the Mountain Rescue people?" asked David. "And how will they find us?"
Half an hour later there was a noise. It was a helicopter. Mr Leinert jumped up and waved to the helicopter and he shouted. But nobody heard or saw them in the dark.
When the helicopter was almost out of sight, Jenny had an idea: she took her camera and shot pictures. The flash light was so bright that the people in the helicopter saw it.
Forty minutes later the Mountain Rescue people got there and saved them.

1 Putting the story together

Look at the pictures. Can you put them in the right order? Example: Picture b) must be first. That's when Mr MacTavish warns the Leinerts about Ben Nevis.

Workshop 1

1 Nessie is a thief: Compound words

There are always two words in a compound word. But look what has happened. Nessie, the Loch Ness monster has taken all the first words.
a) *Can you get them back? Write the compound words down in your exercise book.*

lesson · forecast · soup · salad · cut · light · sport · flat · Lomond · bike · Hostel · Nevis · games · trekking · pipes · pool

b) *Choose five compound words from your list and make sentences with them. Can you make funny sentences, too?*
Example: If Nessie is your pet, you need a swimming pool.

2 Sound track

Say these sentences. Be careful with the [v] *sound in 'of'.*

1. I often dream of horses.
2. Our visitors arrived at half past eleven.
3. Have you found your five pound note?
4. Don't leave your van in front of Alan's car.
5. Have you finished the fruit cake? – No, we've only had half of it.
6. I've never laughed so much in all my life!

3 WORD POWER

Can you find the rhymes? Be careful! Often different letters have the same sound.

1. word
2. trouble
3. eight
4. friend
5. bread
6. laugh
7. through
8. daughter
9. thought

half · shirt · caught · double · said · late · too · spend · water

Workshop 2

BE A FARMER'S FRIEND

Scotland's farmers produce food for you …

… you can help them.

PLEASE
Keep to the paths

Don't walk through cornfields.
You could damage them.
Always walk around them.
Keep to the paths.

PLEASE
Don't leave litter

Litter is dangerous to animals.
Litter could damage farm machines.
Don't leave litter in the fields.
Always take your litter home with you.

PLEASE
Don't damage the fences
People sometimes climb over fences, and damage them.
The animals can get out and run away.
Don't climb over fences.
Always use the gates.

PLEASE
Keep your dog under control

Dogs often run after farm animals.
Always keep your dog under control when you're near a farm.

PLEASE
Leave all gates as you find them

The farmer closes his gates to keep his animals in one field.
He sometimes leaves the gates open, so that the animals can get to water and food.
Always leave gates open or closed as you find them.

1 Getting the facts

Look at the leaflet and find out the facts.
Why mustn't

- people walk through a cornfield?
- people leave litter in the fields?
- people damage farmers' walls?
- dogs run after animals?
- people leave gates open?

Step F

Let's Check

1 WORD POWER

Collect as many words as you can.

Example:
1. There is water in the sea, and in a ...
   – **lake, pond, river.**
2. You can travel by  or 

3. You can stay the night at a **hotel** or at ...
4. On a map of Scotland you can see **islands** and ...
5. When you are on holiday, you can look round **museums** or ...

2 The weather in Scotland

Scotland in the winter ...

... and Scotland in the summer.

3 Talking about things

Find the right words.
Example: 1. *Sarah:* I go out on my bike every day. I love **cycling**.

1. *Sarah:* I go out on my bike every day. I love ... .
2. *Kim:* I enjoy my Saturday job. But I hate ... up early on Saturday morning!
3. *Becky:* Sorry, Maxi. The weather is terrible. It's no good ... you and Mini to the park today.
4. *Simon:* Football on TV is great. But ... football with your friends is better than ... it on TV.
5. *David:* We all enjoyed ... Ben Nevis – but we didn't go all the way to the top.
6. *Mrs Leinert:* I don't want to go in the loch. I can't stand ... in cold water!
7. *Mr Leinert:* What about ... to the cinema? There's a good film on this week.
8. *Mrs MacTavish:* We've got a boat on the loch. Do you like ...?
9. *Jenny:* I love ... letters. But ... to friends on the telephone is nice, too.

4 They've already done it

Example: 1. *Mrs Leinert:* Jenny! Please make your bed now. (✓ – after breakfast)
Jenny: I**'ve** already **made** it, Mum. I **made** it after breakfast.

1. *Mrs Leinert:* Jenny! Please make your bed now. (✓ – after breakfast)
2. *Mrs Penrose:* Colin! Could you repair Mark's cupboard door today? (✓ – yesterday)
3. *Mrs Penrose:* David! Please do your homework now. (✓ – before tea)
4. *Becky:* Simon! Please take Maxi and Mini out. It's your turn! (✓ – half an hour ago)
5. *Robert:* Mum! Could you wash my black jeans this week? (✓ – last week)
6. *Sarah:* Kim! Can you buy that CD for Mum's birthday? (✓ – on Saturday)
7. *Mrs Dixon:* Sarah! Please feed Tabby now. She must be hungry! (✓ – after tea)

Unit 7 Holidays

Step A Holidays in Britain

	°**Britain** ['brɪtn]	Großbritannien	*Britain* = (short for) Great Britain
	north [nɔːθ]	nördlich, Nord-, Norden	
	west [west]	westlich, West-, Westen	
	east [iːst]	östlich, Ost-, Osten	
	south [saʊθ]	südlich, Süd-, Süden	
	to **spend, spent, spent** [spend, spent]	verbringen; ausgeben	
	city ['sɪtɪ]	Großstadt	
	°**Wales** [weɪlz]	Wales	
	own [əʊn]	eigene/r/s	
	°**Welsh** [welʃ]	walisisch	People from *Wales* are *Welsh*.
	hill [hɪl]	Hügel	
	°**Scotland** ['skɒtlənd]	Schottland	
	volleyball ['vɒlɪbɔːl]	Volleyball	Diese Wörter sehen gleich aus wie im Deutschen – achte aber auf die englische Aussprache.
	caravan ['kærəvæn]	Wohnwagen	
	hotel [həʊ'tel]	Hotel	
	°**Isle of Wight** ['aɪl‿əv 'waɪt]	*Insel im Ärmelkanal*	
	beautiful ['bjuːtɪfʊl]	(wunder)schön	
	beach [biːtʃ]	Strand	
	ideal [aɪ'dɪəl]	ideal	
	to travel ['trævl]	reisen	
	island ['aɪlənd]	Insel	There is water all round an *island*.
1	**mountain** ['maʊntɪn]	Berg	
3	**village** ['vɪlɪdʒ]	Dorf	
4	°**museum** [mjuː'zɪəm]	Museum	
⟨5⟩	row [rəʊ]	rudern	
	gently ['dʒentlɪ]	sanft; behutsam	
	stream [striːm]	Bach	
	merrily ['merɪlɪ]	vergnügt	
	life [laɪf]	Leben	

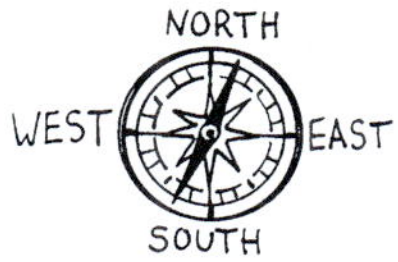

Looking at the UK: Wales

ⓐ	°to **sail** [seɪl]	segeln
	°to **fish** [fɪʃ]	fischen
	°to **pony-trek** ['pəʊnɪtrek]	ausreiten
	°to **surf** [sɜːf]	surfen

Looking at the UK: Scotland

°**Highlands** ['haɪləndz]	Hochland
°**loch** [lɒk]	See *(schottisch)*
°**Loch Linnhe** ['lɒk 'lɪnɪ]	*See in Schottland*
°**North Sea** ['nɔːθ 'siː]	Nordsee
°to **pipe** [paɪp]	pfeifen
bagpipes ['bægpaɪps]	Dudelsack
quickly ['kwɪklɪ]	schnell
stormy ['stɔːmɪ]	stürmisch

Vocabulary

	bank [bæŋk]	Bank	
	°**High Street** ['haɪ ˌstriːt]	*Hauptstraße*	

Step B **Before the Easter holidays**

	°**Easter** ['iːstə]	Ostern	
	to **cycle, cycling** ['saɪkl, 'saɪklɪŋ]	Fahrrad fahren	We take our bikes on holiday – we love *cycling*.
	°**Lake District** ['leɪk ˌdɪstrɪkt]	*Seelandschaft in Nordengland*	
1	to **enjoy** [ɪn'dʒɔɪ]	genießen, gern tun	I *enjoy* climbing mountains.
3	°**character** ['kærəktə]	Charakter	

Step B **From Jenny's travel diary**

	twice [twaɪs]	zweimal	
	°**MacTavish** [mək'tævɪʃ]	*Familienname*	
	°**Scottish** ['skɒtɪʃ]	schottisch	*Scottish*, Welsh and English people come from Great Britain.
	°**Loch Lomond** [ˌlok 'ləʊmənd]	*See in Schottland*	
	garage ['gærɑːdʒ]	Garage	
	to **row** [rəʊ]	rudern	
6	**washing-up** [ˌwɒʃɪŋ 'ʌp]	Abwasch	

Step B **Have you ever?**

	ever ['evə]	je(mals)	
	porridge ['pɒrɪdʒ]	Haferbrei	
8	**kilt** [kɪlt]	Schottenrock	

Step C **At Fort William**

	°**Fort William** [ˌfɔːt 'wɪljəm]	*Ort in Schottland*	
	°**Ben Nevis** [ˌben 'nevɪs]	*(höchster) Berg in Schottland*	
	highest ['haɪɪst]	höchste/r/s	
	it's no good ['nəʊ 'gʊd]	es hat keinen Wert/Sinn	
	hill-walking ['hɪl ˌwɔːkɪŋ]	Wandern	
	forecast ['fɔːkɑːst]	Vorhersage	The *weather forecast* says it will rain.
3	**enjoy yourself** [ɪn'dʒɔɪ jɔː'self]	viel Spaß!	
5	**countryside** ['kʌntrɪsaɪd]	Landschaft, Gegend	
	perhaps [pə'hæps]	vielleicht	
	mistake [mɪ'steɪk]	Fehler	
	longest ['lɒŋgɪst]	längste/r/s	
	pony ['pəʊnɪ]	Pony	
	farmer ['fɑːmə]	Bauer/Bäuerin	
6	to **frighten** ['fraɪtn]	erschrecken	

Step D **On Ben Nevis**

	to **warn** [wɔ:n]	warnen	
	to **change** [tʃeɪndʒ]	(sich) (ver)ändern	
	path [pɑ:θ]	Pfad, Weg	We can't walk up this *path*,
	steep [sti:p]	steil	it's too *steep*.
	slippery ['slɪpərɪ]	rutschig, glatt	In winter the roads are often very *slippery*.
	dark [dɑ:k]	dunkel	
	cloud [klaʊd]	Wolke	Look at those *clouds*.
			– Yes, the weather is changing.
	to **hurry** ['hʌrɪ]	(sich) beeilen	
	°**Mountain Rescue** ['maʊntɪn 'reskju:]	Bergwacht	
	helicopter ['helɪkɒptə]	Hubschrauber	
	sight [saɪt]	Sicht	
	°**flash** [flæʃ]	Blitz	
	bright [braɪt]	hell	

Step E **Workshop 1**

	°**compound word** ['kɒmpaʊnd 'wɜ:d]	zusammengesetztes Wort
	°**Nessie** ['nesɪ]	*Name eines Seemonsters*
	°**Loch Ness** ['lɒk‿'nes]	*See in Schottland*
	hostel ['hɒstl]	Heim, Herberge
	°to **trek** [trek]	trecken
	pipe [paɪp]	Pfeife
2	°**Alan** ['ælən]	*männl. Vorname*
3	**trouble** ['trʌbl]	Schwierigkeiten

Step E **Workshop 2**

to **produce** [prə'dju:s]	erzeugen, herstellen
cornfield ['kɔ:nfi:ld]	Maisfeld
to **damage** ['dæmɪdʒ]	Schaden anrichten
litter ['lɪtə]	Abfall
field [fi:ld]	Feld
fence [fens]	Zaun
gate [geɪt]	Tor
control [kən'trəʊl]	Kontrolle
wall [wɔ:l]	Mauer

no – any – some – every

no books	**any** chairs
no food	**any** wine
nobody	**anybody**
nothing	**anything**
nowhere	**anywhere**
some bottles	**every** house
some milk	**every** pupil
somebody	**everybody**
something	**everything**
somewhere	**everywhere**

Nobody heard the burglar because **everybody** was asleep.

Did you see **anybody** near the house? – Well, I didn't see **anybody** yesterday, but I saw **somebody** in the garden earlier today.

Step F **Let's check**

1	**river** ['rɪvə]	Fluss

Unit 8

A bad week

Step A

The super skater

Last Wednesday Robert, Becky and Simon were outside with their skateboards. Barry Newman was on the other side of the road. When Mrs Croft came home she watched them, then she said, "Hey, not bad. Let me try."
"No, it's too dangerous, Mum," Robert said.
And Becky warned her, "You haven't got a helmet, Mrs Croft."
"Never mind," Mrs Croft answered. "I was a super skater when I was younger. I'll be quite all right."
She jumped on Becky's skateboard, but she tripped and fell.
The children were worried.
"Are you OK, Mum?" Robert asked.
"I'll be all right," his mother said."I'll just go in and lie down."
"Wow! What a super skater!" Barry laughed.
"Go away, Barry!" Robert said and ran into the house.

1 Role play: Are you OK?

Somebody has had an accident.
Ask what is wrong. Work with a partner.

Are you OK?

Have you broken your arm?

broken your leg/hand/...?

– No, I haven't.

What about your head?

How is ...?

– It hurts a bit. But I'll be OK.

I'm quite all right.

Don't worry.

2 WORD POWER

Cut out a picture of somebody in a magazine and write in the parts of the body.

3 Listening practice: Becky's dream

Becky is telling Simon about the monster in her dream.

1. *Write this list in your exercise book. Then listen to the recording and take notes.*
2. *Can you draw the monster?*

The monster

head:
eyes:
mouth:

ears:
arms:
hands:

colour:
T-shirt:
shoes:

Mr and Mrs Dracula are ill

Hi there, I'm Mrs Dracula.
I've got a terrible headache and I'm very ill. The doctor came to our old castle to give me a check-up last night. He took my temperature and examined me. He said, "Don't worry! You've got a bad cold and a temperature, too. But we needn't phone the hospital. You can stay in your old castle, but you must stay in bed for three days."

My son does the shopping for me. He's at the chemist's now. I hope the chemist doesn't give him any nasty medicine. But I must get better soon. Everything is in a mess here! Someone must do the washing-up!

Mr Dracula is ill, too. It's terrible!

4 Mr Dracula

Hello there. I'm Dracula. You know me?
Then you must know my *teeth*, too.
But today I've got a bad *tooth*.
I've got terrible *toothache*.
I must go to the *dentist*.
He must help me.
I need my teeth!

5 Whose are they?

Can you find out?
Number 1 are the ears of a hamster.
Number 2 is …

Cartoon fun

He's got his first tooth now!

Unit 8

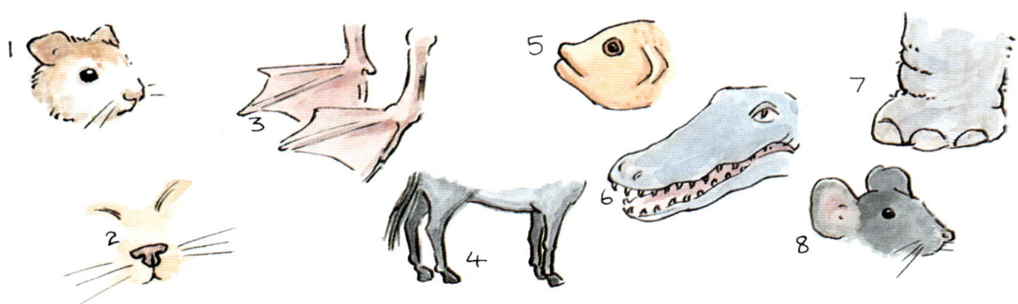

Step B

The next morning ...

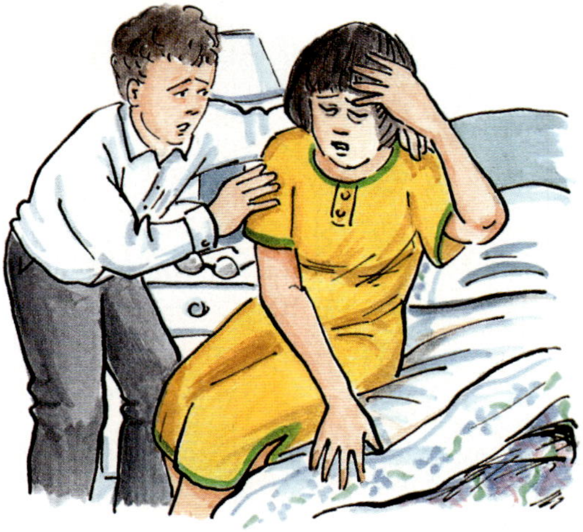

On Thursday Mrs Croft didn't feel well.

Robert: How are you, Mum?
Mrs Croft: I feel ill and I've got a terrible headache.
Robert: Oh dear. Well, you can't go to work today. Go back to bed.
Mrs Croft: I'll just make breakfast for you.
Robert: You needn't do that, Mum. I'll make breakfast.
Mrs Croft: Thanks, Robert. Oh, my head! I think I'll call the doctor.
Robert: I'll phone him for you, Mum. You stay in bed.
Mrs Croft: Thank you, Robert. It's good that you're here.

1 You needn't do that, Mum!

You **needn't** do that.

Robert phones the doctor. He will visit Mrs Croft later.
She must stay in bed, but she wants to do a lot of things.
What does Robert say?

Example: Mrs Croft: I must phone Radio Nottingham.
Robert: You **needn't** phone them, Mum. I can do it.

Your turn 2 What do you think?

Say why. Give reasons with 'must', 'need', 'needn't'.

Do you think it's	good all right nice right OK	that	Robert doesn't go to school Robert makes the breakfast Robert phones the doctor Mrs Croft doesn't go to work Mrs Croft stays in bed Mrs Croft doesn't go to the doctor's Barry Newman laughed	? –	Yes, I do. No, I don't.

Example: It's OK that Robert doesn't go to school because he must look after his mum.

The doctor's visit

Later that morning Dr Patel arrived.

Dr Patel: Good morning, Robert. Where's the patient?
Robert: Hello, Doctor Patel. She's in here. In the bedroom.
Dr Patel: Thank you, Robert. – Good morning, Mrs Croft. No, you mustn't sit up. Robert told me what happened.
Mrs Croft: I feel terrible, doctor.
Dr Patel: Well, you hit your head, so we must be careful. You must go to hospital and they'll examine you there. I'll tell Robert. Don't worry.

You **mustn't** sit up.

3 Oh, no, you mustn't do that!

Mrs Croft is in hospital. She wants to do a lot of things. But the nurse tells her what she *mustn't* do and what she *must* do.

not use the telephone ✓	stay in bed ✓
not do any work	lie down
not get up	sleep a lot
not read	eat only hospital food

Examples:
1. Maybe I can phone the radio station.
   – Oh no, Mrs Croft. You **mustn't** use the telephone.
2. I think I'll visit Mrs Chang. She's here, too.
   – Oh no, Mrs Croft, you **must** stay … .

1. Maybe I can phone the radio station.
2. I think I'll visit Mrs Chang. She's here, too.
3. I've always wanted to read this book.
4. Maybe I'll write a letter to Uncle Arthur.
5. Perhaps I can get a computer and work a bit.
6. I can look through all my old magazines.
7. I'll go for a little walk.
8. I think I'll have a bar of chocolate.

4 Looking at English

You must be quiet here.

You mustn't eat ice cream here.

5 At home

What must you do at home? What needn't you do?
Make a list and compare your list with your partner's list. You can start like this:

You: I must make my bed every morning.
Your partner: Oh, I needn't do that./Yes, I must do that, too.

6 Sound track

t – You mustn't listen to the radio. Mark often makes sandcastles.

l – It's half past four. Walk! Don't talk!

d – On Wednesdays we have sandwiches.

Barry Newman – super skater

Barry Newman knew where his brother's skateboard was. He went into the old shed and took it outside. Then he began to ride around on it. He rode off down the hill. But suddenly the neighbours' dog jumped out in front of him. The skateboard went the wrong way and Barry fell off!

7 Barry's broken leg

Today Barry Newman is in hospital with a broken leg.
The doctor is talking to him.
Read the dialogue and put in 'must', 'mustn't', 'can' or 'can't'.

Doctor: Hello, Barry. How are you today?
Barry: Better, thank you, doctor. … I go back to school soon?
Doctor: It's OK, Barry. You … worry. With a broken leg you … go back to school so soon.
Barry: Oh, good!
Doctor: You … stay here until Friday. Then you … go home. But you … be careful for a few days.
Barry: … I watch TV in the TV room tonight?
Doctor: Well, all right, Barry. You … . But you … stay up too long.
Barry: But the football goes on until 10 o'clock!
Doctor: Football, eh? Well, of course you … miss that. If you … *play* football, then you … *watch* it. Have fun.

8 WORD POWER

One word is wrong in each group. Can you find out which and say why?
a) skateboard, bike, medicine, caravan, van, bus, helicopter, plane
b) ear, nose, knee, dentist, shoulder, foot, ear, finger, leg, hand
c) cow, hen, alligator, guest, hamster, horse, pony, elephant, kangaroo
d) museum, school, guest house, temperature, hotel, hospital, pet shop
e) mountain, lake, hill, supermarket, island, countryside, beach

9 A game

Mike, Simon and Becky visited Barry in hospital. Mike and Simon knew a new game and they played it with Barry and Becky.
Simon: I don't like beans, but I like carrots.
Mike: Apples – yes, but bananas – no!
Barry: What about clothes? Do you like jeans?
Simon: No, but I like pullovers.
Becky: I don't get it. Help us, Simon. What animals do you like?
Simon: I like alligators, and kangaroos, but not frogs.
Mike: Letters – yes, but postcards – no.
Barry: I've got it now. Let me check: You like coffee, but not tea! – And you like sweets and pudding, but not chocolate. You like pizza but not …
Mike: Hey, good. That's right. Well, Becky, have you got it now?
What about you? Have you got it? Then play the game with your friends. Look at the SPELLING of the words. That will help you.

10 Blackout in Nottingham

Example: I was just playing with Mini when the lights went out. *Go on.*
Jenny: I was just … when the lights went out.
Robert: We were just …

past progressive	simple past
He was reading They were playing	when the lights went out

11 Sarah's weekend video

Last Saturday Sarah wanted to make a weekend video with her dad's camcorder. So she visited all her friends and filmed them. Where were they and what were they doing when Sarah came?

1. Robert … clean/bike
2. Becky and Simon … work/garden
3. Maxi and Mini … drink/water
4. David … read/newspaper
5. Mark … feed/birds
6. Mr and Mrs Penrose … go/shopping

Example: Robert was cleaning his bike when Sarah came.
Go on. Becky and Simon were …

12 How good is your memory?

Work with a partner. Ask what he or she was doing at different times yesterday.
Example: You: What were you doing at half past two yesterday?
Your partner: I was waiting for a bus.

At the doctor's

1 Role play: What's the problem?

Act a scene at the doctor's with a partner.

Good morning, … . What's the problem?
Hello, … . What's wrong with you?

I don't feel very well.
I feel terrible/ill/tired.
I've got a bad headache/stomach-ache/flu/… .
I think I've got a temperature.

Let me look at you/your leg/… .
Does this hurt?
Open your mouth, please, and say 'Ah'.

Ouch! That hurts.
No, that doesn't hurt. Ah!

Hmm. I see.

Must I stay in bed?
Can I go to school/play football/…?

You needn't stay in bed, but you must stay at home.
You must take some medicine. Take this prescription to the chemist's.

2 A hospital phrase book

In Britain and other countries you can find little phrase books in hospitals. They help people who can't speak or who don't know the language. The pictures show what the people want to say. Here are some examples:

I would like to…
Ich möchte …
Je voudrais …
…

These pictures mean:

"I'd like to make a telephone call."

"I'd like to listen to …"

"I'd like …"

"I'd like …"

Work with a partner and make your own hospital phrase book in English. Draw pictures and write down what they mean.

3 What does that mean?

You want to visit a friend in hospital in Germany. Your British penfriend goes with you, but doesn't understand all the signs around the hospital. *Can you explain what they mean? Please complete the sentences.*

1. You can visit people every day from … to …
2. That's where the … live.
3. People who have had … go there.
4. You … go through that door.
5. The hospital shop is closed on …
6. We can … there.
7. This entrance … only.
8. That's where the … land.

Laden montags geschlossen

Besuchzeit: täglich 14-18 Uhr

Unfallstation

Zufahrt nur für Krankenwagen

Ausgang

Kein Zutritt

Schwesternwohnheim

Mittwoch nachmittag geschlossen

Hubschrauber-Landeplatz

4 Role play: Helping an injured person

Are you all right?

Can you move it?

Shall I call an ambulance?

I'm not sure. There's something wrong with my arm.

Yes, but it hurts a bit.

No, thanks, I think I'll be all right.

leg/hand/foot/…

No, it hurts too much.

Yes, please do.

Happy Helpers

hey would you like to know hey would you like to know hey would you like to know hey would you like to

Haywood Herald

News and information for pupils, parents and friends of Haywood

Happy Helpers

Don't give your skateboard to your mother, at least, not if she hasn't got a helmet. Robert Croft did, and his mother spent two days in hospital. Her head hurt, but it wasn't too bad.

When Robert and I went to visit her we talked to some of the other patients in the ward. Some of them had problems. We couldn't help them all, but at least we could help some of them.

Shopping

There was a lady in the next bed. It was her last day in hospital. But she still wasn't very well after her operation. She couldn't go shopping. But that was no problem. She told us what she needed and we went to the supermarket for her.

Reading

Another lady wanted to read a letter, but she couldn't. Her eyes were bad after her operation. So I read it to her. But then something funny happened. "That isn't my letter," the lady said and her neighbour in the next bed said "I know, it's my letter." But she wasn't angry and we all laughed. So then I read the right letter.

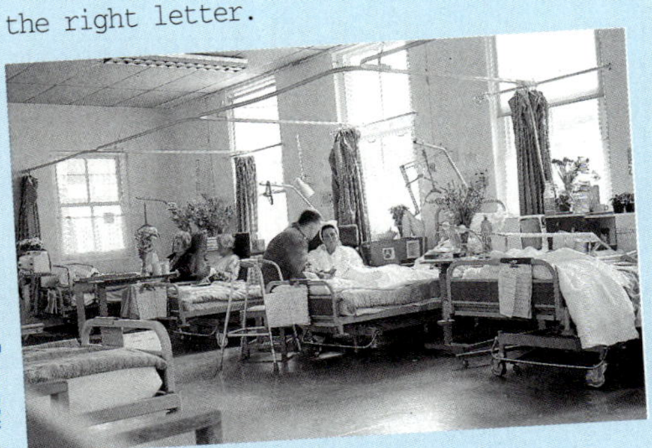

One of the nurses saw me and asked me, "Have you got a little more time?" She took me to the children's ward. There was a little girl there with a story book. She was only four and she couldn't read. I read one of the stories to her and played with her. She was nice.

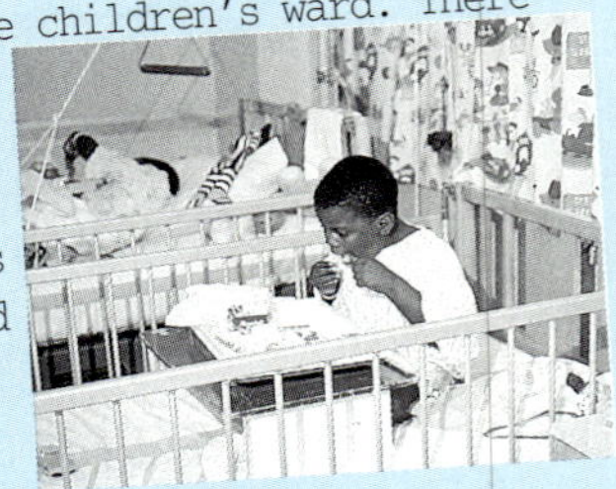

A surprise

And why do you think Haywood is such a quiet and peaceful place? - Barry Newman is in hospital with a broken leg! We visited him, too, and played games with him. And we took all his homework to the hospital for him. He was really happy!!!

The Happy Helpers

Helping people can be really great. Some people go to the hospital every week and help the patients. They're the "Happy Helpers". We've joined them. but they need more young people. So come and join us!

Mrs Croft is at home again now. "I'll never get on a skateboard without a helmet again," she says. So don't forget to wear your helmet, or you'll need a Happy Helper, too.

Becky Burton
Photos: Robert Croft

Unit 8

1 Looking at the report

a) *Find the facts.*
1. Why did Robert and Becky go to the hospital? (mother)
2. How did they help people? (shopping – read letter – children's story)
3. Did anything go wrong? (wrong letter – right letter)

b) *What do you think?*
1. Do you think that Barry was happy when the friends visited him in the hospital? Say why.
2. How did Barry feel about the homework? Say why.

2 New words

These are all new words (nouns) from this unit.
a) *Put all the letters in the right order and write the words down.*
b) *Choose six words and write a sentence with them.*

codrot stechmi horartt dehaahce distent draw
rapmetrute cekpuch demineci stochma

3 Listening practice: Mrs Croft on the radio

When Mrs Croft went back to work, she talked about the Happy Helpers on the radio.
Listen to what Mrs Croft said and make notes about Mr Davis and Sniffy.

The problem	The neighbours	Walks	What Becky can do

Read your notes again. Now write a short report about Mr Davis, Sniffy and Becky.
You can start like this:
There was another patient in the hospital. His name was Mr Davis and he had … .
He had a dog. … *Go on.*

4 ⟨A song: One finger, one thumb⟩

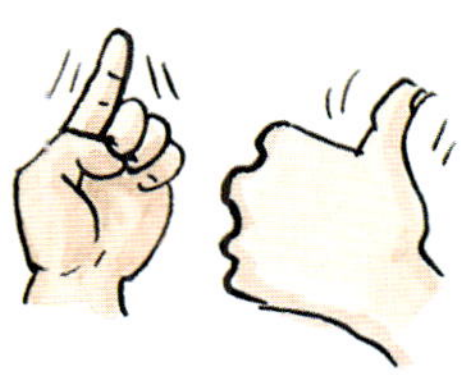

One finger, one thumb keep moving.
One finger, one thumb keep moving.
One finger, one thumb keep moving,
let's all be merry and bright.

One finger, one thumb, one hand keep moving …
One finger, one thumb, one hand, one arm …
One finger, one thumb, one hand, one arm, one leg …
… one nod of the head/stand up – sit down …

Unit 8

Step E

Workshop 1

What happens when you are ill

If you are ill, you must go to bed and rest. In a hospital, doctors and nurses look after you. They find out what is wrong with you.

1 2 3

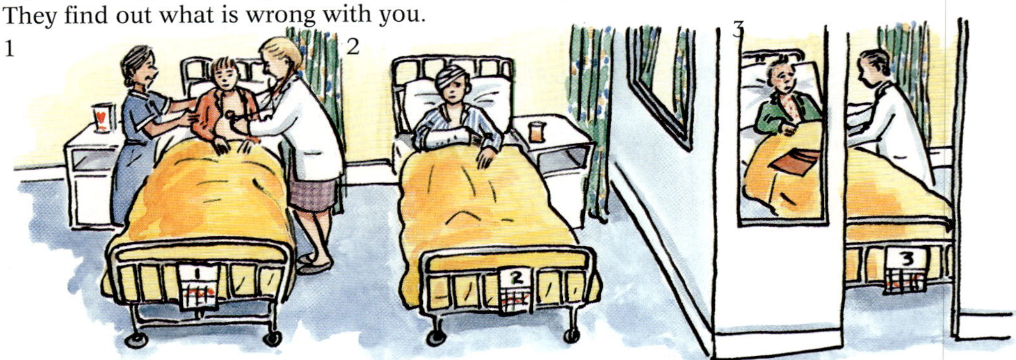

A doctor is listening to one boy's chest to check his heart.

Another boy has had an accident. He has hurt his head and broken his arm.

This boy has lots of spots. He is in a seperate room because he has measles. Other children mustn't visit him!

1 When you are ill

1. What must you do when you are ill?
2. What do the doctors and nurses do with you?
3. What is the doctor listening to in picture 1?
4. What has happened to the boy in picture 2?
5. Why is the boy in picture 3 in a separate room?

2 A word pool

Look at this word pool. Can you sort these words into groups? Here are some examples to help you. Write all the words down in these lists.

head, headache, to break, to hit, shoulder, spot, measles, to trip, to fall, flu, to hurt, dentist, throat, doctor, toothache, chemist, cold, stomach, nurse, patient, finger, knee, ambulance driver, to examine

head	headache	to break	doctor	

3 A hospital quiz

Write down the words.

- This person helps you when you are ill.
- A place where you can get medicine.
- A place where doctors and nurses look after you.
- What you get when you catch a cold.
- What the doctor writes for you.
- What you get when you've got a bad tooth.
- Then you go to a … .
- A person may be … in an accident.

Workshop 2

The broken wing

One day Mark brings a little bird home. It can't fly, so he and David take it to Mrs Blake in the pet shop round the corner.

David: Hello, Mrs Blake. We've got a little bird here.

Mrs Blake: Ah! A budgie. What's his name?

Mark: We don't know. We found him, but he can't fly.

Mrs Blake: Let me see. Ah, yes! Look, his wing is broken.

Mark: Oh dear! Must he go to hospital?

Mrs Blake: No, he needn't go to hospital. I can fix his wing here.

Mark: Can he come and live with us then? Or must we take him to the police station?

Mrs Blake: No, you needn't tell the police but you must try to find his owner. I'll put a notice in the window. And I'll give you a cage for him because he mustn't hop around too much until he is better.

David: Must we give him meat and bread?

Mrs Blake: Oh no. You mustn't feed him things like that. Budgies eat bird seed. Just a minute. I've got a leaflet here about budgies. Take it home and read it. But before that we must fix that wing.

Keeping a budgie

1. **Your budgie must have fresh water every day, and fresh bird seed two or three times a week.**
2. **You must clean the cage and put in fresh sand every week.**
3. **You needn't wash your bird. He can wash himself, so buy a birdbath.**
4. **Your budgie can't fly in his cage. Let him fly round the room. But don't forget to shut all the windows.**
5. **Be a good friend to your budgie and talk to him a lot.**

1 Keeping a pet

Work with a partner and write a leaflet about ponies or hamsters. Say:

- what kinds of room/place your pet needs,
- what you must do and what you needn't do every day,
- what you mustn't do,
- what your pet can do.

Give more information about how to do things.

enough room to run
apples
not bread or biscuits
talk to the pony
brush every week
ill – phone the vet

in a cage
not in a cold room – in a warm room
a piece of carrot or apple
fresh water every day
sand on the floor
clean paper in the cage
clean the cage every week
one hamster in the cage, not two or more together

Step F

Let's check

1 Barry is OK again

Barry must still be quite careful. Here's what he wants to do. Tell him that he *mustn't* … .

Example: 1. Barry, you mustn't eat so many sausages! 2. Barry, … . *Go on, please.*

2 What were they doing

What was everybody doing when David arrived at school yesterday?

Example: 1. Sarah eat a sandwich.
Sarah was eating a sandwich.

1. Sarah eat a sandwich.
2. Robert read a book.
3. Becky watch a bird.
4. Jenny look in her bag.
5. The teacher talk to a boy.
6. Two girls hide behind a tree.
7. Three boys play cards.
8. A group of children play football.

3 Happy Helpers at work

These Happy Helpers are telling their 'patients' what they needn't do.
Can you finish their sentences?
Example: 1. I can get some water for your flowers.
You **needn't** ask the nurse.

2. *Robert:* I can buy a pop magazine for you. You … .
3. *David:* We can help you with your video. You … .
4. *Jenny:* I can help you with your German homework. You … .
5. *Becky:* We can help you with the washing-up. You … .
6. *Simon:* I can buy apples and bananas for you. You … .

phone the TV shop
ask the nurse ✓
go to the shops
phone your German teacher
go to the newsagent's
do all the work in the kitchen
worry about it

4 The children

Barry Newman was at the hospital again last week. What were the children doing when he got there?

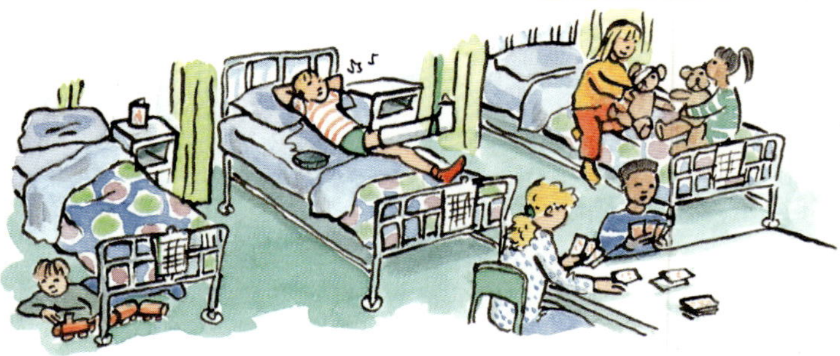

Unit 8 A bad week

Step A The super skater

	skater ['skeɪtə]	Schlitt-/Rollschuhläu-fer/in, Skateboard-fahrer/in	
	skateboard ['skeɪtbɔ:d]	Skateboard	
	to **trip** [trɪp]	stolpern	
1	to **hurt** [hɜ:t]	(sich) verletzen, weh tun	
2	**part** [pɑ:t]	Teil, Stück	

Step A Mr and Mrs Dracula are ill

	ill [ɪl]	krank	
4	°**Dracula** ['drækjʊlə]	*Familienname*	
	headache ['hedeɪk]	Kopfschmerzen	
	temperature ['temprətʃə]	Fieber, (erhöhte) Temperatur	I feel so hot. I think I've got a *temperature*.
	to **examine** [ɪg'zæmɪn]	untersuchen	Vets *examine* pets, doctors *examine* patients.
	chemist ['kemɪst]	Apotheke; Apotheker/in	
	nasty ['nɑ:stɪ]	scheußlich, übel, gemein	
	medicine ['medsn]	Medizin	
	mess [mes]	Unordnung	
5	**tooth** [tu:θ]	Zahn	
	toothache ['tu:θeɪk]	Zahnschmerzen	
	dentist ['dentɪst]	Zahnarzt/ärztin	
	ear [ɪə]	Ohr	You listen and hear with your *ears*.

Vocabulary

Step B The next morning …

1	**doctor** ['dɒktə]	Arzt/Ärztin	
2	**reason** ['ri:zn]	Grund	

Step B The doctor's visit

	°**Patel** [pə'tel]	*Familienname*	
	patient ['peɪʃnt]	Patient/in	
	mustn't ['mʌsnt]	nicht dürfen	
3	°**Arthur** ['ɑ:θə]	*männl. Vorname*	
6	**sandcastle** ['sændkɑ:sl]	Sandburg	You can build *sandcastles* at the seaside.

Step B **Barry Newman – super skater**

7	**a few** [fjuː]	ein paar, einige	
	tonight [tə'naɪt]	heute Abend, heute Nacht	
8	**alligator** ['ælɪgeɪtə]	Alligator	
	hamster ['hæmstə]	Hamster	*Hamsters* are nice pets.
	kangaroo [ˌkæŋgə'ruː]	Känguru	
10	**blackout** ['blækaʊt]	Stromausfall	
	thunderstorm ['θʌndəstɔːm]	Gewitter	
	°**progressive** [prəʊ'gresɪv]	Verlaufsform	
	sweet [swiːt]	süß	
11	**camcorder** ['kæmkɔːdə]	Videokamera	
12	**memory** ['memərɪ]	Gedächtnis	

Step C **At the doctor's**

	°**Suvina** ['sʊvɪnə]	*weibl. Vorname*	
	sore throat ['sɔː 'θrəʊt]	Halsschmerzen	– I've got a *sore throat.*
	stomach-ache ['stʌməkˌeɪk]	Magenschmerzen	Achte auf die Aussprache!
	stomach ['stʌmək]	Magen	
	°**Matthews** ['mæθjuːz]	*Familienname*	
	prescription [prɪ'skrɪpʃn]	Rezept *(vom Arzt)*	You need a *prescription* to get medicine from the *chemist's*.
	Ouch! [aʊtʃ]	Au!	
2	**hospital** ['hɒspɪtl]	Krankenhaus	
	°**phrase** [freɪz]	(Rede-)Wendung	
	language ['læŋgwɪdʒ]	Sprache	
3	**sign** [saɪn]	Schild	
	ambulance ['æmbjʊləns]	Krankenwagen	
	to **land** [lænd]	landen	
4	to **injure** ['ɪndʒə]	verletzen	
	injured ['ɪndʒəd]	verletzt	He has had an accident; he is *injured*.

Step D **Happy Helpers**

	helper ['helpə]	Helfer/in	*Helpers* help people.
	°**Hayward Herald** ['heɪwʊd 'herəld]	*Name eine Schulzeitung*	
	couldn't ['kʊdnt]	konnte(n) nicht	
	at least [ət 'liːst]	wenigstens, mindestens	
	operation [ˌɒpə'reɪʃn]	Operation	
	to **go shopping** ['ʃɒpɪŋ]	einkaufen gehen	
	nurse [nɜːs]	Krankenschwester, Krankenpfleger	
	peaceful ['piːsfʊl]	ruhig	
1	**report** [rɪ'pɔːt]	Bericht, Reportage	
3	to **make notes** [nəʊts]	sich Notizen machen	
	°**Davis** ['deɪvɪs]	*Familienname*	
	°**Sniffy** ['snɪfɪ]	*Name eines Hundes*	
⟨4⟩	thumb [θʌm]	Daumen	
	merry ['merɪ]	fröhlich	
	nod [nɒd]	Nicken	

Step E **Workshop 1**

to **rest** [rest]	ausruhen	
chest [tʃest]	Brust	
heart [hɑːt]	Herz	Your *heart* is in your *chest.*
spot [spɒt]	Fleck, Fickel	
measles [ˈmiːzlz]	Masern	

Step E **Workshop 2**

wing [wɪŋ]	Flügel	A bird has two *wings.*
°**Blake** [bleɪk]	*Familienname*	
owner [ˈəʊnə]	Besitzer	
seed [siːd]	*hier:* Vogelfutter	
fresh [freʃ]	frisch	
sand [sænd]	Sand	
bird-bath [ˈbɜːdˌbɑːθ]	Vogelbad	
brush [brʌʃ]	Bürste	

Step F **Let's check**

3 **flower** [ˈflaʊə] Blume

to be

David **is** very hungry.
Are you sure?
I'm excited/nervous/happy.
Be careful!
Jenny isn't scared of ghosts.
Your shirt is a nice colour.
The radio **is** on.
You're lucky.
It's my birthday today.
Swimming **is** fun.

to have

Have you **had** lunch yet?
Let's **have** a party!
Mark **has** a bath every evening.
Simon **has** new shoes on today.
I **had** a ride/a go on the roundabout.
Have fun/a good time/a nice weekend!

The end of the school year

Step A

The Haywood Fete

The last part of the summer term is usually great fun at Haywood School. And the school always has a summer fete, with a bring-and-buy sale and other activities.

This year there are some German girls and boys in Nottingham. They are members of a band, and they have come for a big concert. But because they are staying with the families of pupils at Haywood, they are happy to play at the school fete, too.

Dear pupils and parents,

Important news! The summer is here - and with it the Haywood Summer Fete. This year the fete will start at 2 o'clock on Saturday 5th July, and there will be a special attraction – a young people's band from Zwickau in Germany.

As always, we need your help with the fete. We already have plans for games and competitions, but we need things for our sale – clothes, books, children's toys (not too old or broken, please!). And we need cakes for the cake stall, too.

We want to collect as much money as we can at the fete. Half will be for the school, and half will go to a charity – because we want to help other people, too.

I hope to see you all on the 5th.

H. Benson

(Head teacher)

1 WORD POWER

These words in the letter are new:
attraction band competition
stall charity

Find them in the letter. What do they mean? Try to guess. Explain them with the ideas on the right.
Start: An attraction …

… is a group of people; they make music together.
… gives help to poor people.
… is what people want to see or hear.
… is when people want to find out who is the best.
… is a table for things in a sale.

2 An activity

Draw a poster for the Haywood School Fete. (You can work with a partner.)
Put the most important information on the poster. Use colours and pictures, too.

3 Listening practice: What's it like in England?

The members of the German band are talking on Radio Nottingham.
Listen to the recording. Find out what is different in England. Is anything the same? Make lists (for your English folder).

in GB	in D
streets little houses gardens …	flats big houses no gardens …

A normal day – an unlucky day

broken · damaged · a shock · sorry · grumpy · unlucky

ⓐ Usually you
- go to a car wash,
- pay for the wash,
- look at the car wash rules,
- check your sunroof (is it open?)

…

And then your car comes out, nice and clean and dry. And you're happy!

ⓑ … But not here! Something has gone wrong. Say what has happened.
- The car has come out …
- It's …
- The driver has had …
- This is an … day for the driver.
- He is very … now.
- The car wash man can only say "…" to the driver.

Drawing by W. Miller © 1979 The New Yorker Magazine, Inc.

4 New words again!

Can you say what goes together?

1. Yesterday was an unlucky day for me! ----→ c)
2. Why are you so grumpy?
3. Rules tell us …
4. It won't rain today!
5. Is this a good car?

a) Oh good. So the weather will be dry!
b) Yes, it's super! It's got a sunroof!
c) I lost my money.
d) Because somebody damaged my bike.
e) … what we may do (what is allowed) and what we mustn't do (what is not allowed).

5 Musical words

How many more words can you find that have something to do with music? (Work with a partner.)

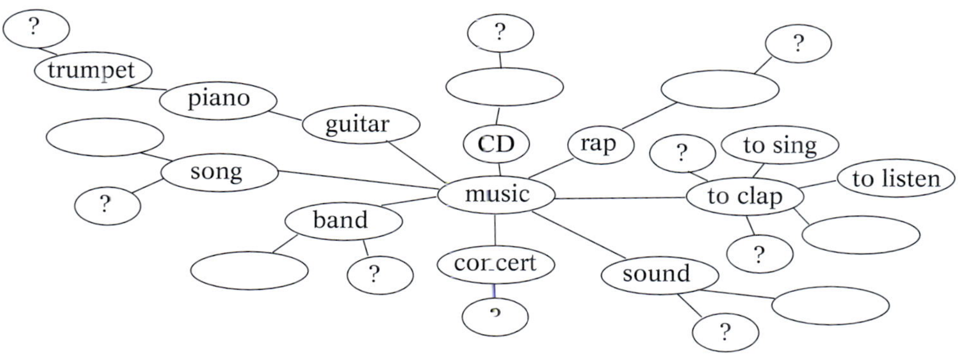

6 The 'bring-and-buy sale' game

Let's play a game: How many things can you buy at the bring-and-buy sale?

Pupil No. 1: I can buy toys there.
Pupil No. 2: I can buy toys and comics there.
Pupil No. 3: I can buy toys and comics and old clothes there.
Pupil No. 4: I can buy toys and comics and old clothes and ??? there.
Pupil No. 5: I can buy …

Step B

Plans for Saturday

It is Thursday – two days before the Haywood Fete.

David: What have you got there, David?
Oh, I like the toy trumpet!
Becky: They're things for the bring-and-buy sale. I'm going to take them to the Assembly Hall before lessons start.
David: We've got a lot of books for the sale. Mum is going to bring them to school in the car tomorrow. Are you going to help at the fete?
Becky: Yes, I am. Jenny and I are going to sell raffle tickets.
David: I'm going to help Mrs Dane with the 'Count the sweets in the bottle' competition.
Becky: Hm. Interesting. Have you already put the sweets in the bottle?
David: Not yet. We're going to do that on Saturday morning. And before you ask, Becky – No! I'm not going to tell you the number!

1 Questions

1. Where is Becky going to take the things for the sale?
   – She is going to take them …
2. What is Mrs Penrose going to bring to school tomorrow?
   – She is going to …
3. How are Becky and Jenny going to help at the fete? – They are …
4. What about David? – He …
5. What are David and Mrs Dane going to do on Saturday morning? – …
6. And what is David *not* going to tell Becky? – …

2 Melanie at the Dixons'

Melanie plays the trumpet in the Zwickau band. She is staying with the Dixons.
Look at the pictures. See what they have got. Then you can say what they are going to do.
1. Melanie has got the telephone in her hand. She is going to phone home.
2. Sarah and Melanie have got some cat food. They …
3. Mr Dixon has got a … . He …
4. Melanie … her … . She …
5. Kim and Mrs Dixon …

take phone
feed make play

Unit 9

3 Your plans

Work with a partner. Talk about your plans. (They can be 'dream' plans, too!)
Example:

What are you going to do at the weekend?

I'm going to play tennis with Superman.

What are you you going to do	tomorrow at the weekend in the summer holidays …	?	I'm going to	see … visit … stay … …

4 Looking at English

a) Be careful! 'Going' isn't always the same tense.
Look at the pair of sentences on the right.
– *Which 'going' is part of a present tense of 'to go'?*
– *Which 'going' is part of a 'going to' future form?*

b) *Make more pairs of sentences like this. Here are some ideas.*
You can start: She is going to the … . She is going to play …

c) *What can you say about the word 'to' in the sentences?*
Which 'to' is part of the verb? Which 'to' is a preposition?

5 Fun at the fete

Can you find their answers?

1. "Mr Stevenson has got all the money from the cake stall."
   – "Oh, I hope he isn't going to run away with it!"
2. "You've got a lot of sweets in that bottle."
   – "Don't worry. I'm not …!"
3. "What's this competition, girls? Guess the hamster's name?"
   – "Yes, but don't ask us. We …!"
4. "Look, your little sister has bought a toy trumpet."
   – "It's OK. She …!"
5. "It's too hot for your jacket? Well, leave it here with me."
   – "I hope you …!"

NOT …

play in the band.

eat them all.

run away with it.

put it on the clothes stall.

tell you its name.

!

Unit 9

Uniforms

Sarah: That feels better! I hate school uniform. – You're lucky, Melanie. You're allowed to wear jeans at school.
Melanie: Yes, but when we play in our band we aren't allowed to wear jeans. We have to wear a special uniform at our concerts.
Kim: I think Melanie's uniform looks great.
Melanie: The Haywood uniform is OK, too.
Kim: At least we don't have to choose different clothes every morning. Remember last month, Sarah? You didn't know *what* you wanted to wear on non-uniform day!
Sarah: OK, OK.
Melanie: Non-uniform day? What's that?
Kim: It was just before you arrived in Nottingham. We had to give 50p for a charity. Then we didn't have to wear uniform. We were allowed to go to school in other clothes.

6 Haywood School

When pupils start at Haywood School, they get this list of rules.
Say what Haywood pupils have to do.

They have to come to school clean and tidy.
They have to …
They …
Go on.

PLEASE REMEMBER THE SCHOOL RULES
- Come to school clean and tidy.
- Wear school uniform.
- Look after things in school.
- Tidy up your classroom.
- Walk in the corridors.
- Think about other people.
- Be polite at all times.

Your turn 7 Your school

What can you say about your school?

We	have to don't have to are allowed to aren't allowed to	wear a uniform eat in lessons talk in lessons	drop litter do homework …

8 Yesterday's lessons

The pupils at Haywood usually have to work in lessons. But it is the end of the summer term, so yesterday they were allowed to do different things …

1. German – have a party
   Jenny/bring some German biscuits

   In German they were allowed to have a …
   Jenny was allowed to bring …

2. English – read comics
   Sarah/tell a funny joke
3. Maths – sing songs
   David/play his guitar
4. History – watch a video
   Robert/choose the video

Unit 9

Looking at the UK: Helping charities

◀ In the UK a lot of people collect money for different charities. Children aren't allowed to collect money in the street. But that isn't a problem – because other activities are more fun!

▲ Sponsored activities are very popular – bike rides, for example. Family and friends give money for every mile.

Schools or youth groups organize sales or concerts or discos. Or they do jobs for other people. ▶

Children often help when there's a charity appeal on TV. Sometimes they collect things, sometimes they send money. Even a few pence can help when everybody works together. ▼

1 Money for charity

1. How can you make money for charities? What ideas can you find on this page? Have you got any more ideas?
2. What can you say about German charities? Do a lot of people organize charity activities? Are there sometimes charity appeals on TV?

Your turn *Have you ever helped a charity? What did you do?*

Step C

The money from the fete

There is an 'ideas box' in the Haywood Assembly Hall this week. It is for pupils' ideas about what they should do with the money from the Summer Fete.

1 The money for Haywood

a) Half the money is for the school.
But everybody wants to buy or get or use the money for something different!
Sarah wants to use the money for a new sports hall.
Robert wants to get … Jenny wants to buy … Becky … David …

b) *Do you like their ideas? Say why or why not.*
Example: I like Jenny's idea because a camcorder is fun.
I don't like …'s idea because …

useful important	…
boring	fun
(not) for everybody	silly

2 Listening practice: Helping others

The pupils want to give half the money to a charity.
What ideas have they got?

Listen to the recording and take notes. You can listen as often as you like, of course.

Unit 9

3 What should they do?

What should the pupils do with the charity money?
Talk about the ideas in your list from exercise 2. (Maybe you have got different ideas.)

I think they should	help … buy … give the money to … …

Yes, I think that's the best idea, too.
Oh no, I think …
I'm not sure. Maybe …

Step D

Lucky weather

"The best car wash in Nottingham! Your car will be nice and clean when you come back to it after the fete!"

Sarah and Robert were in the school car park. They were making money at the summer fete. It was early, but a lot of people – and cars – were already there. It was a good afternoon for the job. Dry, but not too sunny.

Just then Mr Parkinson, one of the teachers, drove into the car park and jumped out of his car.

"Can we wash your car, too, Mr Parkinson?" asked Robert. "It only costs £1."

But Mr Parkinson didn't have much time.

"I'm late for the fete." he answered.

"Please!" said Sarah.

"Oh yes, wash the car. Oh dear, I'm *very* late now!" And with that he hurried away into the school.

"Hm, he got out of bed on the wrong side today," said Robert.

"Oh, he's always a bit grumpy," Sarah laughed. "Come on, Robert. Let's start with these cars."

Washing the cars was fun, but after an hour or so Robert felt a bit tired.

"One more, and then I'm going to have a break," he told Sarah.

"OK. Let's do Mr Parkinson's car. Throw some water over it first, Robert."

Robert picked up a bucket of water and threw it over the car. But then he and Sarah got a shock. The water wasn't only outside. It was inside, too – all over the front seats of the car.

"Oh no, look! He left the sunroof open," Sarah shouted. "What are we going to do now?"

"We have to tell him what we've done," Robert answered. "These seats will never be dry before he comes back. Oh dear, he'll be more than a bit grumpy now!"

Sarah and Robert left the car park and looked for Mr Parkinson. They didn't feel very happy. Even the weather wasn't so nice now. There was a big black cloud over the school.

They found him in the playground. He was organizing pupils and parents. They were carrying stalls from the playground into some classrooms.

"Er – excuse us, Mr Parkinson," Sarah said. "We –" But she wasn't allowed to go on.

"Not now, Sarah," Mr Parkinson told her. "Can't you see we're all busy here? Look at that cloud. We have to get everything into the school before it rains. Oh dear, here are the first drops now. – Don't just stand there, Sarah and Robert. Help with these stalls, please."

A few minutes later everything was inside. Just in time. It was raining hard now.
"Thank you for your help," Mr Parkinson told everyone. "What weather! But the fete can go on in the school." Then he saw Robert and Sarah. "Ah, yes. Now, what did you two want?"
Robert and Sarah thought of the wet seats in the car – and of the rain.
"We wanted to tell you, Mr Parkinson – You left your sunroof open!"

1 Why?

Ask and answer questions.

Why
- were Sarah and Robert washing cars this afternoon
- did Robert say, "He got out of bed on the wrong side today"
- did the water go inside the car
- did they have to carry the stalls into the classrooms
- couldn't Sarah tell Mr Parkinson about the problem right away
- was the weather lucky for Sarah and Robert

?

b) *Ask your partner more questions about the story. You can use the other question words, too.*

What | Who | How much | Where | …

2 Should they?

– *Sarah and Robert tell Mr Parkinson about his sunroof. But what don't they tell him?*
– *Should they tell him everything? Say what you think.*

Yes, they should because … | No, they shouldn't because …

it was his/their mistake | he's a grumpy person | he will/won't be angry | you shouldn't try to hide things | it is/isn't important

3 Sound track: Making different words important

a) *Say the same sentence, but make different words important.*
1. <u>You</u> left your sunroof open.
2. You left <u>your</u> sunroof open.
3. You left your <u>sunroof</u> open.
4. You left your sunroof <u>open</u>.

b) *How can this change the sentence?*
Start: Sentence 1 means "…"
– "You think you closed it – but you didn't."
– "It wasn't anybody else's sunroof."
– "Nobody else left it open."
– "You didn't leave the doors or windows open."

c) *Practise with more sentences from the story. Make different words important.*

Step E

Workshop 1

1 A rope rhyme

Read this rhyme to the beat of a rope.
You can try it out with a rope in the playground.
You can also read it to the beat of some rap music.

Jelly on the plate, jelly on the plate,
Wiggle, woggle, wiggle, woggle,
Jelly on the plate.
Sausage in the pan, sausage in the pan,
Turn it over, turn it over,
Sausage in the pan.
Jam on the shelf, jam on the shelf,
Pull it down, pull it down, jam on the shelf.
Pennies on the floor, pennies on the floor,
Pick them up, pick them up, pennies on the floor.
Dirt in the room, dirt in the room,
Sweep it out, sweep it out, dirt in the room.
Robbers in the house, robbers in the house,
Kick them out, kick them out, robbers in the house.
Apples on the tree, apples on the tree,
Pick them off, pick them off, apples on the tree.
Ants in your pants, ants in your pants,
Scratch them out, scratch them out,
Ants in your pants.

2 The 'going to' game

Let's play a game with 'going to'. Make stories like these:

1. I'm going to go to America!
   What are you going to do in America?
   I'm going to ask an alligator questions about Australia.
2. I'm going to go to Belgium!
   What are you going to do in Belgium?
   I'm going to buy some books at a bring-and-buy sale in Belgium.
3. I'm going to go to Canterville!
   What are you going to do in Canterville?
   I'm going to catch some cows in Canterville.
4. Go on: Denmark/dance/in a disco
   England/eat/eggs
   France/feed/fish
   Glasgow/get/gold
   Holland/?/?
   Italy/?/?
   …

Workshop 2

Thirteen

My sister, Tanya,
has just turned thirteen.
She's grumpy and moody
and terribly mean.
When I ask her to come
and play in the park,
she says "Can't. I'm doing
my homework with Mark."

When the phone rings, she jumps up
and says, "It's for me!"
She never considers
it *mightn't* be!
But it's usually Mark,
and she grins and says, "See!"
She stays on the phone
for HOURS … sometimes THREE!

I say, "I'll tell dad!"
She yells, "You're a bore!"
Then I scream, "I'll tell Mark
that you sniffle and snore!"
She runs out to mum
and says I'm being mean …
I won't be like her
when I turn thirteen!
I hope!

1 Questions, questions, questions

1. How do we know that Tanya is not a very nice sister?
2. What about Tanya and Mark?
3. What do you think the two children did before Mark was Tanya's friend?
4. What does the brother want to tell his dad?
5. What does he want to tell Mark?
6. What does Tanya want to tell her mum? (Does she tell her?)
7. When is a boy or a girl 'mean'? (What does 'mean' mean?)
8. You are 12 or 13 now, too. Do you think that children at this age are like Tanya?
9. What is it like to have a younger/older brother and/or sister? Is it the same in *your* family? Or do you know other children with problems like this? Tell the class about them.
10. Now say what you think about this poem.

2 How people can be

Collect words (adjectives) for how people can be. Make two lists, a 'nice' one and a 'nasty' one.

friendly ***nice*** *…*	***grumpy*** ***moody*** *…*

Step F

Let's Check

1 WORD POWER

Which words go together? Make pairs, and write a sentence with your new word.
Example: The Zwickau band will be a special attraction.

pop, school, car, non-uniform, bring-and-buy, special, charity **+** music, sale, attraction, appeal, day, fete, wash

2 The Dixons' plans

The Dixons are excited about their summer holiday – everybody is talking at the same time!
What can you find out about their holiday plans? Choose from the verbs in the middle.
You can start: They are going to be away for two … . Mr Dixon is going to …

Two weeks holiday – great!

Is the Lake District nice?

I hope you don' t get lost in the hills, Dad!

Your bike can go on top of the car, Sarah.

read	cycle	be away for
stay in	walk	travel by
take		visit

You mustn't forget your camera, Kim.

How many bedrooms has the cottage got?

Don't forget to look for some good books, Mum.

3 What you have to do

You are helping at the summer fete. Tell people what they have to do in these games and competitions. Start: 1. You have to kick the ball through … . 2. You have to … *Go on.*

kick

count

guess

answer

hit

4 What they are allowed to do

Finish the sentences with the ideas on the right.

1. It rained at break yesterday, so the pupils were allowed to …
2. Robert didn't feel well on Friday, so he was …
3. Sarah forgot her Maths homework, but she …
4. Some pupils organized a disco. The teachers' …
5. Last week there was a non-uniform day, so everybody …

wear different clothes
dance at the disco, too
stay inside
go home early
bring it the next day

⟨Revision and fun 3⟩

1 The grammar-time rap

Clap, clap, clap – do the grammar-time rap.
Clap, clap, clap – do the grammar-time rap.

think – thought – thought and buy – bought – bought
ring – rang – rung and sing – sang – sung
throw – threw – thrown and know – knew – known.

Clap, clap, clap – …

teach – taught – taught and catch – caught – caught
hide – hid – hidden and ride – rode – ridden
wake – woke – woken and speak – spoke – spoken

Clap, clap, clap – …

cut – cut – cut and shut – shut – shut
fly – flew – flown and grow – grew – grown
sell – sold – sold and tell – told – told

Clap, clap, clap – …

read – read – read – and say – said – said
see – saw – seen and be – was – been
go – went – gone but do – did – done!

2 Which is which?

a) *Read the sentences and find the right verbs. Say what*
- you do with milk, juice or tea
- happens when you are looking for something and you suddenly see it
- you can do with your ears
- you do when you go away
- you do when you take away somebody else's bag
- you do when you move one thing from one place to another
- you do with dresses, pullovers and shirts

Example: I can drink juice, milk or tea.

b) *Write these irregular verbs down and add the other two forms. Example:* drink – drank – drunk

c) *You can make mobiles like this. It'll help you to remember the verbs.*

3 The fox, the goose and the corn

A farmer had a big problem. He was standing by a river. At his side was a basket of corn, a fox and a goose – and the farmer had to take all three to the other side. But his raft was only big enough for himself and **one** of his belongings. Now he couldn't take the fox and leave the goose alone with the corn. The goose would eat it. And he couldn't leave the fox and the goose alone because the fox was hungry. What could he do? Well, a little later the farmer and all three of his belongings were on the other side of the river.

Can you tell the class how he did it?
First he … . Then …

4 The phone game – what were you doing when I rang?

You need twelve pieces of card or paper.
Draw an activity on each card.
Put the cards on the table (so you can't see the pictures).
Now you can make dialogues with a partner.
Example:
You: What were you doing when I rang last night?
Partner: (take a card) I was playing football.

5 The craziest interviewer

Let's find the craziest interviewer. Ask these questions and then try to find more funny questions. Examples:
Have you ever eaten chicken soup with jam and yoghurt? – Oh no, I haven't.
Have you ever seen a green elephant?
Have you ever cleaned …?
Have you ever cooked …?
Have you ever heard …?
Have you ever …?

6 WORD POWER

Can you make compound words? Write them down.
Example: timetable

7 Cartoon fun

8 Words with 'ch'

Make two lists: one with 'ch' = [k]
one with 'ch' = [tʃ]

[k]	[tʃ]
chemist	beach

sandwich beach child chemist stomach lunch school headache teacher technology

9 Monny's jokes

Q: How do you know that carrots are good for your eyes?
A: I've never seen a rabbit with glasses!

Doctor: Did you take the patient's temperature?
Nurse: No, is it missing?

Doctor: What's the matter with your daughter?
Man: She thinks she's a hen!
Doctor: That's terrible. How long has she been this way?
Man: For three years.
Doctor: Why didn't you bring her to see me sooner?
Man: We needed the eggs.

Q: What did the little green man from space say to the petrol pump?
A: Take your finger out of your ear!

Q: Where do you take a sick horse?
A: To horsepital.

Patient: Doctor, Doctor, I feel like an apple!
Doctor: Well, come over here, I won't bite you.

Unit 9 The end of the school year

Step A The Haywood Fete

fete [feɪt]	Feier, Fest	
term [tɜ:m]	Schuljahresabschnitt	At most schools in Britain the school year has got three *terms*.
°**bring-and-buy sale** ['brɪŋ‿ən 'baɪ 'seɪl]	Wohltätigkeitsbasar	
member ['membə]	Mitglied	
band [bænd]	Kapelle, Musikgruppe	When will the *band* play? – On Saturday, at 4 o'clock.
concert ['kɒnsət]	Konzert	
attraction [ə'trækʃn]	Attraktion	
competition [ˌkɒmpə'tɪʃn]	Wettbewerb	
toy [tɔɪ]	Spielzeug	
°**charity** ['tʃærətɪ]	Wohltätigkeitsverein	
°**Margaret** ['mɑ:gərɪt]	*weibl. Vorname*	

Step A A normal day – an unlucky day

normal ['nɔ:ml]	normal	A *normal* school day at Haywood School begins at 8.50 in the morning.
unlucky [ˌʌn'lʌkɪ]	unglücklich	We were *unlucky* – we didn't win anything.
to **damage** ['dæmɪdʒ]	beschädigen, Schaden anrichten	
°**grumpy** ['grʌmpɪ]	mürrisch, schlecht gelaunt	
to **pay** [peɪ]	zahlen	I like your new shirt. How much did you *pay* for it?
rule [ru:l]	Regel	
sunroof ['sʌnru:f]	Schiebedach	
dry [draɪ]	trocken	*dry* ⟷ wet
4 to **lose, lost, lost** [lu:z, lɒst]	verlieren	
5 **musical** ['mju:zɪkl]	musikalisch	
trumpet ['trʌmpɪt]	Trompete	

Step B Plans for Saturday

to **sell** [sel]	verkaufen	
to **count** [kaʊnt]	zählen	
2 °**Melanie** ['melənɪ]	*weibl. Vorname*	
3 °**Superman** ['su:pəmæn]	*Comicfigur*	
4 °**future** ['fju:tʃə]	Zukunft	
°**library** ['laɪbrərɪ]	Bibliothek	
°**preposition** [ˌprepə'zɪʃn]	Präposition	

Step B Uniforms

°**non-uniform day** ['nɒn‿'ju:nɪfɔ:m ˌdeɪ]	*Tag, an dem keine Schuluniform getragen werden muss*	

Looking at the UK: Helping charities

°to **sponsor** ['spɒnsə]	spenden, sponsern	
sale [seɪl]	Verkauf	
disco ['dɪskəʊ]	Disko, Tanzveranstaltung mit Popmusik	
pence *(pl)* [pens]	*engl. Münze*	
to **work together** ['wɜːk tə'geðə]	zusammenarbeiten	
°**appeal** [ə'piːl]	Aufruf	

Step D **Lucky weather**

°**superclean** ['suːpəkliːn]	blitzsauber	
°**Parkinson** ['pɑːkɪnsn]	*Familienname*	
to **cost, cost, cost** [kɒst]	kosten	
bucket ['bʌkɪt]	Eimer	

Step E **Workshop 1**

1 °**rope** [rəʊp]	Seil	You can jump or climb with a *rope*.
°**jelly** ['dʒelɪ]	Wackelpudding	
°to **wiggle** ['wɪgl]	sich wenden, zappeln	
°to **woggle** ['wɒgl]	wackeln	
°**pan** [pæn]	Topf	
°**jam** [dʒæm]	Marmelade	
°to **pull** [pʊl]	ziehen	
°**penny, pennies** ['penɪ, 'penɪz]	*engl. Münze*	
°**dirt** [dɜːt]	Schmutz	
°to **sweep** [swiːp]	kehren, fegen	
°**robber** ['rɒbə]	Dieb/in	
°**ant** [ænt]	Ameise	
°**pants** [pænts]	Unterhose; Hose	
°to **scratch** [skrætʃ]	kratzen	
2 °**Denmark** ['denmɑːk]	Dänemark	*Denmark* is a country in the north of Europe.
°**alphabetical** [ˌælfə'betɪkl]	alphabetisch	

Vocabulary

Step E **Workshop 2**

°**Tanya** ['tænjə]	*weibl. Vorname*	
moody ['muːdɪ]	launisch	
terribly ['terəblɪ]	schrecklich	
to **consider** [kən'sɪdə]	überlegen	
mightn't (= might not) ['maɪtnt]	könnte (vielleicht) nicht	
to **grin** [grɪn]	lächeln, grinsen	
to **yell** [jel]	schreien	
bore [bɔː]	Langweiler	
to **sniffle** ['snɪfl]	schniefen	
to **snore** [snɔː]	schnarchen	

Step F **Let's check**

cottage ['kɒtɪdʒ]	Cottage, Landhäuschen

⟨Revision and fun 3⟩

1	who cares? [hu: 'kɜəz]	(und) wenn schon?
3	fox [fɒks]	Fuchs
	corn [kɔ:n]	Getreide
	raft [rɑ:ft]	Floß
	belongings [bɪ'lɒŋɪŋz]	Sachen
	even ['i:vən]	auch, selbst
	unwell [ʌn'wel]	krank, schlecht
	rabbit ['ræbɪt]	Kaninchen
	to be down with (flu) ['daʊn wɪð]	krank sein mit
	sooner ['su:nə]	früher
	space [speɪs]	Weltraum
	petrol pump ['petrəl 'pʌmp]	Zapfsäule
	to bite [baɪt]	beißen

to do

Have you **done** your homework yet?
Can you **do** this exercise?
What did you **do** on holiday last year?
What are you **doing** here?
Have you **done** the washing up?

to take

Robert is **taking** a photo of Sarah.
Please listen and **take** notes.
Please **take** off your shoes.
Who has **taken** my pencil?
Grandma **took** the children home.

to make

Mrs Croft has **made** a cake.
Can I **make** a request? Please play 'Help'.
Make notes for a summary, please!

to get

Get well soon!
Last week I **got** lost in Sherwood Forest.
Tabby **got** stuck in a tree yesterday.
What time do you **get** up on Sundays?
Before I go to school I **get** my books ready.
How can I **get** to the city centre?
I always **get** tired when I watch TV.

⟨The story of jeans⟩

1 From Buttenheim to San Francisco

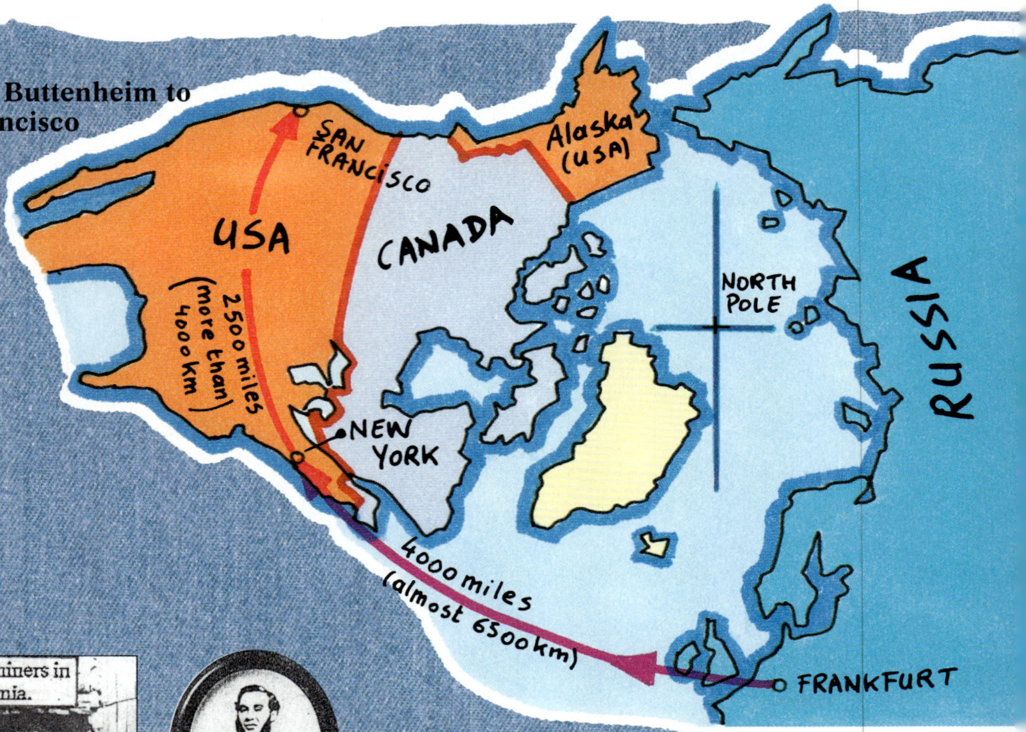

Levi Strauss (1829 – 1902) A German Jew from Buttenheim, near Frankfurt am Main.

- In 1848, Levi Strauss left his home in Buttenheim, near Frankfurt. He went by ship to New York. He was seventeen years old.
- In 1849, someone found gold in California. Thousands of people went west to look for gold.
- In 1853, Strauss travelled west to California. There, he made the first 'jeans' and sold them to the gold miners.

2 From America to the world

German boys and girls in Lederhosen, 1950s.

German kids today.

- When Strauss died in 1902, he was a millionaire. But in Europe nobody wore his jeans.
- American soldiers brought them to Europe after 1945.
- In the 1950s and 1960s more and more boys and girls in Germany wanted to wear 'Nietenhosen'. Parents and teachers didn't like these new American jeans.
- And today? …

3 Levi Strauss gets his great idea

Match the sentences.

Levi wants to sell	don't need tents.
But the gold miners	trousers.
They need	a great idea.
Levi gets	a 'gold mine'.
He can make	tents to miners.
The idea is	trousers out of his tents.

1

2

3

4

5

6

4 Everybody can wear jeans now

Which text goes with which photo? Example: Text a) goes with photo 3.

a) It was a shock (for men) when women started to wear jeans.

b) In the 1960s, jeans were the 'uniform' of young people.

c) In 1853, Levi Strauss made the first jeans for miners in the gold mines of California.

d) Today, everybody wears jeans – from poor kids to the President of the USA.

e) The 1950s, James Dean wore jeans in his films. But parents and teachers told children "You must not wear jeans to school!"

f) At first, jeans were working clothes for people like this cowboy in Texas.

5 A class survey

- *How many people are wearing jeans in your English class today?*
- *Are all the jeans made in the USA.*
- *What colours are they?*

	boys	girls	teacher
jeans			
other trousers			
skirts and dresses			

(A project)

6 ⟨A song: Jeans on⟩ © Text and music: David Dundas/Greenway

1. When I wake up in the morning light,
   I pull on my jeans and I feel all right.
   I pull my blue jeans on,
   I pull my old blue jeans on.
   I pull my blue jeans on,
   I pull my old blue jeans on

2. It's the weekend and I know that you're free,
   So pull on your jeans and come on out with me.
   I need to have you near me, I need to feel you close to me.

3. You and me, we'll go motorbike-riding,
   In the sun and the wind and the rain.
   I got money in my pocket, got a tiger in my tank,
   And I'm king of the road again.

4. I'll meet you in the usual place,
   I don't need anything 'cept your pretty face,
   And I need to have you near me, I need to feel you close to me.
   I need to have you near me, I need to feel you close to me.

7 WORD POWER

a) *You should know these words:*
free, motorbike (think of *bike*), sun (think of *sunny, sun cream*), wind, tank, light (think of the German words), king, usual (think of *usually*).

b) *You know other English words that mean the same:*
close to = near; pull on = put on

c) *Now you only need three words in German:*
rain = Regen; 'cept = außer; pretty = hübsch

8 A jeans joke

Q: Is jeans singular or plural?
A: Well, it's singular at the top and plural at the bottom.

⟨A project⟩

9 Your fashion show

Here's how to do it:

1. Collect old clothes (ask your friends, brothers and sisters, parents and grandparents ...).
Here are some ideas:

2. Who is going to wear what?
3. You need some good music on cassettes or CDs and a cassette recorder or CD player.
And you need a 'DJ'.
4. You need some good texts, too.
What can you say about somebody's 'outfit'? It can be ...

cool · cheap · modern · big · different · fantastic · lovely · warm · new · exciting · smart · small · expensive

And where can you wear these clothes?

in the bed · at the disco · in the kitchen · in the cinema · at the swimming pool · at school · at home · at a pop concert · on the beach

5. Get your classroom (or the assembly hall) ready.
... AND NOW IT'S TIME FOR THE SHOW!

⟨A project⟩

Things to say:

Jennifer Hakan …	looks	fantastic good …	in a black pullover …	with black jeans. …

The This These	exciting dress warm pyjamas … boots	is are …	great for the disco. great for a cold night in a tent.

10 Time for a poem: Boots

© Tony Bradman

When the rain is raining,
When it's raining on the street,
I'm glad I've got my boots on,
My boots upon my feet.

For when the rain is raining,
I can splash and I can stamp,
And while I've got my boots on,
My feet will not get damp.

And when the rain is raining,
I've got my little brolly;
I'll keep it up above my head,
And stay quite dry and jolly.

But when the rain is pouring,
When it comes down very fast,
I think we'd better stay in –
Until the storm is past!

⟨A project⟩

11 Let's dance the Longway

Well, after a fashion show and with nice clothes on, how about a dance … the Longway! The song 'Skip to my Lou' is from America. Listen to it and dance the Longway. It's easy and it's great fun at the end of the school year (and at the end of the project)!

Skip to my Lou

Lost my partner, skip to my Lou, lost my partner, skip to my Lou
lost my partner, skip to my Lou, skip to my Lou my darlin'.
Refrain: Hey, hey, skip … hey, hey, …
hey, hey, …

I'll get another one prettier than you …
Stole my partner, what'll I do? …
I'll get another one quicker than you …

1. Stand in two lines (Girl – Boy – Girl – Boy …) and make a passage like this:

B G B G B G …

G B G B G B …
1 2 3 4 5 6 …

2. When the music starts, the pairs No 1, 3, 5, 7, … walk through the passage. They walk hand in hand. They start with the left foot and go eight steps. On step No. 8 they turn around and walk eight steps back.

3. Now the pairs No. 2, 4, 6, 8, … do the same.

4. Two neighbouring partners always walk hand in hand: they walk eight steps backwards and then eight steps forwards again.
Like this:

5. What other ways can you think of? Can you dance the Longway with changing partners in the middle? Maybe like this:

B G B G B G B G

G B G B G B G B

6. Where can you dance? What clothes can you wear for the dance? Maybe you can all wear nice scarves?

7. There are lots of other things to think of: when you walk hand in hand with a partner, where is your other hand? Don't forget to smile!

8. Try out as many things as you can. And have fun!

⟨A project⟩

⟨Project: The story of jeans⟩

1	°**San Francisco** [ˌsænfrənˈsɪskəʊ]	*Großstadt in den USA*
	gold miner [ˈgəʊld ˌmaɪnə]	Goldgräber
	°**California** [ˌkælɪˈfɔːnjə]	*amerik. Bundesstaat*
	°**Levi Strauss** [ˈliːvaɪ ˈstraʊs]	*Personenname*
	Jew [dʒuː]	Jude
	by ship [baɪ ˈʃɪp]	mit dem Schiff
	°**New York** [ˌnjuː ˈjɔːk]	*Großstadt in den USA*
2	**millionaire** [ˌmɪljəˈneə]	Millionär
	to **wear** [weə]	tragen
	soldier [ˈsəʊldʒə]	Soldat
3	**tent** [tent]	Zelt
4	**shock** [ʃɒk]	Schock
	cowboy [ˈkaʊbɔɪ]	Cowboy
	°**Texas** [ˈteksəs]	*amerik. Bundesstaat*
8	**singular** [ˈsɪŋgjʊlə]	Singular
	plural [ˈplʊərəl]	Mehrzahl
	at the bottom [ˈbɒtəm]	unten
9	**fashion show** [ˈfæʃn ˌʃəʊ]	Modenschau
	fashion [ˈfæʃn]	Mode
	glove [glʌv]	Handschuh
	cap [kæp]	Mütze
	pyjamas [pəˈdʒɑːməz]	Schlafanzug, Pyjama
	outfit [ˈaʊtfɪt]	Kleidung
	smart [smɑːt]	schick
10	to **stamp** [stæmp]	stampfen
	damp [dæmp]	feucht
	brolly [ˈbrɒlɪ]	Regenschirm
	jolly [ˈdʒɒlɪ]	lustig, vergnügt
	to **pour** [pɔː]	gießen
	past [pɑːst]	*hier:* vorbei
11	°**Longway** [ˈlɒŋweɪ]	*Name eines Tanzes*
	passage [ˈpæsɪdʒ]	(Durch-)Gang, Passage
	step [step]	Schritt

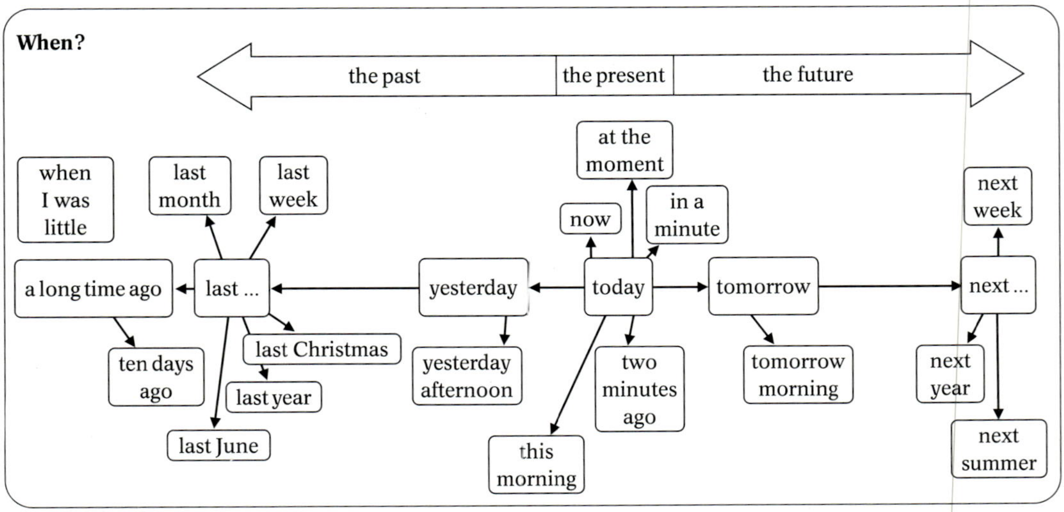

Let's play with words

1 My family

Margaret Miller ∞ Jack Miller — Victoria Hilton ∞ Tom Hilton

David Miller — Mary Miller — Alan Miller ∞ Janet Hilton — Sam Hilton — Audrey Hilton

Michael Miller — Helen Miller — Sarah Miller

Hello, I'm Helen. This is my family. Please find out:

1. *What are my brother's, sister's, father's, mother's, aunts', uncles', grandpas' and grandmas' names?*
2. *How many sons and daughters are there in our family? (Don't forget my grandpas' and my grandmas' children!)*

2 Clothes

Mr Penrose is washing clothes. Mark is helping him. He's thinking: Which clothes go on your arms, which clothes go on your legs? Can you help him?

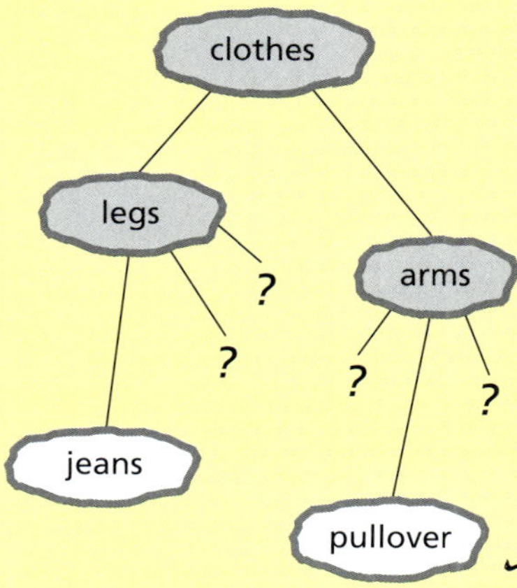

Let's play with words

3 In town

The twinning office of Greentown is working on a nice new map for their town. But, oh dear, their computer has got it all wrong! Can you find out what went wrong? Start like this: Number 1 must be ..., Number 2 ... . So the computer wrote ♠ for the letter ..., ✓ for ... .

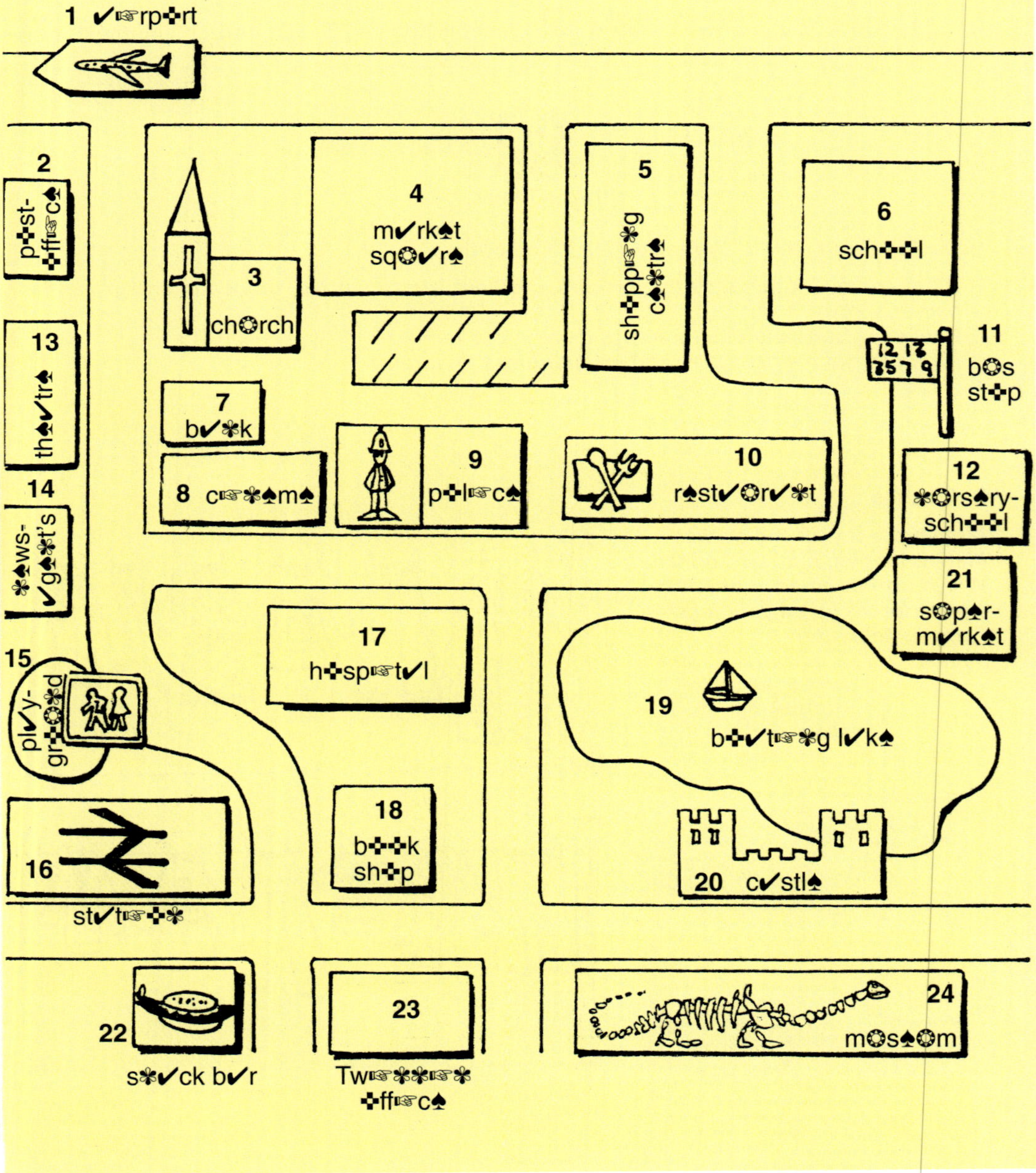

Let's play with words

4 Animal words

Can you find four animals in this word wheel?

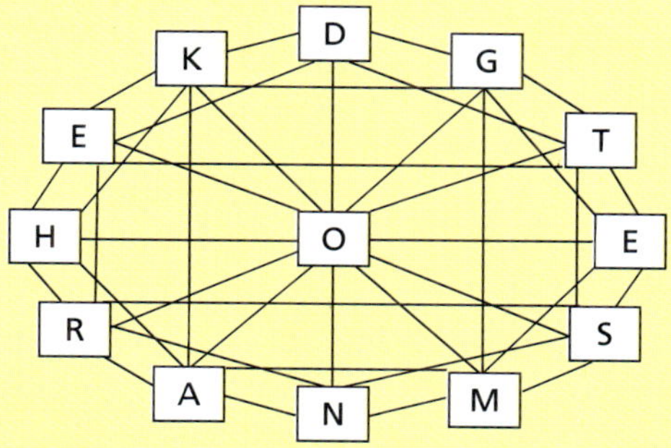

5 Funny pictures

Look at these funny pictures. Can you understand them? Write the sentences in your English folder.

A BRAC is saying hello to a SHIF.

A white OSEMU is running home through the snow.

A NILO has left its cage.

A NEKYMO is asking for a banana.

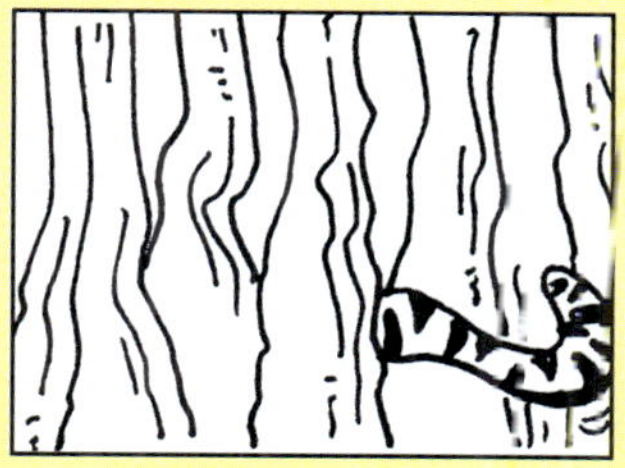

A RIGET is going through the forest.

A BRIBAT doesn't like its carrot.

A black ERAB is talking to his friend, a black HEFESGOD, at night.

An APHELENT is standing in a pond.

Can you make funny pictures for your friends? Put them in your folder, too.

⟨Extra line⟩

1 Robin Hood and the Sheriff

(after Unit 2)

One day, the Sheriff's men caught Will Scarlet, one of the outlaws. They took him to Nottingham. "Ah! One of Robin Hood's men!" said the Sheriff when he saw Will. "Take him to the gallows in the market square tomorrow. Then everyone can see what happens to outlaws!"

That evening Robin and his men heard the news. "We must go to Nottingham at once and save Will!" said one of the outlaws. "Wait," said Robin. "Will is a prisoner in Nottingham Castle. We can't get to him there. But we must save him! What can we do?" "I know the hangman!" said Friar Tuck suddenly. "Good. – Now I've got an idea," said Robin. "Go to Nottingham right away … ." "Can't we all go?" asked another outlaw. "Wait, it's our turn tomorrow!" said Robin.

Early the next morning, Robin was on the way to Nottingham. Twelve of his men were with him. They wore coats over their green clothes, and under their coats they had their bows and arrows.

On the way they met a poor old man in a long black coat with a hood. "Good morning, friend," said Robin. "That's a nice long coat. Can I buy it from you?" "This dirty old thing? You can have it for a pound!" "Thanks," said Robin. He took the coat and gave the old man five pounds. "For you and your family. Take it! Goodbye!" "Five pounds? But that's … ." The old man wanted to thank him, but Robin and his men were already on their way.

At twelve o'clock there were a lot of people in the market square. A man with a rope stood under the gallows. It was Will Scarlet. The Sheriff was there with twenty men. "Well, where's the hangman?" the Sheriff asked his men. But nobody knew. "We can't find him," said one man. "He drank too much last night!" said another, and a lot of people laughed. The Sheriff was angry now. "We need a hangman!" he shouted to the people in the square. "Well? Does nobody want to do the job? For five pounds? For ten pounds?" At first nobody answered. Nobody wanted to help the Sheriff. Then an old man in a black coat with a hood came up to the gallows. "I can do the job for you!" he said. The people in the square were angry when they heard this. A boy threw an apple at the old man. A woman threw an egg.

"Come on! Do the job!" said the Sheriff, and he gave the old man the money. The old man went behind the prisoner.
"What are you doing with that rope?" shouted the Sheriff. "Come on, man! Do your job!"
But suddenly the old man threw off his black coat and stood there – in green clothes now, and with a bow in his hands.
"It's Robin Hood!" a woman shouted. At the same time, Robin's men took off their coats and ran through the crowd with their bows and arrows, ready to help Robin.

"Stop them!" shouted the Sheriff to his men. But the outlaws were ready for them. When the Sheriff's men came after them, Robin shot an arrow from his bow. It went straight into the Sheriff's big hat.
"Be careful, Sheriff!" laughed Robin.

That was enough for the Sheriff. In a minute or two he and all his men were gone. Now Will Scarlet was with his friends again. Robin threw the ten pounds from his purse into the crowd.
"A present from the Sheriff!" he called. Then he and his men were gone – back to their home in Sherwood Forest.

coat [kəʊt] *Mantel*; hood [hʊd] *Kapuze*; rope [rəʊp] *Seil, Strick*; to take off [ˌteɪk_ˈɒf] *ausziehen*; crowd [kraʊd] *Menge, Menschenmenge*; hat [hæt] *Hut*

1 The story

1. The Sheriff's men caught Will Scarlet and … → took him to Nottingham.
2. Robin and the other outlaws were worried when …
3. Friar Tuck knew the hangman, so …
4. Next day Robin and twelve of the others went to Nottingham and …
5. He gave Robin his black coat, and …
6. At 12 o'clock Will Scarlet stood under the gallows, but …
7. "I can do the job!" said an old man, but …
8. "It's Robin Hood!" a woman shouted when …
9. The Sheriff was very scared when …
10. So Robin and his men saved Will, and …

the old man threw off his coat.
people in the crowd threw things at him.
they all went back to Sherwood Forest.
he went to Nottingham right away.
took him to Nottingham.
Robin shot an arrow through his hat.
Robin gave him five pounds for it
on the way they met an old man.
they heard the news.
there was no hangman.

2 A story from Ireland

(after Unit 3)

Long, long ago in Ireland, there was a giant. His name was O'Connor. "I'm the biggest and strongest man in Ireland," he shouted. He climbed the highest mountains. He carried the heaviest stones. He jumped over the highest walls. And he walked through the deepest water. Of course, he needed very long trousers, big pullovers and large shoes.
"And I can tell the best stories in Ireland," O'Connor said. In the evening in the pub he was very noisy. The people of the village did not like him very much.
One afternoon they rushed to O'Connor's house and shouted, "O'Connor! There's a giant from Scotland in the pub. He's bigger and stronger than you. He says he can climb higher mountains than you. He can carry heavier stones than you. And he says he can jump over higher walls and walk through deeper water."

"And what about his clothes?" asked O'Connor.
"His trousers are longer," they answered. "His pullover is bigger and his shoes are larger. He says he can tell better stories than you. And he wants to come and fight you!"
O'Connor was very worried. "What can I do?" he asked his wife. She had an idea, "Quick, jump into the baby's bed," she said. His wife put the baby's bonnet on his head. Just then the Scottish giant rushed in. "Where is that little Irishman?" he shouted. "He's not in," answered O'Connor's wife, "but come and have a look at his baby instead." The Scottish giant did so and looked at the 'baby'. "Let me out, let me out," he shouted. "I don't want to meet this baby's father." And he rushed out of the house and out of the village. The people in the village often laughed about 'O'Connor the Baby'.

story ['stɔːrɪ] *Geschichte, Erzählung*; Ireland ['aɪələnd] *Irland*; giant ['dʒaɪənt] *Riese*; mountain ['maʊntɪn] *Berg*; deep [diːp] *tief*; pub [pʌb] *Kneipe, Wirtschaft*; to rush [rʌʃ] *rasen, stürmen*; to fight [faɪt] *kämpfen*; bonnet ['bɒnɪt] *Mütze, Haube*; head [hed] *Kopf*; Irishman ['aɪrɪʃˌmən] *Ire*; in [ɪn] *zu Hause*; instead [ɪn'sted] *stattdessen*

1 The giant and the baby *Can you say why?*

Why
- did O'Connor need very big clothes
- didn't the people of the village like O'Connor very much
- did they rush to his house one afternoon
- was O'Connor worried
- did the Scottish giant run out of O'Connor's house
- did the people in the village often laugh about O'Connor

?

2 The strongest giant in Ireland *Put adjectives in the right form.*

1. "I'm the … and … giant in Ireland," O'Connor shouted.
2. He climbed the … mountains, and he carried the … stones.
3. He needed … shoes than everyone else.
4. In the pub he was the … giant in Ireland.
5. "And I can tell the … stories," he often said.
6. The people of the village said to O'Connor, "The Scottish giant in the pub is … and … than you!"
7. "He can climb … mountains than you."
8. "He can carry … stones than you."
9. "And his clothes are much … than your clothes."

⟨Extra line⟩

3 The Canterville Ghost

(after Unit 4)

Here is an extract from 'The Canterville Ghost' by Oscar Wilde:

There was thunder and lightning all that night. The next morning, when the American family came down to breakfast, they found the terrible bloodstain on the floor again. "I've tried to clean it," said Washington. "It must be the ghost." He cleaned the floor, but the second morning it was there again. That evening, Mr Otis locked the door and took the key away with him. But the third morning, the stain was there again. All the family were frightened now. The next day was nice and warm. In the evening the family went out for a walk. They came home late in the evening. Then they had dinner. At eleven o'clock they went to bed.

Some time later, Mr Otis heard a strange sound in the corridor outside his room. He got up to see what time it was. It was one o'clock. Then he heard a noise behind the door. He opened it, and there he saw a terrible old man. He had long white hair, his eyes were like fire, and there were heavy chains on his hands and feet.

"My dear sir," said Mr Otis, "you must not make such a noise. Here is some oil for your chains. Tomorrow I can give you some more." And with these words Mr Otis closed his door and went back to bed.

For a short time the Canterville ghost stood quite still. Then he threw the bottle on the floor and ran down the corridor. An awful green light came from him. He came to the end of the corridor. A door opened quietly and someone threw a large pillow at his head. He had to get away, so he went through the wall. Then the house became quiet again. When he got to his little room, he sat down to think.

extract ['ekstrækt] *Auszug*; thunder ['θʌndə] *Donner*; lightning ['laɪtnɪŋ] *Blitz*; bloodstain ['blʌdsteɪn] *Blutfleck*; floor [flɔː] *Fußboden*; to try [traɪ] *versuchen*; to take away [ˌteɪk‿ə'weɪ] *mitnehmen*; strange [streɪndʒ] *merkwürdig*; sound [saʊnd] *Geräusch*; fire ['faɪə] *Feuer*; heavy ['hevɪ] *schwer*; chain [tʃeɪn] *Kette*; must not ['mʌstˌnɒt] *nicht dürfen*; oil [ɔɪl] *Öl*; still [stɪl] *still, reglos*; awful ['ɔːfʊl] *schrecklich*; pillow ['pɪləʊ] *Kissen*

1 Did you understand?

1. What do you find out about the bloodstain?
2. What did Mr Otis hear in the corridor and what did he do?
3. What did the ghost look like?
4. What did the ghost do?

2 Your ghost

a) *Draw a picture of the ghost. Talk about him. Find some adjectives to say what kind of character he is.*

b) *What do you think the ghost can do to frighten the Americans? Make a plan for him.*
Examples: The ghost can … . He could also …

4 The sound of the cricket and the sound of money (after Unit 5)

1. One day an old farmer came to town to visit a friend there. It was very exciting for the old man to walk around the city centre with his friend and to see all the noisy cars and buses and the people. Suddenly, the farmer stopped and said to his friend, "Stop for a moment. Can you hear what I can hear?" – His friend listened, smiled and then answered, "Well, I can hear the cars and buses and the voices of the people. What can you hear?" – "I can hear a cricket. It's chirping under the bush in front of that house over there." His friend listened again. Then he said, "I can't hear anything. You must be wrong. There aren't any crickets here in the city centre." The old farmer walked over to the bush, and there *was* a cricket. Now his friend saw it and could hear it.

2. After a while the farmer's friend said, "Of course you country people can hear better than we townspeople. People from the country have better hearing. Everybody knows that." The farmer smiled and answered, "You're wrong there, my friend. The hearing of a man from the country is no better or worse than the hearing of a man in a town. Pay attention, I will show you something."

3. He took a coin out of his purse and threw it down in the street. It tinkled on the stones and people noticed the sound and turned around. A boy came and picked it up and went away. "You see," said the old farmer, "the sound of the money was no louder than the noise of the cricket. And yet people heard it. But nobody heard the sound of the cricket. That is because we all hear best the things that we like best."

cricket ['krɪkɪt] *Grille*; moment ['məʊmənt] *Augenblick*; to chirp [tʃɜːp] *zirpen*; bush [bʊʃ] *Busch, Strauch*; country ['kʌntrɪ] *Land*; townspeople ['taʊnzˌpiːpl] *Stadtleute, Städter;* hearing ['hɪərɪŋ] *Gehör*; to pay attention [ˌpeɪ‿ə'tenʃn] *aufpassen*; coin [kɔɪn] *Münze*; to tinkle ['tɪŋkl] *hell (er)klingen*; to pick up [ˌpɪk‿'ʌp] *aufheben, in die Hand nehmen*; yet [jet] *trotzdem*

1 Questions about the text

a) *Make two groups. Group A takes section 1, group B looks at sections 2 and 3. Write down three or four questions about your section. Ask: Who? When? What? Where? Why?*
Example: Where did the old farmer come from?

b) *Ask all the questions in class and write down the answers. Now put all the answers in the right order to tell the story again. What are the most important things in the story?*

2 Your opinion

1. What can you hear in a city or a village? Make two lists.
2. An old man or woman from a small village comes to a big city. What can make him or her nervous or worried? What do you think?
3. What do you think about people from the country like the old farmer in this story?
   – Are people from the country like the old farmer in this story?
   – And are people in town like the farmer's friend? Say why or why not.
4. Where would you like to live: in a city or in a village? Say why.

⟨Extra line⟩

5 Have you ever seen a spaghetti bush? (after Unit 6)

You haven't? But perhaps someone has made an April fool of you?
In England, the first day of April is called April Fools' Day. Anyone can make another person an April fool on this day up till twelve o'clock midday. As in Germany, it is a very old tradition, and many of the tricks and jokes are very old, too. But children play these tricks again and again: someone tells you that your shoelace is undone, that there is something wrong with your clothes, or that someone at the door wants to speak to you ... but your shoelace is not undone, your clothes are all right and there is no one at the door. When you get excited, they shout 'April fool!' at you.
At the end of March 1698 someone sent people invitations to watch the washing of the lions at the Tower of London on 1st April. A lot of them went there because they wanted to see the lions, so they were April fools. You can read about this trick in an old London newspaper of 2nd April 1698.
On 1st April 1957 the BBC played a very good trick on their viewers. (At that time not every family had a television.) They showed a film about spaghetti farms in Switzerland. The men on the farms were picking spaghetti from bushes. When the film was over, hundreds of viewers phoned the BBC. Many of them liked the joke very much. Others wanted to know where they could buy spaghetti bushes. And some people were no longer sure that you need flour and water to make spaghetti!
And what about you? Would you like to have a spaghetti bush in your garden?

fool [fu:l] *Narr*; midday ['mɪddeɪ] *Mittag*; tradition [trə'dɪʃn] *Tradition*; joke [dʒəʊk] *Scherz*; shoelace ['ʃu:leɪs] *Schnürsenkel*; undone [ˌʌn'dʌn] *auf*; lion ['laɪən] *Löwe*; Tower ['taʊə] *Turm, Festung*; viewer ['vju:ə] *Zuschauer/in*; television [ˌtelə'vɪʒn] *Fernseher*; Switzerland ['swɪtsəˌlənd] *die Schweiz*; to pick [pɪk] *pflücken*; over ['əʊvə] *vorbei*; flour ['flaʊə] *Mehl*

1 What is it about?

Find good headings for each of the three main paragraphs.

2 Three stories

Read the text again and write down some key words. They will help you to retell the three parts of the text. Example:

1. first day – April Fools' Day, make a person an April fool, a very old tradition, play tricks: shoelace undone, something wrong with clothes, somebody at the door, shout 'April Fool!'

3 A nice trick

a) *Look at this list of tricks and say which one you like best and which you don't like so much. Say why.*

shoelace undone
somebody must go to head teacher
something wrong with clothes
tell somebody that there is a test
spider on your arm
somebody at the door
send somebody to the wrong place
cups and plates broken
...

b) *Which of these tricks have you already played on your friends/parents/teachers ...?*

⟨Extra line⟩

6 The haggis

(after Unit 7)

Kate and Fiona are at a snack bar near their youth hostel. They have got their food, and they are looking for a seat. They see two of the boys from the hostel. There are two empty seats at their table.

Fiona: Hello, you two. Can we sit down here?

Boy: Sure, We're finished. Hey Fiona. Are you Scotch?

Fiona: No, I am *not* Scotch, I'm Scott*ish*.

Boy: Well, if you're Scott*ish*, why are you eating sausages? Why aren't you eating haggis?

Fiona: Why should I? Keep your eyes on your own plate.

2nd boy: All Scots eat haggis. All the time. Everyone knows that. For their breakfast. For their lunch. For their tea. In their sandwiches at school.

Fiona: Ha, ha. Very funny.

2nd boy: They even *look* like haggis.

Fiona: Oh, shut up.

Kate: Leave Fiona alone. You don't even know what a haggis is.

1st boy: Hey, Fiona. Tell us what a haggis is.

Fiona: You mean to say you don't know what a haggis is? Don't they teach you anything in England?

Kate: Come on, Fiona, tell them.

Fiona: Well, a haggis is a small, round animal with four legs, and long hair. It lives in the mountains and it eats grass.

2nd boy: Like a rabbit. We've got lots of those, too.

Fiona: Well, no. Not like a rabbit. You see, a rabbit has two short legs at the front, and two long legs at the back. But the haggis has two short legs on one side, and two long legs on the other side.

1st boy: I've never heard of that before.

Fiona: No, I bet you don't have those in England.

2nd boy: We certainly don't. Are they dangerous?

Fiona: No, not really.

1st boy: How do you catch a haggis?

Fiona: Well, that's very interesting. You see, because their legs on one side are shorter than the other side, they can't walk up and down a mountain. They can only walk round it.

2nd boy: I see. With the short legs on the hill side and the long legs on the valley side.

Fiona: Yes, that's right. And they can only walk round it in one way. So you hide until you see one. Then you jump out in front of it. It turns round, and then of course it falls down because it can't stand. And then you catch it.

1st boy: Are there any near here?

Fiona: I suppose so. High up in the hills. But you don't see them often.

1st boy: Come on, Tom, let's see if we can catch a haggis.

Kate: Hey, they believed you. Aren't they silly?

Fiona: Yes. Typical English. You can tell them anything and they'll believe it.

haggis ['hægɪs] *schottisches Nationalgericht*; youth hostel ['ju:θˌhɒstl] *Jugendherberge*; seat [si:t] *Platz*; Scotch [skɒtʃ] *schottischer Whisky*; to bet [bet] *wetten*; to catch [kætʃ] *fangen*; valley ['vælɪ] *Tal*; I suppose so [sə'pəʊz] *Ich denke schon*; to believe [bɪ'li:v] *glauben*; typical ['tɪpɪkl] *typisch*

1 Comprehension

⟨Extra line⟩

a) Can you answer these questions?
   1. What's the difference between a rabbit and a haggis? 2. How does a haggis walk? 3. How do you catch a haggis? 4. Is a haggis dangerous?

b) 1. Is there an animal like a haggis? 2. Why did Fiona tell the story? 3. Did Kate know the story already? (How do you know?) 4. Why do the boys believe Fiona?

c) Can you tell the story of the haggis in your own words?

7 The shrinking plant

(after Unit 8)

Hannah and Bertie live with their mum and dad in a house in a normal street.
One day a very strange thing happens. Hannah and her brother go into their dad's study, and on the desk Hannah sees a book. Dad has always told the children not to go into his study. But the book looks so interesting. It's title is 'Strange Plants of the World'. There is a picture of a plant with leaves as big as a car!
"Hey, Bertie," Hannah says, "Listen to this. 'The leaves of the Brazilian Dub-Dub plant can make you smaller if you eat them! A man can shrink to the size of an insect! You can only become normal again if you drink a lot of milk!' Look, Bertie!"
Bertie looks at the picture of the fantastic plant. "Don't we have a plant like that downstairs in the living room?"
The children run downstairs into the living room. They find the same plant there!
"Let's eat a leaf and see what happens," says Hannah.

Stop reading! What do you think? Will the children eat a leaf? What will happen?

(b) "I will if you will," says Bertie. And that's what they do. Suddenly, their living room is huge. Above them they can see the Dub-Dub plant. It looks like a big tree now. "Wow!" says Bertie. "We're as small as insects!"
"Let's show Mum! She'll never believe it!"They run through the living-room and into the kitchen. "Mum, Mum!" they shout. "Look at us!" But Mum can't hear them. She is getting something out of a cupboard. Suddenly, Felix the cat comes into the kitchen from the garden through the catflap. He walks over to his milk in the corner."Hello Felix," says Mum. "Are you hungry again? Drink your milk. I'll give you some …" But Felix isn't listening to Mum. He has seen something a lot more interesting than the milk next to the fridge. Something tasty!

Stop reading! What has Felix seen? What will he do?

(c) Yes! Felix has seen the children! Of course, he doesn't know these two little things are Hannah and Bertie. He thinks they are something tasty to eat. His eyes grow bigger and bigger. He runs over to the fridge!
"Oh no!" says Hannah. "He's seen us!"
"Quickly!" says Bertie. "Under the fridge!"
Suddenly there is a terrible noise. It's something electric and very, very noisy …

⟨Extra line⟩

Stop reading!
What is making the noise? What will Felix do?

ⓓ The noise is like a hundred tornadoes. Mum is using the vacuum cleaner on the kitchen floor. Felix hates vacuum cleaners. He runs out through the catflap.
"Oh no! Now the vacuum cleaner is coming this way. Mum can't see us and she always vacuums under the fridge!"
"Wait a minute," says Hannah. "Dad's book said how to become normal again."
"It said, 'Drink milk'," says Bertie. "Lots of milk."
"Well there's milk in the fridge," says Hannah.
"But we're too small to open the fridge door! And the vacuum cleaner is coming!"
"I have an idea!" says Hannah. "Quick, follow me!"

Stop reading!
What is Hannah's idea? What will the children do?

ⓔ They run across the kitchen floor to Felix's milk in the corner. It is as big as a lake! They drink the milk from their hands. Suddenly they are big again!
"Oh, there you are, you two!" says Mum. "It's time to clean your rooms …"
"But Mum!" the children shout. "You'll never believe …"
"No buts!" says Mum. "Your rooms are a mess!"

What do you think? Will Mum believe their story or not? Will they tell Dad?
What will the family do with the Brazilian Dub-Dub plant?

to shrink [ʃrɪŋk] *schrumpfen, eingehen*; plant [plɑ:nt] *Pflanze*; normal ['nɔ:ml] *normal*; study ['stʌdɪ] *Arbeitszimmer*; Brazilian [brə'zɪljən] *brasilianisch*; insect ['ɪnsekt] *Insekt*; huge [hju:dʒ] *riesig, enorm*; catflap ['kætflæp] *Katzentür*; fridge [frɪdʒ] *Kühlschrank*; tasty ['teɪstɪ] *es schmeckt gut*; electric [ɪ'lektrɪk] *elektrisch*; tornado [tɔ:'neɪdəʊ] *Wirbelsturm*; vacuum cleaner ['vækjʊəm 'kli:nə] *Staubsauger*; to vacuum ['vækjʊəm] *staubsaugen*; No buts ['nəʊ 'bʌts] *kein Aber*; mess [mes] *Unordnung*

1 The most important events

Work in small groups. Here are the most important events of the story. Write the sentences in the right order.

a) Mum started to vacuum the kitchen floor.
b) It said that if you eat the leaves of the Dub-Dub plant you shrink.
c) Hannah found an interesting book on Dad's desk.
d) They ran to tell Mum in the kitchen.
e) The children found the plant and ate some leaves.
f) They hid under the fridge.
g) Felix the cat came in and saw them.
h) They remembered how to get back to normal.
i) They drank Felix's milk.
j) They got smaller.

⟨Extra line⟩

8 A Christmas story

Jesus' Christmas Party

There was nothing the innkeeper liked more than a good night's sleep.

But that night there was a knock at the door.

"No room," said the innkeeper. "But we're tired and have a travelled through night and day." "There's only the stable round the back. Here's two blankets. Sign the register," said the innkeeper.

Then he shut the door, climbed the stairs, got into bed, and went to sleep.

But then, later, there was another knock at the door.

"Excuse me, I wonder if you could lend us another, smaller blanket?"

"There. One smaller blanket," said the innkeeper.

Then he shut the door, climbed the stairs, got into bed, and went to sleep. But then a bright light woke him up.

"That's ***all*** I need ," said the innkeeper.

"We are three shepherds."
"Well, what's the matter?
Lost your sheep?"
We 've come to see Mary and Joseph."
"ROUND THE BACK," said the innkeeper.

Then he shut the door, climbed the stairs, got into bed, and went to sleep.

But then there was yet ***another*** knock at the door.

"We are three kings. We've come . . ."

"ROUND THE BACK!"

He slammed the door, climbed the stairs, got into bed, and went to sleep.

But ***then*** a chorus of singing woke him up.

"RIGHT– THAT DOES IT!"

⟨Extra line⟩

So he got out of bed,

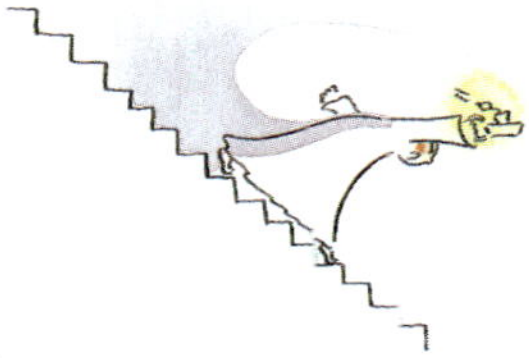

stomped down the stairs,

threw open the door,

went round the back, stormed into the stable, and was just about to speak when –

"Ssshh!"

whispered everybody, "you'll wake the baby!"

"Baby?" said the innkeeper.
"Yes, a baby has this night been born.'
"Oh?" said the innkeeper, looking crossly into the manger.

And just at that moment,
y, amazingly, his
emed to fly away.

"Oh," said the innkeeper, "isn't he ***lovely!"***

In fact, he thought he was so special he woke up ***all*** the guests at the inn, so that they could come and have a look at the baby too.

So no one got much sleep that night!

⟨Extra line⟩

A Christmas story

Christmas ['krismәs] *Weihnachten* – innkeeper ['ɪnki:pә] *Gastwirt* – sleep [sli:p] *Schlaf* – knock [nɔk] *Klopfen* – stable ['steɪbl] *Stall* – blanket ['blæŋkɪt] *Wolldecke* – to sign [saɪn] *unterschreiben* – to wonder ['wʌndә] *sich fragen* – to lend [lend] *ausleihen* – bright [braɪt] *hell* – to draw [drɔ:] *ziehen* – curtain ['kɜ:tn] *Vorhang* – shepherd ['ʃepәd] *(Schaf-)Hirt, Schäfer* – king [kɪŋ] *König* – to slam [slæm] *zuschlagen, zuknallen* – chorus of singing ['kɔ:rәs] *gemeinsames Singen* – That does it! *Das reicht!* – to stomp [stɒmp] *stampfen* – to storm [stɔ:m] *stürmen* – to whisper ['wɪspә] *flüstern* – born [bɔ:n] *geboren* – crossly ['krɒslɪ] *ärgerlich* – manger ['meɪndʒә] *Krippe* – amazingly [ә'meɪziŋlɪ] *verblüffend, erstaunlich* – anger ['æŋgә] *Ärger, Wut* – lovely ['lʌvlɪ] *wunderschön* – in fact [ˌɪn'fækt] *in der Tat, tatsächlich*

⟨Extra line⟩

Grammar

Unit 1

Hallo! Nun geht es weiter mit den Regeln für die englische Sprache. Du weißt ja schon: Das Lernen soll dir wieder leicht gemacht werden. Und es geht auch ziemlich einfach los, nämlich mit Regeln aus dem ersten Buch über ‚Fragen'.

Unit 1 Step A

1 Das Fragewort *which* — The question word *which*

Which lesson have we got next, English or German?
Which lesson finishes at 3.30 on Thursday?
Which is your favourite subject?

- Wenn du nach Dingen aus einer begrenzten Anzahl fragen möchtest, dann kannst du das Fragewort *which* (= welcher, welche, welches) verwenden.

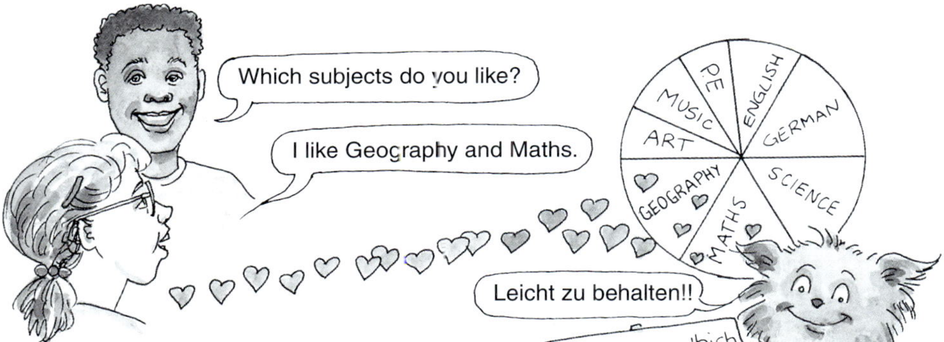

Unit 1 Step B

Zunächst etwas zur Wiederholung:

2 Fragen und verneinte Sätze mit *do/don't* und *does/doesn't*

Questions and negative sentences with *do/don't* and *does/doesn't*

FRAGE			ANTWORT	
Hilfsverb	Vollverb	Ergänzung	Hilfsverb + not	Vollverb
Do you	**know**	the school play?	No, I **don't**	(know it).
Do your teachers	**wear**	school uniform?	No, they **don't**	(wear school uniform).
Does Sarah	**like**	plays?	No, she **doesn't**	(like them).

do	don't
does	doesn't

3 Fragen mit Fragewörtern und *do/does*

Questions with question words and *do/does*

FRAGE					ANTWORT		
Fragewort	Hilfsverb	Subjekt	Vollverb		Subjekt	Vollverb	Ergänzung
What	do	we	need	?	We	need	the Maths books.
Where	does	John	come from		He	comes	from Chicago.
When	does	Robert	have lunch		He	has	lunch at 12.10.
How	do	they	get to school		They	get	there by bike.
Why	does	Becky	go to the play		She	likes	it.

Auf einen Blick

Ihr könnt jetzt auf fünf verschiedene Arten Fragen stellen! Und damit beherrscht ihr sämtliche Fragemöglichkeiten des Englischen. Ist doch super, oder?

1. Betonung	You want to take a role? ↗	Du möchtest eine Rolle übernehmen? ↗
2. Umkehrung	She's lazy. ↔ Is she lazy?	Ist sie faul?
3. Fragewort + Hilfsverb	Where is he?	Wo ist er?
4. Do + Vollverb	Do you like it?	Magst du es?
5. Fragewort + do + Vollverb	What do we need?	Was brauchen wir?

Unit 2

Unit 2 Step B

4 Das *simple past* von *to be* — The simple past of *to be*

Today	I	am	happy, but …	**yesterday**	I was unhappy.
	you	are	nice, but …		you were not nice.
	he	is	in Nottingham, but …		he was in London.
	she	is	back at school, but …		she was at home.
	your bike	is	OK, but …		it was broken.
	we	are	at home, but …		we were in Nottingham.
	you	are	early, but …		you were late.
	my parents	are	in France, but …		they were in Belgium.

Es gibt also zwei verschiedene Formen des *simple past* von *to be*:
WAS – zusammen mit *I, he, she, it*
WERE – zusammen mit *you, we, they*
Ihr müsst ja nur zwei Wörter lernen:
was für die Einzahl und **were** für die Mehrzahl und für *you*.

5 Das *simple past* von *to have* The simple past of *to have*

Das *simple past* von ***to have*** ist noch einfacher. Da gibt es nur das Wort ***had***.

Today	the statue of Robin Hood has an arrow	**but yesterday**	it had no arrow.
	our friends have a leaflet		they had no leaflet.

6 Das *simple past*: regelmäßige Formen The simple past: regular forms

Wenn du über Ereignisse oder Handlungen berichten möchtest, die in der Vergangenheit liegen und abgeschlossen sind, dann kannst du das *simple past* (= die einfache Vergangenheit) benutzen. Das *simple past* braucht man z. B., um Geschichten zu erzählen oder über Erlebnisse zu berichten.

Yesterday ...

I	worked	in the garden.
you	watched	a film.
David	helped	his mother.
Susan	played	a game.
it	rained	in the afternoon.
we	phoned	our friends.
you	stayed	at home.
our friends	arrived	at the station.

- Das *simple past* (die einfache Vergangenheit) von regelmäßigen Verben wird dadurch gebildet, dass man die Endung *-ed* an die Stammform des Verbs (Infinitiv ohne *to*) anhängt. Stammform: *walk* – simple past: *walk + ed = walked*
- Diese Form ist für alle Personen gleich, also: *I walked, you walked, he walked,* usw.

7 Aussprache und Schreibung des *simple past* (regelmäßige Formen)

Bei der Aussprache und beim Schreiben musst du auf folgende Besonderheiten achten:

BEIM SPRECHEN	
phoned stayed lived	Nach Vokalen und nach stimmhaften Konsonanten spricht man [d].
worked helped laughed	Nach stimmlosen Konsonanten spricht man [t].
waited wanted	Nach [d] oder [t] spricht man [ɪd].

BEIM SCHREIBEN	
live – lived phone – phoned like – liked	Ganz bequem: Wenn schon ein ‚e' da ist, dann natürlich nur ein ‚d' dazutun!
try – tried	Verben, die auf Konsonant + *y* enden, erhalten die Endung *-ied*. ABER: *play – played; stay – stayed*
stop – stopped	Nach kurzem, betontem Vokal wird der Endkonsonant verdoppelt.

8 Das *simple past*: unregelmäßige Formen — The simple past: irregular forms

Im Deutschen gibt es regelmäßige Verben (öffnen – öffnete) und unregelmäßige Verben (kommen – kam). Dies ist auch im Englischen so.

to have	had	Yesterday morning we **had** breakfast very early.
to come	came	Yesterday evening my friend **came** and we …
to give	gave	He **gave** me an interesting book.
to sit	sat	Last Friday we **sat** under a big tree.
to go	went	Last Tuesday Becky **went** to the shops.
to get	got	Last Thursday we **got** no homework.
to hear	heard	In my dream I **heard** a terrible noise and …
to throw	threw	I **threw** a ball to Mark.
to see	saw	Yesterday I **saw** my friend Bill. He invited me to a party.
to take	took	Yesterday afternoon I **took** Maxi to the park.
to wake up	woke up	Yesterday morning I **woke up** very late.
to make	made	Last Saturday my dad **made** a wonderful cheese salad.
to meet	met	They **met** at the station.
to say	said	She **said**, "Let's play tennis together."

- Während die regelmäßigen Verben im *simple past* alle auf *-ed* enden, gibt es für die unregelmäßigen Verben keine Bildungsregeln. Die einzelnen Formen musst du dir gut einprägen. Du findest eine Liste dieser Verben auf Seite 207.
- Aber auch bei den unregelmäßigen Verben sind die Formen des *simple past* für alle Personen gleich. (Ausnahme: *to be* – siehe Punkt 4)

Auf einen Blick

9 Der Gebrauch von *you* — The use of *you*

Was das persönliche Fürwort *you* alles heißen kann, das weißt du schon:

you

du	Mark, where are you?
dir	Can I help you, Dad?
dich	Becky, I can see you.
ihr	Yes, children, you can all come!
euch	Maxi and Mini, I can hear you!
Ihnen	I can give you Robert's book, Mrs Croft.
Sie	Yesterday I saw you, Mr Cooper.

Einfach für uns: Ein englisches Wort für sieben deutsch Wörter!
Nicht so einfach für Engländer, die Deutsch lernen wollen!

Nun kommt für uns aber noch eine weitere Bedeutung für das englische *you* hinzu: Das *you* kann auch das unpersönlich ‚man' bedeuten.

So, jetzt steht ihr mit dem *you* auf Du und Du!

GB → You can shoot with a bow and arrow.
D → Man kann mit Pfeil und Bogen schießen.
GB → You can buy souvenirs here.
D → Man kann hier Souvenirs kaufen.

Unit 3 Step B

10 Fragen und Verneinungen mit *was* und *were*
Questions and negative statements with *was* and *were*

Was the weather nice yesterday?	Yes, it was
Were you at the fair?	Yes, I was.
Were Kim and Robert there, too?	Yes, they were.
Was the food good at the fair?	No, it wasn't.

The hot dogs weren't hot and
the lemonade wasn't cold.

Die Verneinung von *was* und *were* funktioniert genauso wie bei *isn't* und *aren't*: Einfach das not ohne o (n't) anhängen, also: *wasn't* / *weren't*.

11 Die Verneinung im *simple past* mit *didn't* Negative sentences with *didn't*

Bei der Verneinung im *simple present* hatten wir *don't* und *doesn't*:
I **don't like** football.
My brother **doesn't like** tennis.

- Im *simple past* verwendet man *didn't* (also *did* + wieder *not ohne o*):
  Sarah waited for me after school. (bejaht)
  But you **didn't wait**. (verneint)

Subjekt	didn't	Infinitiv	
On Sunday it rained all day, so …			
I	didn't	go out	all day.
Sarah	didn't	play	tennis.
Simon	didn't	take	the dogs for a walk.
Mr and Mrs Dixon	didn't	go	to the fair.
We	didn't	like	the weekend.

- Die Form *didn't* ist bei allen Personen gleich.
- Nach *didn't* steht immer der Infinitiv des Vollverbs (Grundform).

12 Entscheidungsfragen mit *did* — Yes/No questions with *did*

Bei Entscheidungsfragen im *simple present* nehmen wir *do* oder *does*:
Does Mark like sweets?

- Im *simple past* nehmen wir *did*.

Did	Subjekt	Infinitiv	restlicher Satz	Kurzantwort
Did	you	watch	'The Adventures of Robin Hood' on TV last night?	Yes I did.
Did	the Sheriff	catch	Robin Hood?	No, he didn't.
Did	Robin and his men	kill	him?	No, they didn't.
Did	the film	show	the gallows and the hangman?	Yes, it did.
Did	you	make	a video?	Yes, I did.

- Die Form *did* ist bei allen Personen gleich.
- Kurzantworten (*Yes, I did.*) klingen etwas höflicher als ein bloßes *Yes* oder *No*.
- Auch hier musst du den Infinitiv des Vollverbs verwenden. Die Vergangenheit wird ja durch *did* ausgedrückt.

13 Die Steigerung von Adjektiven *-er* und *-est*
The comparison of adjectives with *-er* and *-est*

Im Englischen hängt die Art, in der Adjektive gesteigert werden, von ihrer Länge ab. So wird ein kurzes, einsilbiges Adjektiv (z. B. *cold*) anders gesteigert als ein langes, dreisilbiges (z. B. *expensive*). (Vgl. Punkt 15)
Die Steigerung mit *-er* und *-est* ist ganz ähnlich wie im Deutschen (kalt – kälter – am kältesten).

On Friday it was very **cold**.
But yesterday it was **colder**.
And today is the **coldest** day of the month.

- Man bildet die 1. Steigerungsform, indem man *-er* an die Grundform anhängt: cold + **er** → cold**er**.
- Die 2. Steigerungsform wird gebildet, indem man *-est* anhängt: cold + **est** → cold**est**.
- Auf diese Weise werden gesteigert:
  - alle **einsilbigen** Adjektive (*cheap, nice* usw.)
  - alle zweisilbigen Adjektive, die auf **-y** enden (*lazy, easy* usw.)
  - manche zweisilbige Adjektive, z.B. *clever, quiet* und *simple*.

Auf einen Blick

kurze Adjektive	-er	-est
strong	strong**er**	(the) strong**est**
old	old**er**	(the) old**est**
easy	eas**ier**	(the) eas**iest**
clever	clever**er**	(the) clever**est**
small	small**er**	(the) small**est**
poor	poor**er**	(the) poor**est**

Beim Schreiben heißt es: Aufpassen!

1.		2.		3.	
big bi**gg**er (the) bi**gg**est	Der Endkonsonant bei einsilbigen Adjektiven wird verdoppelt, wenn er auf einen betonten, einfachen Vokal folgt.	nice nic**er** (the) nic**est**	Auf ein stummes End-**e** folgt nur **-r** oder **-st**. Also nur ein e!	craz**y** craz**ier** (the) craz**iest**	Bei Adjektiven, die auf **-y** enden, wird das **-y** durch **-i** ersetzt.
Ebenso z. B.: *hot*		Ebenso z. B.: *late*		Ebenso z. B.: *hungry, heavy, silly, early, …*	

Unregelmäßige Steigerung

Wie das Adjektiv ‚gut' im Deutschen wird auch *good* unregelmäßig gesteigert:

These chips are **good**.	gut
But the hot dogs are **better**.	besser
And the salad is the **best** of all.	das beste/am besten

14 Der Vergleich im Satz — Sentences with comparisons

Es gibt drei Grundmuster, mit denen du Gleichheit und Ungleichheit ausdrücken kannst:

Gleichheit

1.	The green ball is **as big as** the red ball.	… so groß wie …

Ungleichheit

2.	The blue ball is not **as big as** the red ball.	… nicht so groß wie …
3.	The red ball is **bigger than** the blue ball.	… größer als …

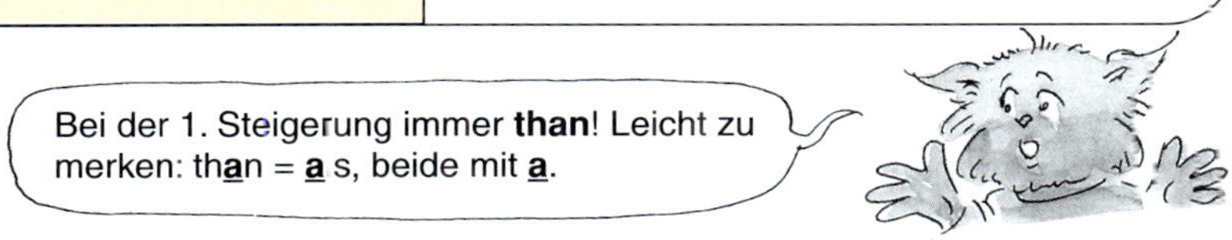

Unit 3 Step D

15 Fragen mit Fragewörtern und *did* — Questions with question words and *did*

Fragewort	did	Subjekt	Infinitiv	restlicher Satz	Antwortsatz
What	did	you	do	in the holidays, Sarah?	We **went** to Skegness.
Where	did	you	stay?		We **stayed** at a guest house.
Why	did	you	go	there?	Because we **wanted** to swim a lot.
How long	did	you	stay	there?	We **stayed** for three weeks.
How	did	Kim	like	it?	She **loved** it. She was in the sea all day.
When	did	you	get back?		We **got** back last Saturday.

- Bei Fragen im *simple past* mit Fragewörtern (*what, when, where, why, how*) wird *did* genommen.
- Bei den Antworten wird dann das Verb im *simple past* genommen (We **went** …/She **loved** it.).

Unit 4

Unit 4 Step B

16 Die Steigerung von Adjektiven mit *more* und *most*

The comparison of adjectives with *more* and *most*

Neben der Steigerung mit *-er* und *-est* (13) gibt es auch noch die Steigerung *more* und *most*.

> Look at these pullovers. They're **expensive**.
> Yes, they are. But these blue ones are **more expensive**.
> And those lovely red ones over there are the **most expensive** in the shop.

- Alle Adjektive, die mehr als zwei Silben haben, werden mit *more* und *most* gesteigert: *expensive* (teuer) – *more expensive* (teuerer) – *the most expensive* (der/die/das teuerste (Teuerste), die teuersten, am teuersten)

Auf einen Blick

lange Adjektive	**more** + Adjektiv	**most** + Adjektiv
terrible	**more** terrible	**most** terrible
expensive	**more** expensive	**most** expensive
popular	**more** popular	**most** popular
fantastic	**more** fantastic	**most** fantastic

- Alle Adjektive, die auf *-ing* enden, werden ebenfalls mit *more* und *most* gesteigert, z. B. *boring – more boring – most boring*.
- Auch die meisten zweisilbigen Adjektiven, die **nicht** auf *-y* enden, werden mit *more* und *most* gesteigert, z. B.: *careful – more careful – most careful*.

Vergleichssätze

Die drei Grundmuster, mit denen du Gleichheit und Ungleichheit ausdrücken kannst, gelten auch für die Adjektive, die mit *more* und *most* gesteigert werden.

The black pullover is **as expensive as** the white pullover.

The grey pullover is **not as expensive as** the white one.

The black pullover is **more expensive than** the grey pullover.

as	ADJECTIVE	as
not as	ADJECTIVE	as
more	ADJECTIVE	than

17 Das *will*-Futur — The *will*-future

Das *will*-Futur kannst du verwenden, wenn du ausdrücken möchtest, was in der Zukunft passieren wird.
Dabei kann es zum einen so sein, dass ein fester Entschluss oder eine feste Verabredung vorliegt.
Zum andern kann es aber auch so sein, dass die Ereignisse nicht zu beeinflussen sind

I will be in England this time next week. Peter will meet me at the airport. We'll have a nice time in London.
The weather will be nice tomorrow. He'll be 19 soon. I'm sure it won't rain.

- Das *will*-Futur wird aus *will* + Infinitiv gebildet.
- *Will* ist in allen Personen gleich.
- Häufig wird statt *will* die Kurzform *'ll* verwendet.
- Die Kurzform der Verneinung *will not* ist *won't*.

I hope I **won't** be late.	– Of course, you **won't**.
Will you **send** me a postcard?	– Yes, I **will**.
Will you **be** back for John's party?	– No, I **won't**.

- Auf Fragen mit *will* klingt die Kurzantwort (*Yes, I will./No, I won't.*) etwas höflicher als bloß *Yes* oder *No*.

18 Nebensätze mit *when*

Clauses with *when*

Nebensatz mit *when* *when clause*	Hauptsatz *main clause*
When I get to the airport, When I write next,	Peter will wait for me there. I'll send you the photos.
simple present	*will-future*

- In einem Satzgefüge (Hauptsatz + Nebensatz), das sich auf die Zukunft bezieht, steht im Hauptsatz das *will*-Futur und im Nebensatz das *simple present*.
- Das Satzgefüge kann, genau wie im Deutschen, auch mit dem Hauptsatz beginnen:
  Will you **collect** us from the station when we **get back**?

Unit 5

Unit 5 Step B

19 *Some* und *any*

Mit *some* und *any* kannst du im Englischen eine unbestimmte Menge oder Anzahl ausdrücken.
Im Deutschen entsprechen *some* und *any* Ausdrücke wie, ‚etwas', ‚einige' oder ‚ein paar'.

 (+)  (?)  (-)

bejahte Aussagen mit *some*	Fragen mit *any*	verneinte Aussagen mit *any*
Let's make **some** sandwiches.	Is there **any** bread?	No, there isn't **any** bread.
Lasst uns ein paar belegte Brote machen.	Gibt es (noch etwas) Brot?	Nein, es ist kein Brot da.
OK. I'll get **some** bread.	Do we need **any** eggs?	Yes, we do. There aren't **any** in the kitchen.
Gut. Ich hole (etwas) Brot.	Brauchen wir (ein paar) Eier?	Ja. In der Küche sind keine.

In bejahten Sätzen verwendet man *some*, in Fragen und verneinten Sätzen meistens *any*.
Im Deutschen bleiben *some* und *any* oft unübersetzt:

Do you need **any** help? – Brauchst du Hilfe?

some – positive Aussagen (und freundliche Fragen)

any – negative Aussagen und Fragen

P O S I T I V E / S O M E

A N Y / N E G A T I V E

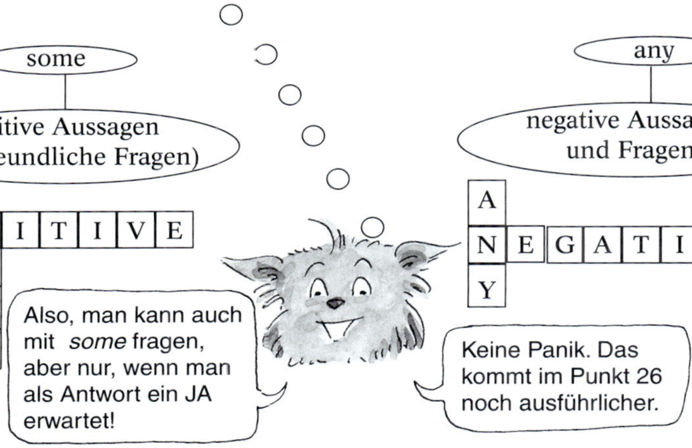

20 Bedingungssätze — Conditional sentences

Mark plays in his room **when it rains**. Mark is in the garden. **If it rains**, he'll go inside.

Aus Unit 4 (vgl. Punkt 18) kennst du schon Satzgefüge aus *when*-Satz und Hauptsatz. Bedingungssätze sind ganz ähnliche Satzgefüge. Sie bestehen aus einem *if*-Satz und einem Hauptsatz.
Der *if*-Satz drückt eine Bedingung (*if it rains*) aus: der Hauptsatz drückt aus, was passiert (*he'll go inside*), falls diese Bedingung erfüllt wird.

if-Satz			Hauptsatz		
If the weather	**is**	nice tomorrow,	we	**'ll go**	swimming.
But if it	**rains,**		we	**won't go.**	
If you	**don't wear**	your anorak,	you	**'ll get**	wet.
simple present			*will-future*		

Der Hauptsatz wird mit dem *will*-Futur gebildet, der *if*-Satz steht im *simple present*. (vgl. Punkt 18)
Bedingungssätze können entweder mit dem *if*-Satz oder dem Hauptsatz beginnen:
If it doesn't rain tomorrow, we'll go swimming.
We'll go swimming tomorrow if it doesn't rain.

If I go to the shops tomorrow, I'll get you a comic. – Falls … (Ich bin mir nicht sicher.)
When I go to the shops tomorrow, I'll get you a comic. – Wenn … (Ich habe es fest vor.)

21 Die Zusammensetzungen von *some* und *any*
The compounds of *some* and *any*

Something, somebody, anywhere usw. sind Zusammensetzungen von *some* und *any*.
Diese zusammengesetzten Wörter werden nach genau denselben Regeln verwendet wie *some* und *any* selbst.

bejahte Aussagen	Fragen	verneinte Aussagen
I want to buy **something** for Jenny's birthday.	Can you think of **anything?**	No, sorry. I ca**n't** think of **anything.**
We must ask **somebody.**	Can you see **anybody?**	I'm sorry. I ca**n't** see **anybody.**
My anorak must be **somewhere.**	Is it **anywhere** in the kitchen?	No, it isn't. I ca**n't** find it **anywhere.**

Unit 6

Unit 6 Step B

22 Das *present perfect*
The present perfect

The boy is washing his pullover.

He **has washed** the pullover. It is clean now.

Es geht häufig um sichtbare und spürbare Resultate von Handlungen, die in der Vergangenheit liegen. Das drückst du dann mit dem *present perfect* aus.

Hier ist die Handlung (das Waschen) vorbei, aber das Ergebnis ist in der Gegenwart noch sichtbar (der Pulli ist sauber).

It's 4.45. The boy has **just** washed his pullover.

Das *present perfect* kannst du auch verwenden, wenn du sagen möchtest, dass eine Handlung gerade erst abgeschlossen ist (häufig in Sätzen mit *just*).

23 Das *present perfect*: regelmäßige Formen
The present perfect: regular forms

	Form von *to have*		*past participle*		
I	've	just	watched	a film on TV.	Was it good?
Mrs Penrose	has		cooked	lunch.	The family can eat now.
Simon and Becky	have		tidied up	their rooms.	The rooms look tidy now.

Das *present perfect* wird gebildet aus *has/have* und dem *past participle* (Partizip Perfekt).

Bei regelmäßigen Verben ist das *past participle* gleich mit der Form des *simple past* (siehe Punkt 2): *watch + ed*.

24 Das *present perfect*: unregelmäßige Formen
The present perfect: irregular forms

	past participle	
The guests have just	come.	
They have	brought	some presents.
I've just	heard	about it.
Jenny has	had	a good lunch.
Mark has never	seen	a ghost.
Grandma Penrose has just	written	a letter.

past participle		Grundform
come	⟵	come
brought	⟵	bring
heard	⟵	hear
had	⟵	have
seen	⟵	see
written	⟵	write

Für die Bildung der unregelmäßigen Formen des *past participle* (*come, brought, heard* usw.) gibt es keine Regel. Deshalb musst du diese Formen wie Vokabeln lernen.

Mini **is eating** her dog biscuits.
Maxi **has** eaten her dog biscuits.

25 Das *present perfect* (Frage, Verneinung und Kurzantwort)
The present perfect (questions, negative sentences and short answers)

Frage					Kurzantwort/Verneinung				
	has/ have	Subjekt	*past participle*			Subjekt	*has/ have*	*past participle*	
	Has	David	made	the fruit salad?	Yes,	he	has.		
	Have	they	eaten	it **yet?**	No,	they	have**n't.**		
	Has	Andreas	tasted	it?		He	has**n't**	seen	it **yet.**
Who	has		done	the washing-up?		Nobody	has.		
						They	have**n't**	finished	lunch **yet.**

Wenn du fragen möchtest, ob etwas schon geschehen ist, kannst du zum *present perfect* noch das Wort *yet* hinzunehmen.
Wenn du ausdrücken möchtest, dass etwas noch nicht geschehen ist, kannst du *not yet* mit dem *present perfect* gebrauchen.

Have you done your homework **yet?**	Hast du **schon** deine Hausaufgaben gemacht?
No, I have**n't** done it **yet.**	Nein, ich habe sie **noch nicht** gemacht.

- *yet* steht immer am Ende des Satzes.

Vergleiche die unterschiedliche Wortstellung im Englischen und im Deutschen:

Has she written the letter?	Yes, she has.	She has written the letter.
Hat sie den Brief geschrieben?	Ja.	Sie hat den Brief geschrieben.

Unit 6 Step C

26 *some* in Fragen — *some* in questions

Im Englischen benutzt man *some* in Fragen, die eigentlich eine höfliche Bitte oder ein höfliches Angebot sind.

Could I have **some** sugar, please?	Könnte ich bitte etwas Zucker haben?
Would you like **some** biscuits?	Möchten Sie (ein paar) Kekse haben?

Unit 7

Unit 7 Step B

27 Das *gerund* The gerund

Normale Hauptwörter (*nouns*) bezeichnen oder benennen ja bekanntlich konkrete Dinge (*a bag*), Personen (*a girl*), Tiere (*a frog*) und dazu auch abstrakte Sachverhalte und Ereignisse (*an invitation, the music*).
Daneben kann man aber auch noch Tätigkeiten wie mit Hauptwörtern benennen: Das Lesen, das Schwimmen, das Wandern, … .
Dieses leistet im Englischen die *ing*-Form des Verbs, eine Form, die du ja zum Glück schon kennst. (Bd. 1, Unit 5) Sie heißt *gerund*.

Auf einen Blick

read + ing = reading kann also zweierlei heißen:
a) *progressive form:* Mark is just reading a comic. (… liest gerade)
b) *gerund:* Reading is fun. ((Das) Lesen macht Spaß.)
Uns geht es jetzt aber nur um das *gerund*.

28 Das *gerund* als Subjekt The gerund as subject

Reading	is fun.
Swimming	is my hobby.
Cycling	all day is great.
Playing	on the beach is wonderful.

Weil das *gerund* die Eigenschaften eines Hauptwortes hat, kann es auch Subjekt eines Satzes sein.

29 Das *gerund* als Objekt The gerund as object

I	like	**reading.**	
Do you	enjoy	**reading,**	too?
We	love	**walking.**	
David doesn't	like	**running.**	
Mrs Leinert	hates	**cooking.**	

Das *gerund* steht, wie du siehst, als Objekt besonders häufig nach Verben der Vorliebe (*like, enjoy, love*) oder der Abneigung (*not like, hate*).

30 Das *gerund* als Subjekt und Objekt
The gerund as subject and object

Auf einen Blick

Subjekt		Objekt
Reading	is fun.	
Playing football	is fun, too.	
Sarah	likes	**cycling.**
I	hate	**cycling** up hills.
Jenny	enjoys	**taking** photos.

Das *gerund* kannst du allein oder mit einem (weiteren) Substantiv als Subjekt oder Objekt benutzen.

31 Gegenüberstellung: Das *present perfect* und die einfache Vergangenheit
Contrast: The present perfect and the simple past

Auf einen Blick

present perfect	*simple past*
Robert **has done** the washing-up. The plates are clean.	He **did** it after breakfast.
Jenny **has made** the tea. We can have it now.	She **made** it half an hour ago.
Have you **ever tried** porridge? **I've already written** six postcards.	Yes, we **had** porridge for breakfast yesterday. I **wrote** them last night.

Hier ist die Handlung (das Abwaschen und Tee zubereiten) zwar vorbei, aber das Ergebnis ist in der Gegenwart noch wirksam (das Geschirr ist sauber, man kann jetzt essen). Wir benutzen das *present perfect*. (Siehe Punkt 22.)

Hier ist die Handlung abgeschlossen und vorbei (Robert hat nach dem Frühstück gespült und das Essen ist schon seit einer halben Stunde fertig). Wir benutzen das *simple past*. (Siehe Punkt 4)

Es gibt übrigens einige Signalwörter *(signal words)*, die dir zeigen, dass man das *present perfect* verwenden muss. Diese Wörter bezeichnen einen Zeitraum, der von der Vergangenheit bis in die Gegenwart reicht. Zwei dieser Wörter sind *ever* (meist in Fragen) und *already*.

Hierfür gibt es auch *signal words*: alle Zeitangaben wie *last week, yesterday, last Friday, two hours ago, after breakfast, last night.*

Have you ever seen a Robin Hood film? – Yes, I saw a good one last month.

I've already seen the new film. – I saw it yesterday.

Unit 7 Step C

32 Das *gerund* nach *what about, it's no good, I can't stand*
The gerund after *what about/it's no good/I can't stand*

Es gibt einige Ausdrücke, nach denen wir das *gerund* verwenden müssen. Hier sind drei davon:

What about **climbing** Ben Nevis today?
It's no good **walking** in the rain all day.
I can't stand **climbing** hills.

Unit 8

Unit 8 Step B

33 *needn't*

Wie du siehst, überlegt sich die Mutter, was sie noch tun muss.
Sie verwendet das Wort *must*.

Ihr Sohn sagt ihr, dass sie etwas nicht zu tun braucht bzw. tun muss.
Er verwendet *needn't*.

	Must	I go to hospital? – No, you	**needn't**	go to hospital,
but you	**must**	stay at home.		
This patient	**must**	stay in bed but that patient	**needn't**	stay in bed.

Needn't kannst du also verwenden, wenn jemand etwas nicht zu tun braucht.
Übrigens: *needn't* ist bei allen Personen gleich.

34 *mustn't*

The children at Haywood School	**must**	walk to school or go by bus.
They	**mustn't**	take their bikes to school.

Mustn't verwenden wir, wenn jemand etwas nicht tun darf.

35 Die Verlaufsform der Vergangenheit The past progressive

Im Englischen gibt es zu jeder Verbzeit eine *simple form* und eine *progressive form*.
So gibt es neben dem *simple past* (siehe *Unit* 2) auch das *past progressive*.

Wenn du ausdrücken willst, dass ein Ereignis in der Vergangenheit längere Zeit dauerte, kannst du das *past progressive* benutzen.
Häufig wird das *past progressive* mit *while*, das *simple past* dagegen mit *when* verbunden.
Es kommen aber nie beide Wörter in einem Satz vor!

gerade ablaufende Handlung	neues Ereignis
past progressive	*simple past*
The Dixons **were** just **having** breakfast	**when** the milkman **came.**
Mrs Dixon **was eating** cornflakes	**when** Sarah **came** in.
While Becky **was working** in the garden,	she suddenly **saw** a mouse.
While the boys **were playing** football,	it **started** to rain.

In diesen Sätzen drückt das *past progressive* aus, dass etwas gerade passierte und noch nicht abgeschlossen war. Das *simple past* drückt aus, dass ein neues Ereignis eintrat.

The Dixons were just having breakfast when the milkman came.
When the milkman came, the Dixons were just having breakfast.

Unit 8 Step C

36 Der bestimmte Artikel — The definite article

Mrs Croft was ill. She spent two days	in		hospital.	
The doctor sent Barry	to		hospital.	
We took all his homework	to	**the**	hospital	for him.
The Happy Helpers work	at	**the**	hospital	every week.

Wenn man an den Zweck von *hospital* denkt (also an einen Ort, an dem Kranke gepflegt werden), dann verwendet man es ohne Artikel: *to hospital.*
Wenn man nur an das Gebäude denkt (in das z. B. auch Besucher gehen), dann verwendet man es mit dem bestimmten Artikel: *to the hospital.*

She's at school.

He's at the school.

Unit 9

Unit 9 Step B

37 Das *going to*-Futur — The *going to* future

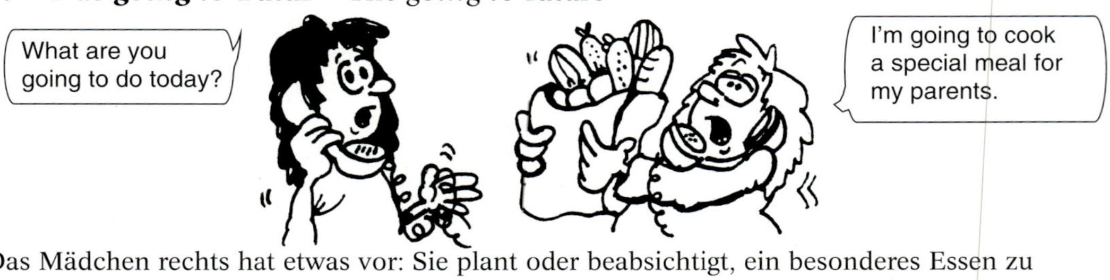

Das Mädchen rechts hat etwas vor: Sie plant oder beabsichtigt, ein besonderes Essen zu kochen. Sie sagt: *I'm going to cook … .*
Wenn du also ausdrücken willst, dass du etwas vorhast oder planst, kannst du das Futur mit *going to* verwenden.

I'm	**going to**	take	these things to the Assembly Hall.
What are you	**going to**	do	today? – I'm going to cook a special meal.
David is	**going to**	take	a photo.
She is	**going to**	phone	home.
We're	**going to**	feed	our cat.
They're	**going to**	play	football.

Das *going to*-Futur wird mit *am/is/are going to* + Infinitiv gebildet.

Going to darfst du nicht mit der Verlaufsform der Gegenwart verwechseln:
Verlaufsform der Gegenwart: **I'm going** home. = Ich gehe (gerade) nach Hause.
Going to: **I'm going to** go home. = Ich habe vor, nach Hause zu gehen.

38 *be allowed to*

Mit *(not) be allowed to* (= dürfen/nicht dürfen) kannst du ausdrücken, dass etwas ganz allgemein erlaubt oder verboten ist.

simple present	**I'm allowed to** listen to music in Maths! You **are allowed to** wear jeans at school. She **is allowed to** go home at 3.30. We**'re allowed to** read comics in English.	They **aren't allowed to** wear rollerskates at school. We **aren't allowed to** drop litter. He **isn't allowed to** use a computer in the lunch break.
simple past	We **were allowed to** have a party in German. He **was allowed to** use a computer in the lunch break.	I **wasn't allowed to** wear jeans. They **weren't allowed to** eat in the classroom.

39 *have to*

In this game you **have to** kick the ball through a hole.

The car **has to** stop.

Have/has to + Infinitiv kannst du verwenden, wenn du ausdrücken möchtest, dass etwas notwendig ist oder getan werden muss.
Die *simple past* heißt bei allen Personen *had to*. Dazu kommt wie im *simple present* ein Infinitiv: *He has to go. – He had to go.*

So, Leute, das war's auch schon! Ihr habt jetzt nach fast zwei Jahren Englisch die wichtigsten Dinge in der Grammatik kennen gelernt. Was im nächsten Jahr noch dazukommt, ist alles ganz harmlos. Ihr werdet das dann bestimmt auch ohne meine Hilfe schaffen. – Ich bin übrigens schon in Ferienstimmung! Ihr auch? Ich sage schon mal Tschüüüsss!

Grammar list

Deutsch/Lateinisch	*Englisch*	*Beispiel*	*Punkt in der Grammatik*
Adjektiv	adjective	nice, terrible	
Steigerung mit -er/-est	comparison with -er/-est	big, bigger, biggest	**13**
Steigerung mit 'more'/'most'	comparison with 'more'/'most'	important, more important, most important	**16**
Adverb	adverb	sometimes, often, etc.	
Artikel	article		
bestimmter Artikel	definite article	the school	**36**
unbestimmter Artikel	indefinite article	a house, an apple	
Auslassungszeichen (Apostroph)	apostrophe	Where's Mini?	
Bedingungssätze (Konditionalsätze)	conditional sentences	If it rains tomorrow, I won't play football.	**20**
Einzahl (Singular)	singular	one house	
Ergänzung (Objekt)	object	She has got a dog.	
Fragen	questions with do/does	Do you know the play? Does Sarah like it?	**2, 3, 4**
Fragewort	which	Which is your favourite subject?	**1**
Gegenwart (Präsens)	present tense		
einfache Form	simple present	I like tennis.	
Verlaufsform	present progressive	He's watching TV	
Gerundium (Gerund)	gerund	reading, cooking	**27**
als Subjekt	as subject	Reading is fun.	**28, 30**
als Objekt	as object	I love swimming.	**29, 30**
nach 'what about'/ 'it's no good'/ 'I can't stand'	after 'what about'/ 'it's no good'/ 'I can't stand'	What about going to the shops?	**32**
Grundform (Infinitiv)	infinitive	to see, to do, etc.	
Hauptwort (Substantiv)	noun	dog, teacher, bike	
Hilfsverb	modal auxiliary		
'Be allowed to'	be allowed to	I'm allowed to go home now!	**38**
'Have to'	have to	I have to do my homework.	**39**
'Mustn't'	mustn't	You mustn't play here!	**34**
'Needn't'	needn't	You needn't stay in bed.	**33**
Mehrzahl (Plural)	plural	two women, five dogs	
Mitlaut (Konsonant)	consonant	b, p, k, l, etc.	
Nebensätze mit 'when'	clauses with 'when'	When Mark is five, he'll start school.	**18**

Deutsch/Lateinisch	*Englisch*	*Beispiel*	*Punkt in der Grammatik*
Selbstlaut (Vokal)	vowel	a, e, i, o, u	
'Some' und 'any'	some and any	Have we got any bread?	**19**
Zusammensetzungen	compounds	something, anything	**21**
'Some' in Fragen	'some' in questions	Would you like some cake?	**26**
Satzgegenstand (Subjekt)	subject	The man was old.	
Tätigkeitswort (Verb)	verb	to go, to see, etc.	
Vergangenheit (Präteritum)	past		
einfache Vergangenheit von 'to be' und 'to have'	simple past of 'to be' and 'to have'	It was cold yesterday but I had fun in the snow.	**31** **4, 5**
regelmäßige Formen	regular forms	David played with Mark.	**6, 7**
unregelmäßige Formen	irregular forms	Jenny went skating.	**8**
verneinte Sätze mit 'wasn't'/'weren't'	negative sentences with 'wasn't'/'weren't'	Robert wasn't at school.	**10**
verneinte Sätze mit 'didn't'	negative sentences with 'didn't'	Sarah didn't go to the shops.	**11**
Fragen mit 'was' und 'were'	questions with 'was' and 'were'	Were you on holiday last week?	**10**
Fragen mit 'did'	questions with 'did'	Did you like the film?	**12, 15**
Verlaufsform der Vergangenheit	past progressive	Kim was watching TV.	**35**
Vergleich im Satz	sentences with comparisons	Mark isn't as old as David.	**14**
Verhältniswort (Präposition)	preposition	in, on, under etc.	
Verneinung	negative sentences with don't/doesn't	I don't know. She doesn't like them.	**2**
Vollendete Gegenwart (Present Perfect)	present perfect	I have just woken up.	**22, 31**
regelmäßige Formen	regular forms	He has cooked lunch.	**23**
unregelmäßige Formen	irregular forms	I've been to China.	**24**
Fragen, Verneinungen und Kurzformen	questions, negative sentences, short forms	Have you ever seen a monster?	**25**
'you'	the use of 'you'	Where are you? You can buy souvenirs here?	**9**
Zukunft (Futur)	future		
going to-Futur	going to future	I'm going to see a film.	**37**
will-Futur	will-future	Robert will be 13 next year.	**17**

Alphabetical word list

In dieser alphabetischen Liste ist das gesamte Vokabular von *Orange Line New 1* und *2* enthalten. Namen werden in gesonderten Listen nach dem Vokabular aufgeführt.
Der Wortschatz aus Übungen und Texten, die in Spitzklammern ⟨ ⟩ stehen, ist wahlfrei.
Der mit ° gekennzeichnete Wortschatz ist rezeptiv.
Die Zahlen verweisen auf das erstmalige Vorkommen der Wörter, z. B.
afternoon [ˌɑːftəˈnuːn] Nachmittag **I** = Band 1
accident [ˈæksɪdənt] Unfall **II 3**, 43 = Band 2, Unit 3, Seite 43

A

a [ə] ein/eine **I**
a few [fjuː] ein paar, einige **II 8**, 126
a hundred years ago [ə ˈhʌndrəd jɪəz əˈgəʊ] vor hundert Jahren **II 4**, 58
a thousand [ˈθaʊznd] (ein)tausend **II 4**, 63
about [əˈbaʊt] über **I**
⟨above⟩ [əˈbʌv] über **II 5**, 78
⟨absurd⟩ [əbˈsɜːd] absurd **II 6**, 94
accident [ˈæksɪdənt] Unfall **II 3**, 43
°to **act** [ækt] spielen **I**
°**activity** [ækˈtɪvɪtɪ] Aktivität **I**
°activities [ækˈtɪvɪtɪz] Aktivitäten **II 1**, 14
°**adjective** [ˈædʒɪktɪv] Adjektiv **II 3**, 42
adventure [ədˈventʃə] Abenteuer **II 2**, 25
to be **afraid** [ˌbiː‿əˈfreɪd] Angst haben **I**
after that [ˌɑːftə ˈðæt] danach **I**
in the **afternoon** [ɪn ðɪ ˌɑːftəˈnuːn] am Nachmittag **I**
again [əˈgen] nochmals, wieder **I**
ago [əˈgəʊ] vor *(zeitlich)* **II 4**, 58
⟨ain't (am not)⟩ [eɪnt] werde nicht **II 5**, 78
at the **airport** [ˈeəpɔːt] am Flughafen **I**
⟨Algebra⟩ [ˈældʒɪbrə] Algebra **II 1**, 9
all [ɔːl] alle, alles **I**
all right [ˌɔːlˈraɪt] in Ordnung **II 2**, 33
All the best [ˈɔːl ðə ˈbest] Alles Gute **II 2**, 27
alligator [ˈælɪgeɪtə] Alligator **II 8**, 126
almost [ˈɔːlməʊst] beinah **II 6**, 89
along [əˈlɒŋ] entlang **I**
°**alphabet** [ˈælfəˌbet] Alphabet **I**
°**alphabetical** [ˌælfəˈbetɪkl] alphabetisch **II 9**, 147
already [ɔːlˈredɪ] schon **II 6**, 96
also [ˈɔːlsəʊ] auch **I**
always [ˈɔːlweɪz] immer **I**
ambulance [ˈæmbjʊləns] Krankenwagen **II 3**, 43
°ambulance driver [ˈæmbjʊləns ˈdraɪvə] Krankenwagenfahrer/in **I**
American [əˈmerɪkən] amerikanisch, Amerikaner/in **II 3**, 41
an [ən] ein/eine **I**
and [ænd] und **I**
angry [ˈæŋgrɪ]° verärgert, böse **I**; wütend **II 2**, 27
animal [ˈænɪml] Tier **I**
°**anorak** [ˈænəræk] Anorak **I**
another [əˈnʌðə] einen weiteren, eine weitere **I**
answer [ˈɑːnsə] Antwort **I**
°**ant** [ænt] Ameise **II 9**, 147
any [ˈenɪ] irgendwelche **II 5**, 74
anybody [ˈenɪbɒdɪ] irgendjemand **II 5**, 75
anyone [ˈenɪwʌn] irgendeine/r **II 5**, 75
anything [ˈenɪθɪŋ] irgendetwas **I**
Anything else? [ˈenɪθɪŋ‿els] Sonst noch etwas? **I**
not ... anything [ˈenɪθɪŋ] nichts **I**
anywhere [ˈenɪweə] irgendwo **II 5**, 75
°**appeal** [əˈpiːl] Aufruf **II 9**, 143
apple [ˈæpl] Apfel **I**
are [ɑː] bist, seid, sind **I**
to have an **argument** [ˌhæv‿ən ˈɑːgjʊmənt] einen Streit, eine Auseinandersetzung haben **II 3**, 41
around [əˈraʊnd] um ... herum **II 5**, 72
to **arrive** [əˈraɪv] ankommen **I**
arrow [ˈærəʊ] Pfeil **II 2**, 25
as [æz] als **II 2**, 26
(not) as ... **as** [əz ... əz] (nicht) so ... wie **II 3**, 46
Art [ɑːt] Kunst **II 1**, 8
to **ask** [ɑːsk] fragen **I**
to ask for [ˈɑːsk fɔː] fragen nach, bitten um **I**
Assembly [əˈsemblɪ] Schulversammlung **II 1**, 8
assistant [əˈsɪstnt] Helfer/in, Assistent/in **I**
shop assistant [ˈʃɒp əˈsɪstənt] Verkäufer/in **II 5**, 74
at [æt] auf **I**
at home [ət ˈhəʊm] zu Hause **I**
at last [ət‿ˈlɑːst] Endlich! **II 2**, 28
at least [ət ˈliːst] wenigstens, mindestens **II 8**, 130
at once [ˌət ˈwʌns] sofort **II 1**, 19
at the airport [ˈeəpɔːt] am Flughafen **I**
⟨at the bottom⟩ [ˈbɒtəm] unten **II 10**, 158
at the bottom of [ˈbɒtm] unten (an) **I**
at the top of ... [ˌæt ðə ˈtɒp‿əv] ganz oben (auf) **I**
attraction [əˈtrækʃn] Attraktion **II 9**, 138
⟨audience⟩ *(pl)* [ˈɔːdɪəns] Zuschauer **II 1**, 17
aunt [ɑːnt] Tante **I**
autumn [ˈɔːtəm] Herbst **II 2**, 28
°**average** [ˈævərɪdʒ] durchschnittlich **I**
away [əˈweɪ] weg **II 1**, 16

B

back [bæk] zurück **I**
back door [ˈbæk dɔː] Hintertür **I**
bad [bæd] böse, schlecht **I**
°**badminton** [ˈbædmɪntən] Badminton **II 1**, 10
bag [bæg] Tasche **I**
bagpipes [ˈbægpaɪps] Dudelsack **II 7**, 109
to **bake** [beɪk] backen **II 6**, 93
baking dish [ˈbeɪkɪŋ ˈdɪʃ] Backform **II 6**, 99
ball [bɔːl] Ball **I**
banana [bəˈnɑːnə] Banane **I**
band [bænd] Kapelle, Musikgruppe **II 9**, 138
bank [bæŋk] Bank **II 7**, 109
bank clerk [ˈbæŋk ˌklɑːk] Bankangestellte(r) **I**
a **bar** of [ˈbɑːr‿əv] eine Tafel (Schokolade) **I**
°to **bark** [bɑːk] bellen **I**
bathroom [ˈbɑːθrʊm] Badezimmer **I**
to **be,** was, were [biː] sein **I**
to be afraid [ˌbiː‿əˈfreɪd] Angst haben **I**
to be good at [biː ˈgʊd‿ət] gut sein in **I**

to be like [laɪk] (ähnlich) sein wie **I**
to be on [bɪ‿'ɒn] eingeschaltet sein **I**
to be proud of [bi: 'praʊd‿əv] stolz sein auf **II 6**, 97
to be wrong about [bi: 'rɒŋ e'bəʊt] Unrecht haben mit **II 1**, 19
beach [bi:tʃ] Strand **I**
°beach ball ['bi:tʃ ˌbɔ:l] Strandball **I**
°beach party ['bi:tʃ ˌpɑ:tɪ] Strandparty **I**
bean [bi:n] Bohne **II 6**, 87
beard [bɪəd] Bart **II 4**, 58
beat [bi:t] Takt **I**
beautiful ['bju:tɪfʊl] (wunder)schön **II 7**, 106
because [bɪ'kɒz] weil **I**
to **become** [bɪ'kʌm] werden **II 5**, 82
bed [bed] Bett **I**
bedroom ['bedrʊm] Schlafzimmer **I**
beef [bi:f] Rindfleisch **II 6**, 88
roast beef ['rəʊst ˌbi:f] Rinderbraten **II 6**, 87
before [bɪ'fɔ:] vor **I**
to **begin** [bɪ'gɪn] beginnen **II 1**, 19
behind [bɪ'haɪnd] hinter **I**
⟨belongings⟩ [bɪ'lɒŋɪŋz] Sachen **II 9**, 151
best [best] best(e) **I**
All the best ['ɔ:l ðə 'best] Alles Gute **II 2**, 27
between [bɪ'twi:n] zwischen **II 5**, 79
big [bɪg] groß **I**
°**Big Wheel** ['bɪg 'wi:l] Riesenrad **II 3**, 47
bike [baɪk] Fahrrad **I**
Biology [baɪ'ɒlədʒɪ] Biologie **II 4**, 59
°**bird** [bɜ:d] Vogel **II 1**, 14
bird-bath ['bɜ:dˌbɑ:θ] Vogelbad **II 8**, 133
°**birdwatcher** ['bɜ:dˌwɒtʃə] Vogelbeobachter/in **II 1**, 14
biro ['baɪərəʊ] Kugelschreiber **I**
birthday ['bɜ:θdeɪ] Geburtstag **I**
Happy Birthday! ['hæpɪ 'bɜ:θdeɪ] Alles Gute zum Geburtstag! **I**
biscuit ['bɪskɪt] Keks **I**
a **bit** [bɪt] ein wenig, ein bisschen **I**
⟨to bite⟩ [baɪt] beißen **II 9**, 152
black [blæk] schwarz **I**
blackberry ['blækbərɪ] Brombeere **II 6**, 99
blackout ['blækaʊt] Stromausfall **II 8**, 127
⟨to blow, blew⟩ [bləʊ, blu:] blasen **II 4**, 63
blue [blu:] blau **I**
°**board** [bɔ:d] Tafel **I**
boat [bəʊt] Boot **I**
°**boating lake** ['bəʊtɪŋ ˌleɪk] See zum Boot fahren **I**
⟨bone⟩ [bəʊn] Knochen **II 2**, 30
book [bʊk] Buch **I**
°**bookshop** ['bʊkʃɒp] Buchhandlung **II 5**, 74
bore [bɔ:] Langweiler **II 9**, 148
°**boring** ['bɔ:rɪŋ] langweilig **I**
a **bottle** of ['bɒtl‿əv] eine Flasche **I**
at the **bottom** of ['bɒtm] unten (an) **I**
bow [bəʊ] Bogen **II 2**, 25
lunch **box** ['lʌntʃ bɒks] Essensbehälter **I**
girls and **boys** (*pl*) [ˌgɜ:lz‿n 'bɔɪz] Mädchen und Jungen **I**
bread [bred] Brot **I**
break [breɪk] Pause **II 1**, 8
breakfast ['brekfəst] Frühstück **I**
bright [braɪt] hell **II 7**, 115
to **bring** [brɪŋ] bringen **I**
°**bring-and-buy sale** ['brɪŋ‿ən 'baɪ 'seɪl] Wohltätigkeitsbasar **II 9**, 138
°**British** ['brɪtɪʃ] britisch **I**
broken ['brəʊkn] gebrochen **I**; kaputt, zerbrochen **I**
⟨brolly⟩ ['brɒlɪ] Regenschirm **II 10**, 160
broomstick ['bru:mstɪk] Besenstiel **II 3**, 51
brother ['brʌðə] Bruder **I**
brown [braʊn] braun **I**
brush [brʌʃ] Bürste **II 8**, 133
bucket ['bʌkɪt] Eimer **II 9**, 145
°**budgie** ['bʌdʒɪ] Wellensittich **I**
to **build** [bɪld] bauen **I**
bully ['bʊlɪ] Tyrann, Schläger **II 1**, 16
to **bully** ['bʊlɪ] tyrannisieren, schikanieren **II 1**, 15
°**burglar** ['bɜ:glə] Einbrecher **I**
bus stop ['bʌs‿stɒp] Bushaltestelle **I**
busy ['bɪzɪ] belebt **I**; beschäftigt **I**
but [bʌt] aber **I**
butter ['bʌtə] Butter **I**
to **buy** [baɪ] kaufen **I**
⟨by ship⟩ [baɪ 'ʃɪp] mit dem Schiff **II 10**, 156
by plane [baɪ‿'pleɪn] mit dem Flugzeug **I**
to go by (*train*) ['gəʊ baɪ] mit (dem Zug) fahren **I**

C

cabbage ['kæbɪdʒ] Kohl **II 6**, 87
°**cage** [keɪdʒ] Käfig **I**
cake [keɪk] Kuchen **I**
calendar ['kæləndə] Kalender **I**
to **call** [kɔ:l] rufen, anrufen **I**
camcorder ['kæmkɔ:də] Videokamera **II 8**, 127
⟨came rolling home⟩ ['rəʊlɪŋ] kam nach Hause **II 2**, 30
camera ['kæmərə] Fotoapparat **I**
can you ['kæn ju:] kannst du, könnt ihr **I**
°**candle** ['kændl] Kerze **I**
can't (= cannot) [kɑ:nt] kann nicht, können nicht **I**
°**canteen** [kæn'ti:n] Kantine **II 1**, 10
⟨cap⟩ [kæp] Mütze **II 10**, 159
car [kɑ:] Auto **I**
car park ['kɑ:ˌpɑ:k] Parkplatz, -haus **II 5**, 72
caravan ['kærəvæn] Wohnwagen **II 7**, 106
card [kɑ:d] Karte **I**
careful ['keəfʊl] vorsichtig **I**
carrot ['kærət] Karotte, Möhre **II 6**, 87
to **carry** ['kærɪ] tragen **I**
case [keɪs] Etui, Hülle **I**
cassette [kə'set] Kassette **II 3**, 47
castle ['kɑ:sl] Burg, Schloss **I**
cat [kæt] Katze **I**
to **catch** [kætʃ] fangen **II 2**, 25
⟨'cause⟩ [kɒz] weil *(Kurzform)* **II 5**, 78
cave [keɪv] Höhle **II 2**, 31
CD player [ˌsi:'di: 'pleɪə] CD-Spieler **I**
centre ['sentə] Zentrum **I**
sports centre ['spɔ:ts ˌsentə] Sportanlage, Sportzentrum **II 1**, 14
chair ['tʃeə] Stuhl **I**
to **change** [tʃeɪndʒ] (sich) (ver)ändern **II 7**, 115
°**character** ['kærəktə] Charakter **II 7**, 110
°**charity** ['tʃærətɪ] Wohltätigkeitsverein **II 9**, 138
cheap [tʃi:p] billig **II 3**, 41
check-out ['tʃek‿aʊt] Kasse **II 5**, 72
°to **check** [tʃek] überprüfen, kontrollieren **I**
cheese [tʃi:z] Käse **I**
Say cheese! [tʃi:z] *Bitte lächeln!* **I**
chemist ['kemɪst] Apotheke; Apotheker/in **II 8**, 123
⟨cherry⟩ ['tʃerɪ] Kirsche **II 6**, 102
chest [tʃest] Brust **II 8**, 132
chicken ['tʃɪkɪn] Huhn **II 6**, 87
child, children [tʃaɪld, 'tʃɪldrən] Kind, Kinder **I**
Chinese ['tʃeɪni:z] chinesisch **II 5**, 82

Vocabulary

chips [tʃɪps] Pommes frites **II 6**, 87
chocolate ['tʃɒklət] Schokolade **I**
to **choose** [tʃu:z] auswählen **II 5**, 76
°**church** ['tʃɜ:tʃ] Kirche **I**
cinema ['sɪnɪmə] Kino **I**
cinnamon ['sɪnəmən] Zimt **II 6**, 99
city ['sɪtɪ] Großstadt **II 7**, 106; Stadt **I**
to **clap** [klæp] klatschen **II 4**, 64
class [klɑ:s] Klasse **I**
°**classmate** ['klɑ:smeɪt] Klassenkammerad/in **I**
classroom ['klɑ:sru:m] Klassenzimmer **I**
to **clean** [kli:n] reinigen **I**; ⟨sauber machen⟩ **II 6**, 101
clean [kli:n] sauber **II 4**, 58
clever ['klevə] schlau, klug **I**
°to **climb** up ['klaɪm‿ʌp] klettern, steigen **I**
°**climbing** ['klaɪmɪŋ] Bergsteigen, Klettern **II 1**, 14
clock [klɒk] Uhr **II 5**, 72
to **close** [kləʊz] (sich) schließen **I**
clothes ['kləʊðz] Kleidung **I**
cloud [klaʊd] Wolke **II 7**, 115
°**club** [klʌb] Klub, Verein **I**
coat [kəʊt] Mantel **II 3**, 51
°**coconut** ['kəʊkənʌt] Kokosnuss **II 3**, 47
°coconut shy ['kəʊkənʌt 'ʃaɪ] Wurfbude **II 3**, 47
°**code** [kəʊd] Code **I**
coffee ['kɒfɪ] Kaffee **I**
coke [kəʊk] Cola **I**
cold [kəʊld] kalt **I**
to **collect** [kə'lekt] sammeln **I**
collection [kə'lekʃn] Sammlung **II 5**, 81
colour ['kʌlə] Farbe **I**
comes [kʌmz] kommt **I**
Come on! ['kʌm‿ɒn] Kommt! **I**
to come back [kʌm 'bæk] zurückkommen **I**
to come off [kʌm‿'ɒf] ab-, herunterrutschen **II 4**, 64
to come up to s.o. [kʌm‿'ʌp tʊ] auf jdn. zukommen/-gehen **II 3**, 51
comic ['kɒmɪk] Comicheft **I**
to **compare** [kəm'peə] vergleichen **II 3**, 45
competition [ˌkɒmpə'tɪʃn] Wettbewerb **II 9**, 138
°to **complete** [kəm'pli:t] vervollständigen **II 5**, 74
°**compound word** ['kɒmpaʊnd 'wɜ:d] zusammengesetztes Wort **II 7**, 116
computer [kəm'pju:tə] Rechner, Computer **I**
concert ['kɒnsət] Konzert **II 9**, 138
to **consider** [kən'sɪdə] überlegen **II 9**, 148
control [kən'trəʊl] Kontrolle **II 7**, 117
to **cook** [kʊk] kochen **II 6**, 87
⟨corn⟩ [kɔ:n] Getreide **II 9**, 151
corner ['kɔ:nə] Ecke **II 5**, 72
cornfield ['kɔ:nfi:ld] Maisfeld **II 7**, 117
°**cornflakes** ['kɔ:nfleɪks] Cornflakes **II 6**, 98
to **correct** [kə'rekt] korrigieren **II 2**, 36
corridor ['kɒrɪdɔ:] Korridor, Gang **II 1**, 17
to **cost**, cost, cost [kɒst] kosten **II 9**, 145
°**costume** ['kɒstju:m] Kostüm **II 4**, 60
cottage ['kɒtɪdʒ] Cottage, Landhäuschen **II 9**, 149
⟨could be⟩ [kʊd] könnte sein **II 1**, 9
couldn't ['kʊdnt] konnte(n) nicht **II 8**, 130
to **count** [kaʊnt] zählen **II 9**, 140
countryside ['kʌntrɪsaɪd] Landschaft, Gegend **II 7**, 114
court [kɔ:t] Hof **II 5**, 73
cousin ['kʌzn] Cousine, Cousin **I**
cow [kaʊ] Kuh **II 6**, 87
⟨cowboy⟩ ['kaʊbɔɪ] Cowboy **II 10**, 157
°**Crash!** [kræʃ] Krach! **I**
crayon ['kreɪən] Buntstift **I**
crazy ['kreɪzɪ] verrückt **I**
cream [kri:m] Sahne **II 6**, 96
cricket ['krɪkɪt] Kricket *(engl. Schlagballspiel)* **II 4**, 67
town **crier** ['taʊn 'kraɪə] Ausrufer/in **II 2**, 32
crisps [krɪsps] (Kartoffel-)Chips **II 6**, 97
⟨to cross⟩ [krɒs] überqueren **II 6**, 101
crumble ['krʌmbl] Streusel **II 6**, 99
to **cry** [kraɪ] weinen **II 5**, 80
cup [kʌp] Tasse **II 6**, 93
cupboard ['kʌbəd] Schrank **II 4**, 58
°**curry** ['kʌrɪ] Curry *(indisches Gericht)* **II 6**, 96
to **cut**, cut [kʌt] schneiden **II 5**, 76
°to cut up ['kʌt‿ʌp] schneiden **II 6**, 89
to **cycle**, cycling ['saɪkl, 'saɪklɪŋ] Fahrrad fahren **II 7**, 110

D

Dad [dæd] Papa, Vati **I**
to **damage** ['dæmɪdʒ] beschädigen **II 9**, 139; Schaden anrichten **II 7**, 117
⟨damp⟩ [dæmp] feucht **II 10**, 160
to **dance** [dɑ:ns] tanzen **I**
dangerous ['deɪndʒərəs] gefährlich **II 3**, 48
dark [dɑ:k] dunkel **II 7**, 115
date [deɪt] Datum **I**
daughter ['dɔ:tə] Tochter **II 4**, 58
day [deɪ] Tag **I**
°for the day [fə ðə 'deɪ] für den Tag **I**
from day to day [frəm 'deɪ‿tʊ‿'deɪ] von Tag zu Tag **II 2**, 36
°**dead** [ded] tot **I**
Dear … [dɪə] Liebe(r) … **II 2**, 27
Dear me! [ˌdɪə 'mi:] Meine Gute! **II 5**, 72
to **deceive** [dɪ'si:v] täuschen, betrügen **II 5**, 80
dentist ['dentɪst] Zahnarzt/ärztin **II 8**, 123
department store [di:'pɑ:tmənt 'stɔ:] Warenhaus **II 5**, 72
desk [desk] Pult; Schreibtisch **I**
dessert [dɪ'zɜ:t] Nachtisch **II 6**, 99
detail ['di:teɪl]° Detail, Einzelheit **II 1**, 14
dialogue ['daɪəlɒg] Dialog **II 1**, 8; °Gespräch **I**
°**diary** ['daɪərɪ] Tagebuch **I**
°**dice** [daɪs] Würfel **I**
°to **dictate** [dɪk'teɪt] diktieren **I**
⟨dictionary⟩ ['dɪkʃənrɪ] Wörterbuch **II RF1**, 53
°picture dictionary ['pɪktʃə 'dɪkʃənrɪ] Bilderwörterbuch **I**
°to **die** [daɪ] sterben **I**
⟨difference⟩ ['dɪfrəns] Unterschied **II RF1**, 53
different ['difrənt] anders, verschieden **I**
difficult ['dɪfɪkəlt] schwierig **II 1**, 14
to **dig** [dɪg] graben **I**
dinner ['dɪnə] Abendessen **II 6**, 88
°**dirt** [dɜ:t] Schmutz **II 9**, 147
dirty ['dɜ:tɪ] dreckig, schmutzig **II 3**, 45
disco ['dɪskəʊ] Disko, Tanzveranstaltung mit Popmusik **II 9**, 143
dish [dɪʃ] Gericht **II 6**, 87
to **do** [du:] tun, machen **I**
to do a trick [trɪk] einen Trick machen **I**
°to do an interview [ˌdu: ən 'ɪntəvju:] ein Interview machen **I**
doctor ['dɒktə] Arzt/Ärztin **II 8**, 124; °Doktor **I**
dodgem car ['dɒdʒəm ˌkɑ:] Autoscooter **II 3**, 43
dog [dɒg] Hund **I**
dog biscuit ['dɒg ˌbɪskɪt] Hundekuchen **I**
°dog-free ['dɒgfri:] hundefrei **I**

door [dɔː] Tür **I**
°**double** ['dʌbl] doppelt **I**
doughnut ['dəʊnʌt] Krapfen, Berliner **II 5**, 75
⟨to be down with (*flu*)⟩ ['daʊn wɪð] krank sein mit **II 9**, 152
downstairs [ˌdaʊn'steəz] unten **I**
dragon ['drægən] Drachen **II 3**, 51
drama ['drɑːmə] Drama, Theater- **II 1**, 7
°to **draw** [drɔː] zeichnen **I**
dream [driːm] Traum **II 1**, 8
dress [dres] Kleid **I**
drink [drɪŋk] Getränk **II 2**, 29
to **drink** [drɪŋk] trinken **I**
to **drive**, drove, driven ['drɪvn] fahren **I**
driver ['draɪvə] Fahrer/in **I**
to **drop** [drɒp] fallen(lassen) **II 6**, 97
dry [draɪ] trocken **II 9**, 139

E

each [iːtʃ] jede(r) **II 2**, 25
ear [ɪə] Ohr **II 8**, 123
early ['ɜːlɪ] früh **II 3**, 43
east [iːst] östlich, Ost-, Osten **II 7**, 106
°**Easter** ['iːstə] Ostern **II 7**, 110
easy ['iːzɪ] leicht **I**
to **eat** [iːt] essen **I**
PE (= Physical **Education**) [ˌpiː 'iː/'fɪzɪkl ˌedjʊ'keɪʃn] Sportunterricht **II 1**, 7
°sound **effect** ['saʊnd ɪˌfekt] Geräusch(effekt) **II 4**, 64
egg [eg] Ei **I**
°**elephant** ['elɪfənt] Elefant **I**
else [els] sonst (noch) **I**
empty ['emptɪ] leer **II 5**, 80
ending ['endɪŋ] Ausgang **II 3**, 49; °Endung, Ende **I**
enemy ['enəmɪ] Feind **II 2**, 25
to **enjoy** [ɪn'dʒɔɪ] genießen **I**; gern tun **II 7**, 110
enjoy yourself [ɪn'dʒɔɪ jɔː'self] viel Spaß! **II 7**, 113
enough [ɪ'nʌf] genug **I**
°**er** [ɜː] nun **I**
escalator ['eskəleɪtə] Rolltreppe **II 5**, 72
even ['iːvən] auch, selbst **II 4**, 58
evening ['iːvnɪŋ] Abend **I**
in the evening ['iːvnɪŋ] abends, am Abend **I**
ever [evə] je(mals) **II 7**, 112
every ['evrɪ] jeder, jede, jedes **I**
every day ['evrɪ 'deɪ] jeden Tag **I**
everybody ['evrɪˌbɒdɪ] alle, jede/r **II 4**, 64
everyone ['evrɪwʌn] jeder **I**
everything ['evrɪθɪŋ] alles **I 4**, 66
to **examine** [ɪg'zæmɪn] untersuchen **II 8**, 123
°**example** [ɪg'zɑːmpl] Beispiel **I**
excited [ɪk'saɪtɪd] aufgeregt **II 2**, 28
°**exciting** [ɪk'saɪtiŋ] aufregend **I**
Excuse me! [ɪk'skjuːz mɪ] Entschuldigung! **I**
expensive [ɪk'spensɪv] teuer **II 3**, 41
to **explain** [ɪks'pleɪn] erklären **II 6**, 100
extra ['ekstrə] zusätzlich **II 2**, 29

F

face [feɪs] Gesicht **I**
in **fact** [ɪn‿'fækt] tatsächlich **I**
fair [feə] Volksfest, Jahrmarkt **II 2**, 31
to **fall over** [ˌfɔːl‿'əʊvə] hinfallen **II 5**, 76
family ['fæmɪlɪ] Familie **I**
family name ['fæməlɪ ˌneɪm] Familienname **II 4**, 67
fan [fæn] Fan **II 1**, 14
⟨fancy that⟩ ['fænsɪ 'ðæt] so was **II 6**, 94
fantastic [fæn'tæstɪk] phantastisch **II 3**, 41
⟨far⟩ [fɑː] weit **II 5**, 78
farm [fɑːm] Farm, Bauernhof **I**
farmer ['fɑːmə] Bauer/Bäuerin **II 7**, 114
⟨fashion⟩ ['fæʃn] Mode **II 10**, 159
⟨fashion show⟩ ['fæʃn ˌʃəʊ] Modenschau **II 10**, 159
fast [fɑːst] schnell **II 5**, 76
fat [fæt] dick **I**
father ['fɑːðə] Vater **I**
favourite ['feɪvərɪt] Lieblings- **I**
fax [faks] Fax **II 6**, 87
°to **feed** [fiːd] füttern **I**
to **feel** fine [faɪn] sich gut fühlen **II 4**, 64
to feel like ['fiːl laɪk] sich fühlen wie **I**
to feel sick [sɪk] sich schlecht/krank fühlen **II 3**, 41
°**fellow** ['feləʊ] Kerl, „Typ“ **I**
fence [fens] Zaun **II 7**, 117
ferry ['ferɪ] Fähre **II 2**, 29
to **fetch** [fetʃ] holen **I**
fete [feɪt] Feier, Fest **II 9**, 138
a **few** [fjuː] ein paar, einige **II 8**, 126
field [fiːld] Feld **II 7**, 117
film [fɪlm] Film **II 2**, 25
to **find** [faɪnd] finden **I**
°Find the answer. [ˌfaɪnd ðɪ 'ɑːnsə] Finde die Antwort. **I**
to feel **fine** [faɪn] sich gut fühlen **II 4**, 64
finger ['fɪŋgə] Finger **I**
to **finish** ['fɪnɪʃ] beenden **I**
°**fire brigade** ['faɪə brɪ'geɪd] Feuerwehr **I**
fireman ['faɪəmən] Feuerwehrmann **II 2**, 32
first [fɜːst] zuerst **II 1**, 12
first name ['fɜːst ˌneɪm] Vorname **II 4**, 67
fish [fɪʃ] Fisch **I**
fish finger ['fɪʃ 'fɪŋgə] Fischstäbchen **I**
°to **fish** [fɪʃ] fischen **II 7**, 108
⟨fjord⟩ [fjɔːd] Fjord **II 6**, 102
°**flash** [flæʃ] Blitz **II 7**, 115
flat [flæt] Wohnung **I**
flat tyre [ˌflæt 'taɪə] Plattfuß **I**
floor [flɔː] Fußboden **I**; Stockwerk/Etage **II 5**, 72
flour ['flaʊə] Mehl **II 6**, 99
flower ['flaʊə] Blume **II 8**, 134
°**flowerpot** ['flaʊəˌpɒt] Blumentopf **I**
flu [fluː] Grippe **II 4**, 64
⟨fly⟩ [flaɪ] Fliege **II 6**, 94
to **fly** [flaɪ] fliegen **I**
°to **fold** [fəʊld] falten **II 4**, 65
folder ['fəʊldə] Mappe; Schnellhefter **I**
°to **follow** ['fɒləʊ] folgen **I**
food [fuːd] Essen, Nahrung **II 6**, 87; Lebensmittel **II 5**, 73
foot [fʊt] Fuß **II 2**, 35
football ['fʊtbɔːl] Fußball **I**
football match ['fʊtbɔːl ˌmætʃ] Fußballspiel **I**
⟨footprint⟩ ['fʊtprɪnt] Fußabdruck **II 6**, 102
for [fɔː] für **I**
for example [fər‿ɪg'zɑːmpl] zum Beispiel **I**
°for the day [fə ðə 'deɪ] für den Tag **I**
⟨Ford⟩ [fɔːd] *Automarke* **II 5**, 78
forecast ['fɔːkɑːst] Vorhersage **II 7**, 113
forest ['fɒrɪst] Wald **II 2**, 25
to **forget**, forgot [fə'get, fə'gɒt] vergessen **II 4**, 60
fork [fɔːk] Gabel **II 6**, 96
form [fɔːm] Form **I**

°**fortune** ['fɔːtʃuːn] Weissagung **II 4**, 65
°fortune teller ['fɔːtʃuːn ˌtelə] Wahrsager/in **II 4**, 65
⟨fox⟩ [fɒks] Fuchs **II 9**, 151
free [friː] frei **I**
to **freeze**, froze, frozen ['friːz] gefrieren, tiefkühlen **II 6**, 99
⟨French⟩ [frentʃ] Französisch **II 1**, 9
fresh [freʃ] frisch **II 8**, 133
⟨fridge⟩ [frɪdʒ] Kühlschrank **II 6**, 102
friend [frend] Freund/in **I**
friendly ['frendlɪ] freundlich **I**
to **frighten** ['fraɪtn] erschrecken **II 7**, 114
frightening ['fraɪtnɪŋ] erschreckend, Furcht erregend **II 4**, 58
frog [frɒg] Frosch **I**
from [frɒm/frəm] aus, von **I**
from day to day [frəm 'deɪ‿tʊ‿'deɪ] von Tag zu Tag **II 2**, 36
front door ['frʌnt 'dɔː] Haustür **I**
in **front of** [ɪn 'frʌnt‿əv] vor **I**
fruit [fruːt] Obst **II 5**, 77
full of ['fʊl‿əv] voll mit **II 3**, 43
fun [fʌn] Spaß **I**
it's great fun ['greɪt fʌn] es macht großen Spaß **II 1**, 12
funny ['fʌnɪ] lustig, komisch **I**
°**future** ['fjuːtʃə] Zukunft **II 9**, 141

G

gallows ['gæləʊz] Galgen **II 2**, 26
game [geɪm] Spiel **I**
garage ['gærɪdʒ] Garage **I**
garden ['gɑːdn] Garten **I**
gate [geɪt] Tor **II 7**, 117
⟨gently⟩ ['dʒentlɪ] sanft; behutsam **II 7**, 107
Geography [dʒɪ'ɒgrəfɪ] Erdkunde **II 1**, 7
German ['dʒɜːmən] deutsch **I**
German teacher ['dʒɜːmən 'tiːtʃə] Deutschlehrer/in **I**
to **get** [get] holen **I**
to get away [ˌget‿ə'weɪ] entkommen **II 2**, 36
⟨to get down⟩ [ˌget 'daʊn] hinunterbekommen **II RF1**, 53
to get on [get‿'ɒn] einsteigen **I**
to get s.th ready ['redɪ] etw. fertig machen, vorbereiten **II 4**, 62
to get something out ['get sʌmθɪŋ 'aʊt] etw. herausholen **I**
°to get stuck [get 'stʌk] feststecken, stecken bleiben **I**
to get the bus [ˌget ðə 'bʌs] den Bus nehmen **I**
to get there ['get‿ðeə] hinkommen **I**
to get up [ˌget‿'ʌp] aufstehen **I**; ⟨heraufkommen⟩ **II RF1**, 53
Get well! ['get 'wel] Gute Besserung! **I**
°**Get Well card** ['get 'wel 'kɑːd] Gute-Besserungs-Karte **I**
ghost ['gəʊst] Geist **II 4**, 58
°**ghost train** ['gəʊst 'treɪn] Geisterbahn **II 3**, 47
girls and boys (*pl*) [ˌgɜːlz‿n 'bɔɪz] Mädchen und Jungen **I**
to **give** [gɪv] geben **I**
to give away [ˌgɪv‿ə'weɪ] verschenken **II 3**, 45
to give s.o. a lift [lɪft] jdn. im Auto mitnehmen **I**
glass [glɑːs] Glas **II 6**, 87
glasses ['glɑːsɪz] Brille **II 5**, 82
⟨glove⟩ [glʌv] Handschuh **II 10**, 159
to **go** [gəʊ] gehen **I**
°Go on. [gəʊ‿'ɒn] Mach(t) weiter. **I**
to go for a walk ['gəʊ‿fər‿ə‿'wɔːk] spazieren gehen **I**
to go round [ˌgəʊ 'raʊnd] herumgehen **I**
to go shopping [ˌgəʊ 'ʃɒpɪŋ] einkaufen gehen **II 8**, 130
to go swimming [ˌgəʊ 'swɪmɪŋ] schwimmen gehen **I**
to go to the shops [ˌgəʊ tə ðə 'ʃɒps] einkaufen gehen **I**
to have a go [ˌhæv‿ə'gəʊ] (es) probieren **II 3**, 47
goal [gəʊl] Tor **I**
gold [gəʊld] Gold **II 2**, 33
⟨gold miner⟩ ['gəʊld ˌmaɪnə] Goldgräber **II 10**, 156
gold pieces ['gəʊld 'piːsɪs] Goldstücke **II 2**, 33
⟨to be gone⟩ [gɒn] weg(gegangen) sein **II 4**, 63
⟨gonna (= going to)⟩ ['gɒnə] werde **II 5**, 78
good [gʊd] gut **I**
to be good at [biː 'gʊd‿ət] gut sein in **I**
it's no good ['nəʊ 'gʊd] es hat kein Wert/Sinn **II 7**, 113
Good luck! ['gʊd 'lʌk] Viel Glück! **II 4**, 67
Good morning. [ˌgʊd 'mɔːnɪŋ] Guten Morgen. **I**
Goodbye. [ˌgʊd'baɪ] Auf Wiedersehen. **I**
goose, geese (*pl*) [guːs, giːs] Gans, Gänse **II 2**, 31
I've **got** [aɪv'gɒt] ich habe **I**
she hasn't got [ʃiː 'hæznt gɒt] sie hat kein **I**
grandma ['grænmɑː] Oma, Großmutter **I**
grandpa ['grænpɑː] Opa, Großpapa **I**
great [greɪt] groß, großartig **I**
°**Greek** [griːk] griechisch, Grieche/Griechin **I**
green [griːn] grün **I**
⟨to grieve⟩ [griːv] trauern **II 5**, 78
to **grin** [grɪn] lächeln, grinsen **II 9**, 148
°**group** [gruːp] Gruppe **I**
to **grow,** grew [grəʊ, gruː] (an)pflanzen, wachsen **II 6**, 87
°**grumpy** ['grʌmpɪ] mürrisch, schlecht gelaunt **II 9**, 139
to **guess** [ges] (er)raten **II 5**, 78
guest [gest] Gast, Besucher/in **II 6**, 90
°guest house ['gesthaʊs] Gästehaus **I**
guitar [gɪ'tɑː] Gitarre **I**

H

hair [heə] Haar **II 3**, 51
half [hɑːf] halb **I**
hall [hɔːl] Flur **I**
ham [hæm] Schinken **I**
hamster ['hæmstə] Hamster **I**
hand [hænd] Hand **II 2**, 35
hangman ['hæŋmən] Henker **II 2**, 26
to **happen** ['hæpn] passieren, geschehen **I**
Happy Birthday! ['hæpɪ 'bɜːθdeɪ] Alles Gute zum Geburtstag! **I**
to work **hard** [hɑːd] hart/schwer arbeiten **II 6**, 96
she **hasn't** got [ʃiː 'hæznt gɒt] sie hat kein **I**
to **hate** [heɪt] hassen, nicht ausstehen können **II 1**, 12
to **have**, had [hæd] hatte **I**
to have a bath [ˌhæv‿ə'bɑːθ] baden **I**
to have a go [ˌhæv‿ə'gəʊ] (es) probieren **II 3**, 47
to have a good time [ˌhæv‿ə'gʊd taɪm] sich gut amüsieren **II 3**, 41
to have a ride ['hæv‿ə'raɪd] fahren **II 3**, 47
to have an argument [ˌhæv‿ən 'ɑːgjʊment] einen Streit, eine Auseinandersetzung haben **II 3**, 41
headache ['hedeɪk] Kopfschmerzen **II 8**, 123
headline ['hedlaɪn] Schlagzeile **I**
headmaster [ˌhed'mɑːstə] Schulleiter **II 1**, 15
to **hear** [hɪə] hören **II 2**, 25
heart [hɑːt] Herz **II 8**, 132
°to **heat** [hiːt] erhitzen, heiß machen **II 6**, 89
⟨heaven⟩ ['hevn] Himmel **II 5**, 78

heavy ['hevɪ] schwer **II 2**, 33
helicopter ['helɪkɒptə] Hubschrauber **II 7**, 115
Hello. [hə'ləʊ] Hallo./Guten Tag. **I**
helmet ['helmɪt] Helm **II 2**, 33
to **help** [help] helfen **I**
Help! [help] Hilfe! **I**
helper ['helpə] Helfer/in **II 8**, 130
hen [hen] Henne **II 6**, 87; °Huhn **I**
her [hɜː] ihr/ihre **I**
here [hɪə] hier **I**
here you are ['hɪə juː ˌɑː] bitte schön **I**
hero ['hɪərəʊ] Held/in **II 2**, 36
he's (= he is) [hiːz] er ist **I**
he's got (= he has got) ['hiːz gɒt] er hat **I**
Hey! [heɪ] Hey! **I**
Hi! [haɪ] Hallo! **I**
to **hide** [haɪd] (sich) verstecken **II 1**, 16
highest ['haɪɪst] höchste/r/s **II 7**, 113
°**Highlands** ['haɪləndz] Hochland **II 7**, 109
hill [hɪl] Hügel **I**
hill-walking ['hɪl ˌwɔːkɪŋ] Wandern **II 7**, 113
him [hɪm] ihm, ihn **I**
⟨himself⟩ [hɪm'self] (er) selbst **II RF1**, 53
his [hɪz] sein/seine **I**
History ['hɪstərɪ] Geschichte **II 1**, 7
to **hit**, hit [hɪt, hɪt] treffen, schlagen **II 3**, 48
°**Hmm.** [m] Hm./Tja. **I**
°**hockey** ['hɒkɪ] Hockey **I**
⟨what a hog⟩ [ˌwɒt‿ə 'hɒg] was für ein Schwein **II 6**, 94
hole [həʊl] Loch **I**
to make a hole ['meɪk‿ə 'həʊl] ein Loch graben **I**
holiday ['hɒlɪdeɪ] Urlaub, Ferien **I**
home [həʊm] Heim, Zuhause **I**
at home [ət 'həʊm] zu Hause **I**
homework ['həʊmwɜːk] Hausaufgaben **I**
to **hope** [həʊp] hoffen **II 4**, 60
horse [hɔːs] Pferd **I**
hospital ['hɒspɪtl] Krankenhaus **I**
hostel ['hɒstl] Heim, Herberge **II 7**, 116
hot [hɒt] heiß **I**
hot dog ['hɒt 'dɒg] Hotdog *(heißes Würstchen in einem Brötchen)* **II 3**, 41
hotel [həʊ'tel] Hotel **II 7**, 106
house [haʊs] Haus **I**
°**housekeeper** ['haʊsˌkiːpə] Haushälter/in **II 4**, 64
°**hovercraft** ['hɒvəˌkrɑːft] Luftkissenboot **I**
how [haʊ] wie **I**
How many …? [haʊ 'menɪ] Wie viele …? **I**
How much is …? [ˌhaʊ 'mʌtʃ‿ɪz] Wie viel kostet …? **I**
How old are you? [haʊ 'əʊld] Wie alt bist du? **I**
hug [hʌg] Umarmung **II 2**, 28
a **hundred years ago** [ə 'hʌndred jɪəz ə'gəʊ] vor hundert Jahren **II 4**, 58
I'm **hungry.** [ˌaɪm 'hʌŋgrɪ] Ich bin hungrig. **I**
to **hurry** ['hʌrɪ] (sich) beeilen **II 7**, 115
to **hurt** [hɜːt] (sich) verletzen, weh tun **II 8**, 122; °schmerzen **I**

I

I [aɪ] ich **I**
⟨I do know that⟩ ich weiß doch, dass **II 1**, 9
I haven't (= I have not) [aɪ'hævnt] ich habe kein **I**
I spy with my little eye … *engl. Kinderspiel* **II 1**, 19
I think so. [aɪ 'θɪŋk ˌsəʊ] Ich denke schon. **II 4**, 59
⟨I took⟩ (das) ich hatte/nahm **II 1**, 9
I'd like … [aɪd 'laɪk] Ich hätte gern … **II 5**, 75
ice cream ['aɪs kriːm] Eiskrem **I**
ice-skating ['aɪsˌskeɪtɪŋ] Schlittschuhlaufen **II 3**, 41
idea [aɪ'dɪə] Idee **II 7**, 106; Einfall **I**
ideal [aɪ'dɪəl] ideal **II 7**, 106
if [ɪf] wenn, ob **II 5**, 76
ill [ɪl] krank **II 8**, 123
I'll (= I will) [aɪl, aɪ 'wɪl] ich werde **II 4**, 60
I'm (= I am) [aɪm] ich bin **I**
I'm at Haywood School. [ˌaɪm‿ət 'heɪwʊd ˌskuːl] Ich gehe auf die Haywood School. **I**
I'm hungry. [ˌaɪm 'hʌŋgrɪ] Ich bin hungrig. **I**
I'm lucky. ['lʌkɪ] Ich habe Glück. **I**
I'm not sure. [ˌaɪm nɒt 'ʃʊə] Ich bin nicht sicher. **I**
to **imagine** [ɪ'mædʒɪn] sich vorstellen **II 3**, 51
important [ɪm'pɔːtənt] wichtig **II 1**, 10
in [ɪn] in **I**
in a minute ['mɪnɪt] in einer Minute **I**
in fact [ɪn‿'fækt] tatsächlich **I**
in front of [ɪn 'frʌnt‿əv] vor **I**
in the afternoon [ɪn ðɪ ˌɑːftə'nuːn] am Nachmittag **I**
in the evening ['iːvnɪŋ] abends, am Abend **I**
in the morning [ɪn ðə 'mɔːnɪŋ] am Vormittag **I**
°**Indian** ['ɪndjən] indisch, Inder/in **II 5**, 73
information [ˌɪnfə'meɪʃn]° Information **I**; Auskunft **II 5**, 72
to **injure** ['ɪndʒə] verletzen **II 8**, 129
inside ['ɪnsaɪd] drinnen **I**
interesting ['ɪntrɪstɪŋ] interessant **II 1**, 12
°**interview** ['ɪntəvjuː] Interview **I**
into ['ɪntʊ] in … hinein **II 1**, 10
invitation [ˌɪnvɪ'teɪʃn] Einladung **I**
to **invite** [ɪn'vaɪt] einladen **I**
°**irregular** [ɪ'regjʊlə] unregelmäßig **II 2**, 28
is [ɪz] ist **I**
Is she …? ['ɪz ʃɪ] Ist sie …? **I**
island ['aɪlənd] Insel **II 7**, 106
°**isn't it** ['ɪznt‿ɪt] nicht wahr **II 1**, 7
she isn't [ʃiː 'ɪznt] sie ist nicht **I**
it [ɪt] es **I**
It doesn't say. [ɪt ˌdʌznt 'seɪ] Das steht nicht darauf. **II 1**, 11
it's [ɪts] es ist **I**
it's fun [fʌn] es macht Spaß **I**
it's great fun ['greɪt fʌn] es macht großen Spaß **II 1**, 12
°**Italian** [ɪ'tælɪən] italienisch, Italiener/in **I**
its [ɪts] sein, seine/ihr, ihre **I**
I've got [aɪv'gɒt] ich habe **I**

J

jacket ['dʒækɪt] Jacke **II 4**, 58
°**jam** [dʒæm] Marmelade **II 9**, 147
jeans [dʒiːnz] Jeans **I**
°**jelly** ['dʒelɪ] Wackelpudding **II 9**, 147
⟨jumbo jet⟩ ['dʒʌmbəʊ ˌdʒet] Jumbojet **II 5**, 78
⟨Jew⟩ [dʒuː] Jude **II 10**, 156
job [dʒɒb] Job, Arbeit **I**
to **join** [dʒɔɪn] Mitglied werden **II 2**, 30
joke [dʒəʊk] Witz **II 1**, 15
⟨jolly⟩ ['dʒɒlɪ] lustig, vergnügt **II 10**, 160
juice [dʒuːs] Saft **II 6**, 93
⟨jumbo jet⟩ ['dʒʌmbəʊ ˌdʒet] Jumbojet **II 5**, 78
to **jump** [dʒʌmp] springen **II 3**, 48
junior ['dʒuːnjə] Unterstufen-, junger **II 4**, 58
just [dʒʌst] gerade; nur **I**

K

kangaroo [ˌkæŋgəˈruː]° Kängeru **I**; Känguru **II 8**, 126
to **keep s.o. away** [ˌkiːp‿əˈwaɪ] jdn. zurück halten **II 3**, 51
to **kick** [kɪk] kicken **I**
kilt [kɪlt] Schottenrock **II 7**, 112
kind of [ˈkaɪnd‿əv] Art (von) **II 4**, 67
kitchen [ˈkɪtʃn] Küche **I**
° **kite** [kaɪt] Drache **I**
° **kiwi** [ˈkiːwiː] Kiwi **II 6**, 88
knife, knives [naɪf, naɪvz] Messer **I**
to **know** [nəʊ] wissen **II 1**, 7
⟨I do know that⟩ ich weiß doch, dass **II 1**, 9
to **know**, knew, known [nəʊn] wissen, kennen **II 6**, 98
knee [niː] Knie **II 8A** 122

L

° **ladder** [ˈlædə] Leiter **I**
lady [ˈleɪdɪ] Dame **II 5**, 79
° **lamb** [læm] Lamm **I**
° **lambing shed** [ˈlæmiŋ ˈʃed] Schafpferch, Schafstall **I**
to **land** [lænd] landen **II 8**, 129
language [ˈlæŋgwɪdʒ] Sprache **II 8**, 129
last [lɑːst] letzte/r/s **II 1**, 8
late [leɪt] spät **I**
to **laugh** [lɑːf] lachen **I**
to laugh at s.o. [ˈlɑːf‿ət] lachen über jdn. **II 3**, 48
lazy [ˈleɪzɪ] faul **I**
leaflet [ˈliːflɪt] Prospekt, Informationsblatt **II 2**, 25
° to **learn** [lɜːn] lernen **I**
to **leave** [liːv] abfahren, weggehen **I**; lassen, verlassen **II 1**, 19
⟨left⟩ [left] linke/r/s **II 3**, 49
on the left [left] auf der linken Seite, links **I**
leg [leg] Bein **I**
lemon [ˈlemən] Zitrone **II 6**, 99
lemonade [ˌlemənˈeɪd] Limonade **I**
to **lend** [lend] (aus) leihen **II 5**, 83
less [les] weniger **II 5**, 82
lesson [ˈlesn] Stunde, Unterricht **II 1**, 7
° **Let's start.** [ˌlets ˈstɑːt] Lasst uns anfangen. **I**
letter [ˈletə] Buchstabe **I**; Brief **I**
° **library** [ˈlaɪbrərɪ] Bibliothek **II 9**, 141
to **lie** [laɪ] liegen **I**
⟨life⟩ [laɪf] Leben **II 7**, 107
lift [lɪft] Fahrstuhl **II 5**, 72
lightning [ˈlaɪtnɪŋ] Blitz **II 4**, 64
to **like** [laɪk] mögen **I**
I'd like … [aɪd ˈlaɪk] Ich hätte gern … **II 5**, 75
° like that [laɪk ˈðæt] so, auf diese Weise **I**
Would you like …? [ˌwʊd jʊ ˈlaɪk] Hättest du/Hätten Sie gern …? **II 5**, 75
to **listen** [ˈlɪsn] hören **I**
° **listening practice** [ˈlɪsnɪŋ ˌpræktɪs] Hörverständnisübung **I**
litter [ˈlɪtə] Abfall **II 7**, 117
little [ˈlɪtl] klein **I**
to **live** [lɪv] leben, wohnen **I**
living-room [ˈlɪvɪŋrʊm] Wohnzimmer **I**
° **loch** [lɒk] See *(schottisch)* **II 7**, 109
° **locked** [lɒkt] verschlossen **I**
a **long** way [ˈlɒŋ ˈweɪ] weit **I**
longest [ˈlɒŋgɪst] längste/r/s **II 7**, 114
Look. [lʊk] Schau mal./Schaut mal. **I**
to look for [ˈlʊk fɔː] suchen **II 1**, 16
to look like [ˈlʊk laɪk] aussehen (wie) **II 1**, 16
to look nice [lʊk ˈnaɪs] nett/schön aussehen **II 3**, 41
⟨Lord⟩ [lɔːd] Herr **II 5**, 78
lorry [ˈlɒrɪ] Lastwagen **II 3**, 43
to **lose**, lost, lost [luːz, lɒst] verlieren **II 9**, 139
a **lot** of [əˈlɒt‿əv] viel(e) **I**
lots of [ˈlɒts‿əv] viele **I**
loud [laʊd] laut **I**
love [lʌv] Liebe **II 1**, 15
⟨to love⟩ [lʌv] lieben **II 1**, 9
lower [ˈləʊə] der/die/das untere **II 5**, 72
Good **luck!** [ˈgʊd ˈlʌk] Viel Glück! **II 4**, 67
I'm **lucky.** [ˈlʌkɪ] Ich habe Glück. **I**
lunch [lʌntʃ] Mittagessen **II 1**, 8
lunch box [ˈlʌntʃ bɒks] Essensbehälter **I**
lunchtime [ˈlʌntʃtaɪm] Mittagspause **II 1**, 14

M

magazine [ˌmægəˈziːn] Zeitschrift **I**
to **make** a hole [ˈmeɪk‿ə ˈhəʊl] ein Loch graben **I**
° to make a request [ˈmeɪk‿ə rɪˈkwest] sich ein Lied wünschen **I**
° **Make a poster.** [ˌmeɪk‿ə ˈpəʊstə] Mach(t) ein Poster. **I**
man, men [mæn, men] Mann, Männer **I**
manager [ˈmænɪdʒə] Geschäftsführer **II 5**, 82
many [ˈmenɪ] viele **I**
map [mæp] Karte **I**
market [ˈmɑːkɪt] Markt **I**
street market [ˈstriːt ˈmɑːkɪt] Straßenmarkt **II 5**, 77
football **match** [ˈfʊtbɔːl ˌmætʃ] Fußballspiel **I**
mate [meɪt] Kumpel **II 5**, 80
Maths [mæθs] Mathe(matik) **II 1**, 7
What's the matter with you? [ðə ˈmætə] Was ist mit dir los? **II 3**, 51
⟨may⟩ [meɪ] dürfen **II 6**, 101
maybe [ˈmeɪbiː] vielleicht **I**
me [miː] mir, mich **I**
meal [miːl] Mahlzeit, Essen **II 6**, 87
to **mean** [miːn] bedeuten **II 5**, 80
measles [ˈmiːzlz] Masern **II 8**, 132
meat [miːt] Fleisch **II 6**, 87
medicine [ˈmedsn] Medizin **II 8**, 123
to **meet** [miːt] treffen **I**
meeting [ˈmiːtɪŋ] Treffen, Besprechung **II 1**, 10
member [ˈmembə] Mitglied **II 9**, 138
memory [ˈmemərɪ] Gedächtnis **II 8**, 127
⟨merrily⟩ [ˈmerɪlɪ] vergnügt **II 7**, 107
⟨merry⟩ [ˈmerɪ] fröhlich **II 8**, 131
mess [mes] Unordnung **II 8**, 123
middle [ˈmɪdl] Mitte **II 4**, 65
mightn't (= might not) [ˈmaɪtnt] könnte (vielleicht) nicht **II 9**, 148
mighty [ˈmaɪtɪ] gewaltig **II 5**, 80
⟨mile⟩ [maɪl] Meile **II 4**, 63
milk [mɪlk] Milch **I**
⟨millionaire⟩ [ˌmɪljəˈneə] Millionär **II 10**, 156
° **mince** [mɪns] Hackfleisch **II 6**, 96
mind map [ˈmaɪnd mæp] Gedankennetzwerk **II 1**, 18
Never mind! [ˈnevə ˈmaɪnd] Macht nichts! **II 2**, 28
⟨gold miner⟩ [ˈgəʊld ˌmaɪnə] Goldgräber **II 10**, 156
minute [ˈmɪnɪt] Minute **I**
in a minute [ˈmɪnɪt] in einer Minute **I**
⟨to miss⟩ [mɪs] verpassen **II 4**, 63
° **missing** [ˈmɪsɪŋ] fehlend **I**
mistake [mɪˈsteɪk] Fehler **II 7**, 114

mixture ['mɪkstʃə] Mischung **II 6**, 99
⟨mobile⟩ ['məʊbaɪl] Mobile **II RF1**, 54
pocket **money** ['pɒkɪt ˌmʌnɪ] Taschengeld **I**
monster ['mɒnstə] Ungeheuer **II 2**, 32
month [mʌnθ] Monat **I**
moody ['mu:dɪ] launisch **II 9**, 148
more [mɔ:] mehr **I**; noch etwas **I**
in the **morning** [ɪn ðə 'mɔ:nɪŋ] am Vormittag **I**
most [məʊst] am meisten **II 4**, 59
mother ['mʌðə] Mutter **I**
mountain ['maʊntɪn] Berg **II 7**, 106
°Mountain Rescue ['maʊntɪn 'reskju:] Bergwacht **II 7**, 115
mouse [maʊs] Maus **I**
mouth [maʊθ] Mund **II 2**, 35
Mrs ['mɪsɪz] Frau *(als Anrede)* **I**
much [mʌtʃ] viel **I**
Mum [mʌm] Mama, Mutti **I**
°**museum** [mju:'zɪəm] Museum **II 7**, 107
music ['mju:zɪk] Musik **I**
musical ['mju:zɪkl] musikalisch **II 9**, 139
must [mʌst] müssen **I**
mustn't ['mʌsnt] nicht dürfen **II 8**, 125
my [maɪ] mein/meine **I**

N

name [neɪm] Name **I**
°My name is … [maɪ 'neɪm‿ɪz] Ich heiße … **I**
nasty ['nɑ:stɪ] scheußlich, übel, gemein **II 8**, 123
near [nɪə] in der Nähe von, bei **I**
nearly ['nɪəlɪ] beinahe, fast **II 2**, 36
to **need** [ni:d] brauchen, benötigen **I**
neighbour ['neɪbə] Nachbar/in **I**
nervous ['nɜ:vəs] aufgeregt, nervös **II 4**, 60
never ['nevə] niemals **I**
Never mind! ['nevə 'maɪnd] Macht nichts! **II 2**, 28
new [nju:] neu **I**
news [nju:z] Nachricht(en) **II 2**, 33
newsagent's ['nju:zˌeɪdʒənts] Laden für Zeitungen, Zeitschriften, Tabakwaren, Süßigkeiten, etc. **II 5**, 72
newspaper ['nju:sˌpeɪpə] Zeitung **II 2**, 32
⟨next⟩ [nekst] nächste/r/s **II 1**, 17
nice [naɪs] nett **I**
Nice to meet you! ['naɪs tə 'mi:t ju:] Schön dich kennen zu lernen! **I**
night [naɪt] Nacht **II 2**, 26
no [nəʊ] nein **I**
nobody ['nəʊbədɪ] niemand **I**
⟨nod⟩ [nɒd] Nicken **II 8**, 131
noise [nɔɪz] Geräusch **I**
noisy ['nɔɪzɪ] laut, lärmend **II 3**, 41
°**non-uniform day** ['nɒn‿'ju:nɪfɔ:m ˌdeɪ] *Tag, an dem keine Schuluniform getragen werden muss* **II 9**, 142
normal ['nɔ:ml] normal **II 9**, 139
north [nɔ:θ] nördlich, Nord-, Norden **II 7**, 106
⟨Norwegian⟩ [nɔ:'wi:dʒən] norwegisch; Norweger/in **II 6**, 102
°**nosy** ['nəʊzɪ] neugierig **I**
not [nɒt] nicht **I**
not … anything ['enɪθɪŋ] nichts **I**
not so bad ['nɒt‿səʊ‿'bæd] nicht so schlimm **I**
not … yet [jet] noch nicht **I**
nose [nəʊz] Nase **II 8A** 122
notebook ['nəʊtbʊk] Notizheft **II 3**, 46
to make **notes** [nəʊts] sich Notizen machen **II 8**, 131
nothing ['nʌθɪŋ] nichts **II 2**, 33

notice ['nəʊtɪs] Aushang, Schild **II 1**, 11; Mitteilung **II 1**, 10
to **notice**, noticed ['nəʊtɪs] merken, sehen **II 2**, 33
°**noun** [naʊn] Substantiv, Nomen **II 3**, 42
now [naʊ] jetzt **I**
nurse [nɜ:s] Krankenschwester, Krankenpfleger **II 8**, 130
nursery school ['nɜ:sərɪ ˌsku:l] Kindergarten **II 2**, 30

O

°**oak** [əʊk] Eiche **II 2**, 31
rolled **oats** ['rəʊld 'əʊts] Haferflocken **II 6**, 99
of [ɒv/əv] von **I**
of course [əv‿'kɔ:s] natürlich **I**
°police **officer** [pə'li:s 'ɒfɪsə] Polizist/in **I**
often ['ɒfn] oft **I**
°**oh** [əʊ] oh **I**
OK ['əʊˌkeɪ] richtig, gut, in Ordnung **I**
old [əʊld] alt **I**
on [ɒn] auf **I**
on Fridays [ɒn 'fraɪdeɪz] freitags **II 1**, 8
on the left [left] auf der linken Seite, links **I**
on the radio [ɒn] im Radio **I**
on the right [raɪt] auf der rechten Seite, rechts **I**
on the telephone [ˌɒn‿ðə‿'telɪfəʊn] am Telefon **I**
the blue **one** [wʌn] das Blaue **II 1**, 13
only ['əʊnlɪ] nur **I**
°**Oops!** [u:ps] *Ausruf* **I**
operation [ˌɒpə'reɪʃn] Operation **II 8**, 130
°**opinion** [ə'pɪnɪən] Meinung **I**
°**opposite** ['ɒpəzɪt] Gegenteil; gegenüber **I** Gegensatz **II 1**, 19
or [ɔ:] oder **I**
orange ['ɒrɪndʒ] orange **I**
°**order** ['ɔ:də] Reihenfolge **I**
other ['ʌðə] ander(e) **I**
Ouch! [aʊtʃ] Au! **II 8**, 128
our ['aʊə] unser, unsere **I**
⟨outfit⟩ ['aʊtfɪt] Kleidung **II 10**, 159
outlaw ['aʊtlɔ:] Gesetzlose/r, Vogelfreie/r, Bandit/in **II 2**, 25
outside ['aʊtsaɪd] draußen **I**
over ['əʊvə] über **I**; zu Ende **II 1**, 7
over there [ˌəʊvə 'ðeə] da drüben **I**
⟨overhead projector⟩ ['əʊvəˌhed prə'dʒektə] Tageslichtprojektor **II 1**, 17
own [əʊn] eigene/r/s **II 7**, 106
owner ['əʊnə] Besitzer **II 8**, 133

P

a **packet** of ['pækɪt‿əv] ein Paket **I**
Please look at page … ['lʊk‿ət peɪdʒ] Schau/Schaut bitte auf Seite … **I**
to **paint** [peɪnt] (be)malen; streichen **II 3**, 41
°**pair** [peə] Paar **I**
pale [peɪl] blass **II 3**, 51
°**pan** [pæn] Topf **II 9**, 147
°**pants** [pænts] Unterhose; Hose **II 9**, 147
paper ['peɪpə] Papier **II 5**, 78
parents ['peərənts] Eltern **I**
park [pɑ:k] Park **I**
part [pɑ:t] Teil **II 3**, 41; Stück **II 8**, 122
°past **participle** ['pɑ:st 'pɑ:tɪsɪpl] Partizip Perfekt **II 6**, 98
°**partner** ['pɑ:tnə] Partner/in **I**

to **pass** [pɑːs] reichen **I**
⟨passage⟩ [ˈpæsɪdʒ] (Durch-)Gang, Passage **II 10**, 161
⟨past⟩ [pɑːst] vorbei **II 10**, 160; nach **I**
° past participle [ˈpɑːst ˈpɑːtɪsɪpl] Partizip Perfekt **II 6**, 98
path [pɑːθ] Pfad, Weg **II 7**, 115
patient [ˈpeɪʃnt] Patient/in **II 8**, 125
to **pay** [peɪ] zahlen **II 9**, 139
PE (= Physical Education) [ˌpiː ˈiː/ˈfɪzɪkl ˌedjʊˈkeɪʃn] Sportunterricht **II 1**, 7
peaceful [ˈpiːsfʊl] ruhig **II 8**, 130
⟨pear⟩ [peə] Birne **II 6**, 102
° to **peel** [piːl] schälen **II 6**, 89
pen [pen] Füller **I**
pence (*pl*) [pens] *engl. Münze* **II 9**, 143
pencil [ˈpensl] Bleistift **I**
pencil case [ˈpenslkeɪs] Federtasche **I**
° **penny**, pennies [ˈpenɪ, ˈpenɪz] *engl. Münze* **II 9**, 147
people [ˈpiːpl] Leute **I**
perhaps [pəˈhæps] vielleicht **II 7**, 114
° **person** [ˈpɜːsn] Person **I**
pet [pet] Haustier **I**
pet shop [ˈpet ʃɒp] Tierhandlung, Zoohandlung **I**
⟨petrol pump⟩ [ˈpetrəl ˈpʌmp] Zapfsäule **II 9**, 152
to **phone** [fəʊn] anrufen, telefonieren **I**
to **take a photo** [ˈteɪk‿ə‿ˈfəʊtəʊ] ein Foto machen **I**
° **phrase** [freɪz] (Rede-)Wendung **II 8**, 129
° **piano** [pɪˈænəʊ] Klavier **II 1**, 14
to **pick** [pɪk] nehmen, pflücken, auswählen **II 4**, 63
to pick s.th. up [pɪk‿ˈʌp] etwas aufheben **I**
picture [ˈpɪktʃə] Bild **I**
° **picture dictionary** [ˈpɪktʃə ˈdɪkʃənrɪ] Bilderwörterbuch **I**
piece [piːs] Stück **II 5**, 76
pig [pɪg] Schwein **II 3**, 41
⟨pill⟩ [pɪl] Tablette **II RF1**, 53
pillow [ˈpɪləʊ] Kissen **II 4**, 64
° **pilot** [ˈpaɪlət] Pilot/in **I**
pint of [ˈpaɪnt‿əv] 0,47 Liter **II 4**, 63
pipe [paɪp] Pfeife **II 7**, 116
° to **pipe** [paɪp] pfeifen **II 7**, 109
pizza [ˈpiːtsə] Pizza **II 5**, 73
place [pleɪs] Platz, Ort **II 1**, 19; Stelle **I**
to **plan** [plæn] planen **II 4**, 65
by **plane** [baɪ‿ˈpleɪn] mit dem Flugzeug **I**
plate [pleɪt] Teller **II 6**, 96
play [pleɪ] Theaterstück **II 1**, 11
to **play** [pleɪ] spielen **I**
playground [ˈpleɪgraʊnd] Schulhof; Spielplatz **I**
Please look at page ... [ˈlʊk‿ət peɪdʒ] Schau/Schaut bitte auf Seite ... **I**
plenty [ˈplentɪ] eine Menge **II 5**, 80
° **plural** [ˈplʊərəl] Mehrzahl, Plural **I**
pocket money [ˈpɒkɪt ˌmʌnɪ] Taschengeld **I**
° **police** [pəˈliːs] Polizei **I**
° police officer [pəˈliːs ˈɒfɪsə] Polizist/in **I**
policeman [pəˈliːsmən] Polizist **I**
° **Polish** [ˈpəʊlɪʃ] polnisch, Pole/Polin **I**
polite [pəˈlaɪt] höflich **II 6**, 94
pond [pɒnd] Teich **I**
pony [ˈpəʊnɪ] Pony **II 7**, 114
° to **pony-trek** [ˈpəʊnɪtrek] ausreiten **II 7**, 108
poor [pʊə] arm **II 2**, 28
pop music [ˈpɒp ˌmjuːzɪk] Popmusik **I**
popcorn [ˈpɒpkɔːn] Popcorn **II 3**, 41
pop (= **popular**) [ˈpɒpjʊlə] beliebt **I**
porridge [ˈpɒrɪdʒ] Haferbrei **II 7**, 112
post office [ˈpəʊst‿ɒfɪs] Postamt **I**
postcard [ˈpəʊstkɑːd] Postkarte **I**
° **Make a poster.** [ˌmeɪk‿ə ˈpəʊstə] Mach(t) ein Poster. **I**
potato(es) [pəˈteɪtəʊ] Kartoffel(n) **I**
a **pound of** [ˈpaʊnd‿əv] ein Pfund **I**
⟨to pour⟩ [pɔː] gießen **II 10**, 160
° **power** [ˈpaʊə] Kraft, Stärke **I**
practice [ˈpræktɪs]° Übung **I**; Training **II 1**, 14
° listening practice [ˈlɪsnɪŋ ˌpræktɪs] Hörverständnisübung **I**
to **prepare** [prɪˈpeə] vorbereiten, zubereiten **II 6**, 96
° **preposition** [ˌprepəˈzɪʃn] Präposition **II 9**, 141
prescription [prɪˈskrɪpʃn] Rezept *(vom Arzt)* **II 8**, 128
present [ˈpreznt] Geschenk **I**
° present perfect [ˈpreznt ˈpɜːfɪkt] Perfekt **II 6**, 92
pretty [ˈprɪtɪ] hübsch **II 4**, 58
price [praɪs] Preis **II 5**, 72
prison [prɪzn] Gefängnis **II 2**, 33
prisoner [ˈprɪznə] Gefangene/r **II 2**, 36
prize [praɪz] Preis **II 3**, 44
probably [ˈprɒbəblɪ] wahrscheinlich **II 1**, 19
problem [ˈprɒbləm] Problem **I**
to **produce** [prəˈdjuːs] erzeugen, herstellen **II 7**, 117
programme [ˈprəʊgræm] Sendung, Programm **I**
° **progressive** [prəʊˈgresɪv] Verlaufsform **II 8**, 127
° **project** [ˈprɒdʒekt] Projekt **II 4**, 62
⟨overhead projector⟩ [ˈəʊvəˌhed prəˈdʒektə] Tageslichtprojektor **II 1**, 17
prompter [ˈprɒmptə] Souffleur, Souffleuse (*Stichwortgeber/in beim Theater*) **II 4**, 58
to be **proud of** [biː ˈpraʊd‿əv] stolz sein auf **II 6**, 97
° to **pull** [pʊl] ziehen **II 9**, 147
pullover [ˈpʊlˌəʊvə] Pullover **I**
pump [pʌmp] Pumpe **I**
pupil [ˈpjupl] Schüler/in **II 1**, 10
° **puppet** [ˈpʌpɪt] Marionette **II 4**, 62
purple [ˈpɜːpl] lila **I**
purse [pɜːs] Geldbeutel, Portemonnaie **II 1**, 15
° to **put** [pʊt] (ein)setzen, legen **I**
⟨put your whole self in⟩ [ˈhəʊl ˈself] macht einen Schritt vorwärts **II 3**, 49
⟨pyjamas⟩ [pəˈdʒɑːməz] Schlafanzug, Pyjama **II 10**, 159

Q

quarter [ˈkwɔːtə] Viertel **I**
° **queen** [kwiːn] Königin **I**
° **question** [ˈkwestʃn] Frage **I**
quick [kwɪk] schnell **II 1**, 19
quickly [ˈkwɪklɪ] schnell **II 7**, 109
quiet [ˈkwaɪət] ruhig, leise **I**
° **quiz** [kwɪz] Fragespiel, Quiz **I**

R

⟨rabbit⟩ [ˈræbɪt] Kaninchen **II 9**, 152
radio [ˈreɪdɪəʊ] Radio **I**
on the radio [ɒn] im Radio **I**
° radio request [ˈreɪdɪəʊ rɪˈkwest] Musikwunsch im Radio **I**
° **raffle** [ˈræfl] Verlosung, Tombola **II 4**, 59
⟨raft⟩ [rɑːft] Floß **II 9**, 151
to **rain** [reɪn] regnen **I**
° **rainbow** [ˈreɪnbəʊ] Regenbogen **I**
° **rap-rhyme** [ˈræpˈraɪm] Rapvers **I**
rat [ræt] Ratte **II 3**, 51
° to **read** [riːd] lesen **I**

°to read out [ˈriːd‿aʊt] vorlesen **I**
ready [ˈredɪ] fertig **I**
really [ˈrɪəlɪ] wirklich **I**
reason [ˈriːzn] Grund **II 8**, 124
recipe [ˈresɪpɪ] (Koch-)Rezept **II 6**, 87
red [red] rot **I**
°**register** [ˈredʒɪstə] Namensliste **II 1**, 10
regular [ˈregjʊlə] regelmäßig **II 2**, 30
to **remember** [rɪˈmembə] merken, sich erinnern an **II 1**, 15
to **repair** [riːˈpeə] reparieren **I**
report [rɪˈpɔːt] Bericht, Reportage **II 8**, 131
°radio **request** [ˈreɪdɪəʊ rɪˈkwest] Musikwunsch im Radio **I**
°to make a request [ˈmeɪk‿ə‿rɪˈkwest] sich ein Lied wünschen **I**
°Mountain **Rescue** [ˈmaʊntɪn ˈreskjuː] Bergwacht **II 7**, 115
to **rest** [rest] ausruhen **II 8**, 132
restaurant [ˈrestərɒnt] Restaurant **I**
°**rhyme** [raɪm] Reim **I**
°rhyme-time [ˈraɪm ˌtaɪm] Zeit für Reime **II 6**, 98
rhythm [ˈrɪðəm] Rhythmus **II 6**, 88
to **ride**, rode, ridden [ˈrɪdn] reiten **II 6**, 98
to have a ride [ˈhæv‿əˈraɪd] fahren **II 3**, 47
right [raɪt] richtig **I**
all right [ˌɔːlˈraɪt] in Ordnung **II 2**, 33
on the right [raɪt] auf der rechten Seite, rechts **I**
right away [ˌraɪt‿əˈweɪ] jetzt sofort **I**
⟨right hand out⟩ rechte Hand nach hinten **II 3**, 49
ring [rɪŋ] Ring **I**
river [ˈrɪvə] Fluss **II 7**, 118
roast beef [ˈrəʊst ˌbiːf] Rinderbraten **II 6**, 87
°**robber** [ˈrɒbə] Dieb/in **II 9**, 147
rock [rɒk] Felsen, Stein **II 2**, 31
°**role** [ˈrəʊl] Rolle **II 1**, 11
°role play [ˈrəʊl pleɪ] Rollenspiel **I**
rolled oats [ˈrəʊld ˈəʊts] Haferflocken **II 6**, 99
roof [ruːf] Dach **II 5**, 77
room [ruːm] Zimmer **I**
°**rope** [rəʊp] Seil **II 9**, 147
rough [rʌf] hart, rau **II 5**, 80
round [raʊnd] herum **I**; um … herum **I**
°**roundabout** [ˈraʊndəbaʊt] Karussell **II 3**, 47
to **row** [rəʊ] rudern **II 7**, 111
rule [ruːl] Regel **II 9**, 139
to **run** [rʌn] rennen, laufen **II 1**, 16
to run off, ran off [ˈrʌn‿ɒf, ræn] wegrennen **II 3**, 48
⟨runway⟩ [ˈrʌnweɪ] Start- und Landebahn **II 5**, 78

S

°to **sail** [seɪl] segeln **II 7**, 108
salad [ˈsæləd] Salat **I**
°**salami** [səˈlɑːmɪ] Salami **II 6**, 87
sale [seɪl] Verkauf **II 9**, 143
⟨salt⟩ [sɔːlt] Salz **II 6**, 102
same [seɪm] gleich **I**
sand [sænd] Sand **II 8**, 133
sandcastle [ˈsændkɑːsl] Sandburg **II 8**, 125
sandwich [ˈsænwɪdʒ] belegtes Brot **II 5**, 73
saucepan [ˈsɔːspən] Topf **II 6**, 96
sausage [ˈsɒsɪdʒ] Wurst, Würstchen **I**
to **save** [seɪv] sparen **I**
°to **say** [seɪ] sagen **I**
It doesn't say. [ɪt ˌdʌznt ˈseɪ] Das steht nicht darauf. **II 1**, 11
Say cheese! [tʃiːz] *Bitte lächeln!* **I**
to be **scared of** [ˈskeəd‿əv] Angst haben vor **II 2**, 27
scene [siːn] Szene **II 1**, 16
school [skuːl] Schule **I**
school bag [ˈskuːlbæg] Schultasche **I**
Science [ˈsaɪəns] Naturwissenschaft; Wissenschaft **II 1**, 8
°**Scottish** [ˈskɒtɪʃ] schottisch **II 7**, 111
°to **scratch** [skrætʃ] kratzen **II 9**, 147
to **scream** [skriːm] schreien **II 6**, 88
°**seaside** [ˈsiːsaɪd] Küste, See **I**
seat [siːt] Sitz **II 3**, 48
°**section** [ˈsekʃn] Abschnitt **II 4**, 64
to **see** [siː] sehen **I**
I see. [aɪ‿ˈsiː] Ich verstehe. **I**
°See you later, alligator! [ˈsiː jə ˈleɪtə ˈælɪgeɪtə] Bis später! **I**
seed [siːd] Vogelfutter **II 8**, 133
⟨put your whole self in⟩ [ˈhəʊl ˈself] macht einen Schritt vorwärts **II 3**, 49
to **sell** [sel] verkaufen **II 9**, 140
to **send**, sent [send, sent] schicken **II 6**, 87
°**sentence** [ˈsentəns] Satz **I**
⟨shake it all about⟩ [ˈʃeɪk ɪt‿ɔːl əˈbaʊt] schüttelt sie fest aus **II 3**, 49
she isn't [ʃiː ˈɪznt] sie ist nicht **I**
°**shed** [ʃed] Schuppen, Stall **I**
°**sheep** [ʃiːp] Schaf(e) **I**
°**sheepdog** [ˈʃiːpdɒg] Schäferhund **I**
shelf, shelves [ʃelf, ʃelvz] Regal, Regale **I**
sheriff [ˈʃerɪf] Sheriff **II 2**, 25
she's (= she is) [ʃiːz] sie ist **I**
she's got (= she has got) [ˈʃiːz gɒt] sie hat **I**
⟨by ship⟩ [baɪ ˈʃɪp] mit dem Schiff **II 10**, 156
shirt [ʃɜːt] Hemd **I**
⟨shock⟩ [ʃɒk] Schock **II 10**, 157
shoe [ʃuː] Schuh **I**
to **shoot** [ʃuːt] schießen **II 2**, 25
shop [ʃɒp] Laden, Geschäft **I**
shop assistant [ˈʃɒp əˈsɪstənt] Verkäufer/in **II 5**, 74
shopping list [ˈʃɒpɪŋ ˈlɪst] Einkaufsliste **I**
shopping centre [ˈʃɒpɪŋ ˈsentə] Einkaufszentrum **I**
short [ʃɔːt] kurz **II 4**, 58
short for [ˈʃɔːt‿fɔː] die Kurzform von **II 1**, 7
to **shout** [ʃaʊt] rufen, schreien **II 2**, 28
to **show** [ʃəʊ] zeigen **I**
to feel **sick** [sɪk] sich schlecht/krank fühlen **II 3**, 41
side [saɪd] Seite **II 4**, 64
sight [saɪt] Sicht **II 7**, 115
sign [saɪn] Schild **II 8**, 129
shoulder [ˈʃəʊldə] Schulter **II 8A 122**
°**signal** [ˈsɪgnl] Signal **II 6**, 92
silly [ˈsɪlɪ] dumm, albern, blöd **I**
simple [ˈsɪmpl] einfach **II 6**, 99
to **sing** [sɪŋ] singen **I**
to sing out [ˈsɪŋ‿aʊt] (lautstark) singen **I**
⟨singular⟩ [ˈsɪŋgjʊlə] Singular **II 10**, 158
sister [ˈsɪstə] Schwester **I**
to **sit** [sɪt] sitzen **I**
skateboard [ˈskeɪtbɔːd] Skateboard **I**
skater [ˈskeɪtə] Schlitt-/Rollschuhläufer/in, Skateboardfahrer/in **II 8**, 122
°**skin** [skɪn] Fell, Haut **I**
skirt [skɜːt] Rock **II 4**, 58
sleep [sliːp] schlafen **I**
⟨slide rule⟩ [ˈslaɪd ˌruːl] Rechenschieber **II 1**, 9
slippery [ˈslɪpərɪ] rutschig, glatt **II 7**, 115
small [smɔːl] klein **II 1**, 13
⟨smart⟩ [smɑːt] schick **II 10**, 159

snack [snæk] Imbiss **II 2**, 29
snack bar ['snækbɑː] Imbissstube **II 2**, 29
to **sniffle** ['snɪfl] schniefen **II 9**, 148
to **snore** [snɔː] schnarchen **II 9**, 148
so [səʊ] nun, also **II 1**, 8; so **II 1**, 16
So do I. ['səʊ duː 'aɪ] Ich auch. **II 1**, 12
sock [sɒk] Socke **II 5**, 73
⟨soldier⟩ ['səʊldʒə] Soldat **II 10**, 156
some [sʌm] einige **II 1**, 7
somebody ['sʌmbədɪ] jemand **II 3**, 45
someone ['sʌmwʌn] jemand **II 5**, 75
something ['sʌmθɪŋ] etwas **I**
sometimes ['sʌmtaɪmz] manchmal **I**
somewhere ['sʌmweə] irgendwo **II 5**, 72
son [sʌn] Sohn **I**
song [sɒŋ] Lied **I**
soon [suːn] bald **I**
⟨sooner⟩ ['suːnə] früher **II 9**, 152
sore throat ['sɔː 'θrəʊt] Halsschmerzen **II 8**, 128
Sorry! ['sɒrɪ] Entschuldigung!/Tut mir Leid. **I**
to be sorry ['sɒrɪ] bedauern **II 4**, 64
° **sound track** ['saʊndtræk] Tonspur **I**
° sound effect ['saʊnd ɪˌfekt] Geräusch(effekt) **II 4**, 64
to **sound** ['saʊnd] klingen **II 1**, 7
soup [suːp] Suppe **II 6**, 87
south [saʊθ] südlich, Süd-, Süden **II 7**, 106
souvenir [ˌsuːvə'nɪə] Andenken, Souvenir **II 2**, 26; ° Souvenir, Andenken **I**
⟨space⟩ [speɪs] Weltraum **II 9**, 152
spade [speɪd] Schaufel, Spaten **I**
° **Spanish** ['spænɪʃ] spanisch, Spanier/in **I**
to **speak** [spiːk] sprechen **I**
special ['speʃl] Spezialität des Hauses **I**
special ['speʃl] besondere/r/s **II 2**, 28
to **spell** [spel] buchstabieren **I**
to **spell**, spelt, spelt [spelt] buchstabieren **II 6**, 98
to **spend**, spent, spent [spend, spent] verbringen; ausgeben **II 7**, 106
⟨spider⟩ ['spaɪdə] Spinne **II 6**, 94
° to **sponsor** ['spɒnsə] spenden, sponsern **II 9**, 143
spoon [spuːn] Löffel **I**
sports [spɔːts] Sport **II 1**, 7
sports centre ['spɔːts ˌsentə] Sportanlage, Sportzentrum **II 1**, 14
spot [spɒt] Fleck, Pickel **II 8**, 132
spring [sprɪŋ] Frühling **I**
to **sprinkle** ['sprɪŋkl] streuen **II 6**, 99
to **spy** [spaɪ] spionieren **II 1**, 19
I spy with my little eye … *engl. Kinderspiel* **II 1**, 19
square [skweə] Platz **I**; Quadrat, Platz **II 4**, 65
stage [steɪdʒ] Bühne **II 4**, 60
stall [stɔːl] Stand **II 3**, 48
⟨to stamp⟩ [stæmp] stampfen **II 10**, 160
to **stand** [stænd] stehen **I**
° **star** [stɑː] Star, Stern **I**
° to **start** [stɑːt] anfangen **I**
° Let's start. [ˌlets 'stɑːt] Lasst uns anfangen. **I**
station ['steɪʃn] Bahnhof **I**
° **statue** ['stætʃuː] Statue **I**
to **stay** [steɪ] wohnen, bleiben **I**
to **steal**, stole [stiːl, stəʊl] stehlen **II 2**, 33
steep [stiːp] steil **II 7**, 115
step [step] ⟨Schritt⟩ **II 10**, 161; ° Lektion **I**
° **stick** [stɪk] Stock **I**
still [stɪl] noch **II 3**, 45
stomach ['stʌmək] Magen **II 8**, 128
stomach-ache ['stʌməkˌeɪk] Magenschmerzen **II 8**, 128
stone [stəʊn] Stein **I**
to **stop** [stɒp] (an)halten **I**
Stop it! ['stɒp‿ɪt] Hör/Hört auf! **II 1**, 16
store [stɔː] Geschäft, Laden **II 5**, 72
stormy ['stɔːmɪ] stürmisch **II 7**, 109
story ['stɔːrɪ] Geschichte **II 1**, 17
straight on ['streɪt 'ɒn] geradeaus **I**
strange [streɪndʒ] seltsam, merkwürdig **II 3**, 51
⟨stream⟩ [striːm] Bach **II 7**, 107
street [striːt] Straße **I**
street market ['striːt 'mɑːkɪt] Straßenmarkt **II 5**, 77
strong [strɒŋ] stark **II 5**, 80
° to get **stuck** [get 'stʌk] feststecken, stecken bleiben **I**
subject ['sʌbdʒɪkt] Fach **II 1**, 7
suddenly ['sʌdnlɪ] plötzlich **II 1**, 19
sugar ['ʃʊgə] Zucker **I**
° **summary** ['sʌmərɪ] Zusammenfassung **II 4**, 65
summer ['sʌmə] Sommer **I**
sunny ['sʌnɪ] sonnig **I**
sunroof ['sʌnruːf] Schiebedach **II 9**, 139
super ['suːpə] super **II 5**, 74
° **superclean** ['suːpəkliːn] blitzsauber **II 9**, 145
° **superdog** ['suːpədɒg] Superhund **I**
° **superkid** ['suːpəˌkɪd] Superkind **I**
supermarket ['suːpəˌmɑːkɪt] Supermarkt **II 5**, 73
sure [ʃʊə] sicher **I**
I'm not sure. [ˌaɪm nɒt 'ʃʊə] Ich bin nicht sicher. **I**
° to **surf** [sɜːf] surfen **II 7**, 108
surprise [sə'praɪz] Überraschung **I**
⟨to swallow⟩ ['swɒləʊ] (hinunter)schlucken **II 6**, 94
sweatshirt ['swetʃɜːt] Sweatshirt **II 3**, 41
° to **sweep** [swiːp] kehren, fegen **II 9**, 147
sweet [swiːt] süß **II 8**, 127
sweets [swiːts] Süßigkeiten **I**
to **swim** [swɪm] schwimmen **I**
to go **swimming** [ˌgəʊ 'swɪmɪŋ] schwimmen gehen **I**
swimming-pool ['swɪmɪŋ ˌpuːl] Schwimmbecken **I**

T

T-shirt ['tiː ˌʃɜːt] T-Shirt **I**
table [teɪbl] Tisch **I**
table tennis ['teɪbl ˌtenɪs] Tischtennis **II 1**, 14
to **take** out [teɪk 'aʊt] herausholen, -nehmen **II 1**, 19
to take a photo ['teɪk‿ə‿'fəʊtəʊ] ein Foto machen **I**
to take off ['teɪk‿ɒf] abnehmen **II 2**, 33
to take s.o. to ['teɪk] jdn. mitnehmen **II 2**, 25
to take with me [teɪk 'wɪð miː] mitnehmen **I**
takeaway ['teɪkəˌweɪ] Essen zum Mitnehmen **II 5**, 82; Imbissstube, Schnellgaststätte mit Straßenverkauf **II 6**, 95
tale [teɪl] Geschichte, Sage **II 2**, 25
talk [tɔːk] Gespräch, Plauderei **I**
to talk about ['tɔːk‿əbaʊt] über etwas reden **I**
tall [tɔːl] groß **II 3**, 51
to **taste** [teɪst] schmecken; probieren **II 6**, 87
tea [tiː] Tee; Teemahlzeit **I**
° to **teach** [tiːtʃ] beibringen; unterrichten **I**
teacher ['tiːtʃə] Lehrer/in **I**
German **teacher** ['dʒɜːmən 'tiːtʃə] Deutschlehrer/in **I**
team [tiːm] Team, Mannschaft **I**
teaspoon ['tiːspuːn] Teelöffel **II 6**, 99
Technology [tek'nɒlədʒɪ] Technik; Informatik **II 1**, 8
teddy ['tedɪ] Teddybär **II 3**, 45
teeth [tiːθ] Zähne **II 3**, 51
telephone ['telɪfəʊn] Telefon **I**
on the telephone [ˌɒn‿ðə‿'telɪfəʊn] am Telefon **I**

to **tell** [tel] sagen, erzählen **I**
to tell the time ['tel‿ðə‿'taɪm] die Zeit sagen **I**
to tell the way ['tel ðə 'weɪ] den Weg beschreiben **I**
temperature ['temprətʃə] Fieber, (erhöhte) Temperatur **II 8**, 123
° **tennis** ['tenɪs] Tennis **I**
⟨tent⟩ [tent] Zelt **II 10**, 157
term [tɜ:m] Schuljahresabschnitt **II 9**, 138
terrible ['terɪbl] schrecklich **I**
terribly ['terəblɪ] schrecklich **II 9**, 148
than [ðæn] als **II 3**, 45
Thank you! ['θæŋkju:] Danke! **I**
Thanks. [θæŋks] Danke. **I**
That looks fun! Das sieht spaßig aus. **II 3**, 47
that's (= that is) [ðæts] das ist **I**
That's great. [ðæts 'greɪt] Das ist großartig. **I**
that's me [ðæts 'mi:] das bin ich **I**
⟨that's what it's all about⟩ [ˌɔ:l‿ə'baʊt] so wird's gemacht **II 3**, 49
the [ðə] der, die, das **I**
the blue one [wʌn] das Blaue **II 1**, 13
theatre ['θɪətə] Theater **II 4**, 62
their [ðeə] ihr **I**
them [ðem] ihnen/sie **I**
then [ðen] dann, also **II 1**, 11
there [ðeə] dort **I**
there are ['ðeər‿ə] es gibt, da sind **I**
there's (= there is) [ðeəz] es gibt, da ist **I**
these [ði:z] diese **I**
they aren't (= are not) [ðeɪ 'ɑ:nt] sie sind nicht **I**
they won't (= they will not) [ðeɪ 'wəʊnt, ðeɪ wɪl 'nɒt] sie werden nicht **II 4**, 60
they're (= they are) [ðeə] sie sind **I**
thief, thieves [θi:f, θi:vz] Dieb/in, Diebe **II 2**, 25
thin [θɪn] dünn **II 3**, 51
thing [θɪŋ] Sache, Ding **I**
to **think** [θɪŋk] denken, meinen **I**
I think so. [aɪ 'θɪŋk ˌsəʊ] Ich denke schon. **II 4**, 59
to think of ['θɪŋk‿əv] an etw. denken **I**
thirsty ['θɜ:stɪ] durstig **II 6**, 93
this [ðɪs] diese/dieser **I**
this afternoon [ˌðɪs‿ɑ:ftə'nu:n] heute Nachmittag **I**
those [ðəʊz] jene **I**
a thousand ['θaʊznd] (ein)tausend **II 4**, 63
through [θru:] durch **I**
throw [θrəʊ] Wurf **II 3**, 48
to **throw**, threw, thrown [θrəʊn] werfen **II 6**, 98
⟨thumb⟩ [θʌm] Daumen **II 8**, 131
thunder ['θʌndə] Donner **II 4**, 64
thunderstorm ['θʌndəstɔ:m] Gewitter **II 8**, 127
ticket ['tɪkɪt] Fahrkarte **I**
to **tidy** (up) ['taɪdɪ] aufräumen **II 3**, 44
° **tiger** ['taɪgə] Tiger **I**
tights (*pl*) [taɪts] Strumpfhose **II 4**, 58
till [tɪl] bis **I**
time [taɪm] Zeit **I**
timetable ['taɪmteɪbl]° Fahrplan **I**; Stundenplan **II 1**, 7
tired ['taɪəd] müde **I**
title ['taɪtl] Titel **II 4**, 64
to [tə] mit **I**; vor **I**; nach **I**
° **toast** [təʊst] Toast **II 6**, 88
today [tə'deɪ] heute **I**
toe [təʊ] Zehe **II 8**, 122
⟨toenail⟩ ['təʊneɪl] Zehennagel **II 6**, 102
together [tə'geðə] zusammen **I**
toilet ['tɔɪlɪt] Toilette **I**
tomato(es) [tə'mɑ:təʊ] Tomate(n) **I**
tomorrow [tə'mɒrəʊ] morgen **II 4**, 61
tonight [tə'naɪt] heute Abend, heute Nacht **II 8** 126
too [tu:] auch **I**; zu **II 2**, 33
⟨I took⟩ (das) ich hatte/nahm **II 1**, 9
tooth [tu:θ] Zahn **II 8**, 123
toothache ['tu:θeɪk] Zahnschmerzen **II 8**, 123
at the **top** of [ˌæt ðə 'tɒp‿əv] ganz oben (auf) **I**
tough [tʌf] hart, knallhart **II 5**, 80
tourist ['tʊərɪst] Tourist/in **I**
towards [tə'wɔ:dz] auf … zu **II 1**, 19
town crier ['taʊn 'kraɪə] Ausrufer/in **II 2** 32
toy [tɔɪ] Spielzeug **II 9**, 138
° **tractor** ['træktə] Traktor **I**
train [treɪn] Zug **I**
to **train** [treɪn] trainieren **I**
trainers ['treɪnəz] Sportschuhe **II 5**, 74
⟨transparency⟩ [træns'pærənsɪ] Folie **II 1**, 17
to **travel** ['trævl] reisen **II 7**, 106
tree [tri:] Baum **I**
° to **trek** [trek] trecken **II 7**, 116
° to **trick** [trik] überlisten **I**
to do a trick [trɪk] einen Trick machen **I**
⟨Trigonometry⟩ [trɪgə'nɒmətrɪ] Trigonometrie **II 1**, 9
trip [trɪp] Ausflug **II 3**, 43
to **trip** [trɪp] stolpern **II 8**, 122
° **trolley** ['trɒlɪ] Einkaufswagen **II 5**, 72
trouble ['trʌbl] Schwierigkeiten **II 7**, 116
trousers ['traʊzəz] Hose(n) **I**
true [tru:] wahr **II 5**, 82
trumpet ['trʌmpɪt] Trompete **II 9**, 139
to **try** [traɪ] (aus)probieren, versuchen **II 1**, 14
to try on [ˌtraɪ‿'ɒn] anprobieren **I**
tunnel ['tʌnl] Tunnel **II 2**, 31
to **turn** left [ˌtɜ:n 'left] nach links gehen **I**
⟨to turn around⟩ [ˌtɜ:n‿ə'raʊnd] herumdrehen **II 3**, 49
to turn round [ˌtɜ:n 'raʊnd] (sich) umdrehen **II 1**, 15
to watch **TV** ['wɒtʃ‿ˌti:'vi:] fernsehen **I**
twice [twaɪs] zweimal **II 7**, 111
° **twin town** ['twɪn 'taʊn] Partnerstadt **I**
° **Twinning Office** ['twɪnɪŋ ˌɒfɪs] Städtepartnerschafts-büro **I**
flat **tyre** [ˌflæt 'taɪə] Plattfuß **I**

U

uncle ['ʌŋkl] Onkel **I**
under ['ʌndə] unter **I**
⟨Underground⟩ ['ʌndəgraʊnd] Untergrundbahn **II 5**, 78
to **understand** [ˌʌndə'stænd] verstehen **II 3**, 49
unhappy [ˌʌn'hæpɪ] unglücklich **I**
° **uniform** ['ju:nɪfɔ:m] Uniform **I**
° **unit** ['ju:nɪt] Einheit, Kapitel **I**
unlucky [ˌʌn'lʌkɪ] unglücklich **II 9**, 139
until [ən'tɪl] bis **II 2**, 28
⟨unwell⟩ [ʌn'wel] krank, schlecht **II 9**, 152
upper ['ʌpə] der/die/das obere **II 5**, 72
upstairs [ˌʌp'steəz] oben **I**
us [ʌs] uns **I**
⟨to use⟩ [ju:z] benutzen **II 1**, 17
useful ['ju:sfʊl] nützlich **II 4**, 58
usually ['ju:ʒʊəlɪ] gewöhnlich **I**

V

vampire ['væmpaɪə] Vampir **II 3**, 51
van [væn] Lifer-, Möbelwagen **II 2**, 29
vanilla [və'nɪlə] Vanille **II 6**, 99

vegetable ['vedʒtəbl] Gemüse **II 5**, 77
°**verb** [vɜ:b] Verb **II 2**, 28
very ['verɪ] sehr **I**
vet [vet] Tierarzt/Tierärztin **I**
video ['vɪdɪəʊ] Video **II 1**, 8
village ['vɪlɪdʒ] Dorf **II 7**, 107
violet ['vaɪələt] violett **I**
visit ['vɪzɪt] Besuch, Besichtigung **I**
to **visit** ['vɪzɪt] besuchen, besichtigen **II 3**, 41
voice [vɔɪs] Stimme **II 4**, 60
volleyball ['vɒlɪbɔ:l] Volleyball **II 7**, 106

W

to **wait**, waited [weɪt] warten **II 2**, 33
to wait for [weɪt] warten auf **I**
waiter ['weɪtə] Ober **II 6**, 87
to **wake up** [weɪk‿'ʌp] aufwachen, wecken **I**
walk [wɔ:k] Spaziergang **I**
to go for a walk ['gəʊ‿fər‿ə‿'wɔ:k] spazieren gehen **I**
wall [wɔ:l] Mauer **II 7**, 117
walnut ['wɔ:lnʌt] Walnuss **II 6**, 99
to **want**, wanted ['wɒntɪd] wollen, wünschen **II 2**, 32
to want to [wɒnt] wollen **I**
warm [wɔ:m] warm **I**
to **warn** [wɔ:n] warnen **II 7**, 115
to **wash** [wɒʃ] (sich) waschen **I**
to wash up [ˌwɒʃ‿'ʌp] abwaschen **I**
washing-up [ˌwɒʃɪŋ 'ʌp] Abwasch **II 7**, 111
to **watch** [wɒtʃ] (zu)schauen **I**
to watch TV ['wɒtʃ‿ˌti:'vi:] fernsehen **I**
water ['wɔ:tə] Wasser **II 2**, 36
way [weɪ] Weg **I**
to **wear** [weə] tragen **I**
weather ['weðə] Wetter **I**
week [wi:k] Woche **I**
weekend [ˌwi:k'ənd] Wochenende **I**
welcome to ['welkəm] willkommen bei **I**
well [wel] gesund **I**; tja, nun **I**
Well done! ['wel 'dʌn] Gut gemacht! **II 3**, 48
°**Welsh** [welʃ] walisisch **II 7**, 106
we're ['wɪə] wir sind **I**
west [west] westlich, West-, Westen **II 7**, 106
wet [wet] nass **I**
what [wɒt] Was **I**
What a … ['wɒt‿ə] Was für ein(e) … **I**
⟨what a hog⟩ [ˌwɒt‿ə 'hɒg] was für ein Schwein **II 6**, 94
What about …? [ˌwɒt‿ə'baʊt] Was ist mit …? **I**
What colour is …? [ˌwɒt 'kʌlər‿ɪz] Welche Farbe hat …? **I**
°What goes together? ['wɒt gəʊz tə'geðə] Was passt zusammen? **I**
What time is it? [taɪm] Wie spät ist es? **I**
what's (= what is) [wɒts] was ist **I**
What's her name? ['wɒts hɜ: 'neɪm] Wie heißt sie? **I**
What's on? [ˌwɒts‿'ɒn] Was gibt's? **I**
What's that in English? [wɒts'ðæt‿ɪn‿'ɪŋglɪʃ] Wie heißt das auf Englisch? **I**
What's the date? [deɪt] Den Wievielten haben wir (heute)? **I**
What's the matter with you? [ðə 'mætə] Was ist mit dir los? **II 3**, 51
What's your name? [ˌwɒts jɔ: 'neɪm] Wie heißt du?/ Wie heißen Sie? **I**
What's yours? [jɔ:z] Wie heißt du? **I**
wheel [wi:l] Rad **II 3**, 47
when [wen] wann, wenn **I**
where [weə] wo **I**
Where are you from? ['weər‿ə ju: 'frɒm] Woher kommst du? **I**
which [wɪtʃ] welche(r) **I**
while [waɪl] während **II 6**, 96
⟨whistle⟩ ['wɪsl] Pfeife **II 4**, 63
white [waɪt] weiß **I**
who [hu:] wer **I**
⟨who cares?⟩ [hu: 'kɜəz] (und) wenn schon? **II 9**, 150
⟨put your whole self in⟩ ['həʊl 'self] macht einen Schritt vorwärts **II 3**, 49
⟨whole self out⟩ einen Schritt rückwärts **II 3**, 49
whose [hu:z] wessen **II 1**, 20
why [waɪ] warum **I**
°to **wiggle** ['wɪgl] sich wenden, zappeln **II 9**, 147
°**wild** [waɪld] wild **I**
to **win**, won [wɪn, wʌn] gewinnen **II 3**, 45
window ['wɪndəʊ] Fenster, Schaufenster **II 5**, 74
°**windy** ['wɪndɪ] windig **I**
°**wine** [waɪn] Wein **II 6**, 87
wing [wɪŋ] Flügel **II 8**, 133
winter ['wɪntə] Winter **I**
witch [wɪtʃ] Hexe **II 3**, 51
with [wɪð] bei; mit **I**
with her ['wɪð‿hɜ:] mit ihr **I**
without [wɪ'ðaʊt] ohne **I**
°to **woggle** ['wɒgl] wackeln **II 9**, 147
woman, women ['wʊmən, 'wɪmɪn] Frau, Frauen **I**
wonderful ['wʌndəfʊl] wunderbar **I**
°**Woof!** [wʊf] Wau, wau! *(Hundebellen)* **I**
°**word** [wɜ:d] Wort **I**
°word power ['wɜ:d ˌpaʊə] Wortschatz **II 1**, 7
°to **work** [wɜ:k] arbeiten **I**
to work hard [hɑ:d] hart/schwer arbeiten **II 6**, 96
to work late [ˌwɜ:k 'leɪt] bis spät arbeiten **I**
to work together ['wɜ:k tə'geðə] zusammenarbeiten **II 9**, 143
⟨world⟩ [wɜ:ld] Welt **II 1**, 9
°**worried** ['wʌrɪd] besorgt **II 1**, 16; beunruhigt **I**
to **worry** ['wʌrɪ] sich Sorgen machen **II 1**, 16
worst [wɜ:st] schlechteste/r/s **II 3**, 45
⟨would be⟩ [wʊd] wäre **II 1**, 9
Would you like …? [ˌwʊd jʊ 'laɪk] Hättest du/Hätten Sie gern …? **II 5**, 75
°**Wow!** [waʊ] Mensch, toll! **I**
⟨to wriggle⟩ ['rɪgl] sich schlängeln, zappeln **II 6**, 94
to **write**, wrote, written [raɪt, rəʊt, 'rɪtn] schreiben **II 6**, 87
wrong [rɒŋ] falsch **I**
to be wrong about [bi: 'rɒŋ e'bəʊt] Unrecht haben mit **II 1**, 19

Y

year [jɪə] Jahr, Jahrgang **I**
to **yell** [jel] schreien **II 9**, 148
yellow ['jeləʊ] gelb **I**
yes [jes] ja **I**
yesterday ['jestədeɪ] gestern **II 3**, 41
yoghurt ['jɒgət] Joghurt **II 6**, 99
Yorkshire pudding ['jɔ:kʃə 'pʊdɪŋ] Yorkshire pudding *(engl. Gericht aus Mehl, Milch usw.)* **II 6**, 100
you [ju:] man **II 2**, 25
you [ju:] du, ihr, Sie **I**
you two ['ju: 'tu:] ihr beide **I**
⟨You put your right hand in⟩ [raɪt hænd] Streckt eure rechte Hand nach vorne **II 3**, 49

young [jʌŋ] jung **II 3**, 41
your [jɔː/jə] dein, deine **I**
°Your turn! ['jɔː tɜːn] Du bist an der Reihe./Ihr seid dran. **I**
you're (= you are) [jʊə] du bist **I**
You're ten. [jʊə 'ten] Du bist zehn Jahre alt. **I**
youth centre ['juːθ ˌsentə] Jugendzentrum **II 4**, 62

Z

°**zone** [zəʊn] Zone **I**

Boys' names

°**Alan** ['ælən]
°**Arthur** ['ɑːθə]
°**Barry** ['bærɪ]
°**Benny** ['benɪ]
°**Boris** ['bɒrɪs]
°**Christian** ['krɪstɪən]
°**Colin** ['kɒlɪn]
°**David** ['deɪvɪd]
°**Eddy** ['edɪ]
°**Gary** ['gærɪ]
°**Jack** [dʒæk]
°**Jurek** ['juːrek]
°**Lenny** ['lenɪ]
°**Mike** [maɪk]
°**Robert** ['rɒbət]
°**Simon** ['saɪmən]
°**Washington** ['wɒʃɪŋtən]

Girls' names

°**Annabel** ['ænəbel]
°**Becky** ['bekɪ]
°**Daisy** ['deɪzɪ]
°**Ilona** [ɪ'ləʊnə]
°**Jane** [dʒeɪn]
°**Janet** ['dʒænɪt]
°**Jenny** ['dʒenɪ]
°**Kim** [kɪm]
°**Laura** ['lɔːrə]
°**Liza** ['laɪzə]
°**Margaret** ['mɑːgərɪt]
°**Maria** [mə'riːə]
°**Melanie** ['melənɪ]
°**Melina** [mə'liːnə]
°**Nora** ['nɔːrə]
°**Sally** ['sælɪ]
°**Sarah** ['seərə]
°**Shabina** [ʃə'biːnə]
°**Suvina** ['sʊvɪnə]
°**Tanya** ['tænjə]
°**Victoria** [vɪk'tɔːrɪə]
°**Virginia** [və'dʒɪnjə]
°**Wendy** ['wendɪ]
°**Wilma** ['wɪlmə]

Surnames

°**Benson** ['bensn]
°**Blackwell** ['blækwəl]
°**Blake** [bleɪk]
°**Broadwood** ['brɔːdwʊd]
°**Burton** ['bɜːtn]
°**Cooper** ['kuːpə]
°**Dane** [deɪn]
°**Davis** ['deɪvɪs]
°**Dixon** ['dɪksn]
°**Dracula** ['drækjʊlə]
°**Hod** [hɒd]
°**Ismaili** [ɪzmɑː'iːlɪ]
°**Jessop** ['dʒesəp]
°**MacTavish** [mək'tævɪʃ]
°**Matthews** ['mæθjuːz]
°**Miller** ['mɪlə]
°**Morris** ['mɒrɪs]
°**Newman** ['njuːmən]
°**Nosy** ['nəʊzɪ]
°**Otis** ['əʊtɪs]
°**Parkinson** ['pɑːkɪnsn]
°**Patel** [pə'tel]
°**Penrose** [pen'rəʊz]
°**Richards** ['rɪtʃədz]
°**Singh** [sɪŋ]
°**Spook** [spuːk]
°**Stevenson** ['stiːvnsn]
°**Umney** ['ʌmnɪ]
°**Underwood** ['ʌndəwʊd]
°**Wood** [wʊd]

Geographical names

°**America** [ə'merɪkə]
°**Angel Row** ['eɪndʒəl 'rəʊ]
°**Arndale Road** ['ɑːndeɪl ˌrəʊd]
°**Arnot Hill Park** ['ɑːnət hɪl 'pɑːk]
°**Beastmarket Hill** ['biːstmɑːkɪt]
°**Beeston** ['biːstən]
°**Belgium** ['beldʒəm]
°**Ben Nevis** [ˌben 'nevɪs]
°**Berlin** [bɜː'lɪn]
°**Bestwood** ['bestwʊd]
°**Britain** ['brɪtn]
°**California** [ˌkælɪ'fɔːnjə]
°**Canterville** ['kæntəvɪl]
°**Castle Gate** ['kɑːsl 'geɪt]
°**Channel Tunnel** ['tʃænl 'tʌnl]
°**Chicago** [ʃɪ'kɑːgəʊ]
°**Denmark** ['denmɑːk]
°**Edward's Lane** ['edwədz 'leɪn]
°**England** ['ɪŋglənd]
⟨Europe⟩ ['jʊərəp]
°**Fort William** [ˌfɔːt 'wɪljəm]
°**France** [frɑːns]
°**Friar Lane** ['fraɪə 'leɪn]
°**Germany** ['dʒɜːmənɪ]
°**Heathrow** ['hiːθrəʊ]
°**High Street** ['haɪ ˌstriːt]
°**Holland** ['hɒlənd]
°**Isle of Wight** ['aɪl‿əv 'waɪt]
°**Lake District** ['leɪk ˌdɪstrɪkt]
°**Larwood Grove** ['lɑːwʊd 'grəʊv]
°**Loch Linnhe** ['lɒk 'lɪnɪ]
°**Loch Lomond** ['lɒk 'ləʊmənd]
°**Loch Ness** ['lɒk‿'nes]
°**London** ['lʌndən]
°**Major Oak** [ˌmeɪdʒə 'əʊk]
°**Mansfield Road** ['mænsfiːld ˌrəʊd]
°**Mortimer's Hole** ['mɔːtɪməz 'həʊl]
°**Mount Street** ['maʊnt ˌstriːt]
°**New York** [ˌnjuː 'jɔːk]
°**North Sea** ['nɔːθ 'siː]
°**Northern Ireland** [ˌnɔːðn 'aɪələnd]
°**Nottingham** ['nɒtɪŋəm]
°**San Francisco** [ˌsænfrən'sɪskəʊ]
°**Scotland** ['skɒtlənd]
°**Sherwood** ['ʃɜːwʊd]
°**Sherwood Forest** ['ʃɜːwʊd 'fɒrɪst]
°**Skegness** [ˌskeg'nes]
°**Texas** ['teksəs]
°**UK** (= **United Kingdom**) [ˌjuː'keɪ]
°**Wales** [weɪlz]
°**Yorkshire** ['jɔːtʃə]

Other names

°**Blackstone Castle** ['blækstəʊn]
°**Blacky** ['blækɪ]
°**Broad Marsh Centre** ['brɔːd ˌmɑːʃ 'sentə]
°**Canterville Chase** ['kæntəvɪl 'tʃeɪs]
°**Food Court** ['fuːd ˌkɔːt]
°**Goose Fair** ['guːs 'feə]
°**Harris** ['hærɪs]
°**Hayward Herald** ['heɪwʊd 'herəld]
°**Haywood School** ['heɪwʊd ˌskuːl]
°**Levi Strauss** ['liːvaɪ 'straʊs]
°**Longway** ['lɒŋweɪ]
°**Maid Marian** [ˌmeɪd 'mærɪən]
°**Maxi** ['mæksɪ]
°**Mini** ['mɪnɪ]
°**Monny** ['mɒnɪ]
Mr Bean [biːn]
°**Nessie** ['nesɪ]
°**Puddles** ['pʌdlz]
°**Radio 1** ['reɪdɪəʊ 'wʌn]
°**Radio Nottingham** ['reɪdɪəʊ 'nɒtɪŋəm]
°**Robin Hood** ['rɒbɪn 'hʊd]
°**Sneinton Market** ['sniːntən 'mɑːkɪt]
°**Sniffy** ['snɪfɪ]
°**Springfield Farm** ['sprɪŋfiːld]
°**St Peter's Church** [snt 'piːtəz 'tʃɜːtʃ]
°**Superman** ['suːpəmæn]
°**Tabby** ['tæbɪ]
°**Teens** [tiːnz]
°**The Spider** [ðə 'spaɪdə]
°**The Taj Mahal Restaurant** [ðə ˌtɑːdʒ mə'hɑːl 'restərɒŋ]
°**The Tales of Robin Hood** [ðə 'teɪlz‿əv 'rɒbɪn 'hʊd]
°**Tweety** ['twiːtɪ]
°**Two'n'Two** ['tuː‿n‿'tuː]

List of irregular verbs

infinitive	simple past	past participle	German
be [bi:]	was [wɒz]	been [bi:n]	sein
begin [bɪ'gɪn]	began [bɪ'gæn]	begun [bɪ'gʌn]	beginnen
bend [bend]	bent [bent]	bent [bent]	(sich) bücken, biegen
bring [brɪŋ]	brought [brɔ:t]	brought [brɔ:t]	bringen
buy [baɪ]	bought [bɔ:t]	bought [bɔ:t]	kaufen
catch [kætʃ]	caught [kɔ:t]	caught [kɔ:t]	fangen
choose [tʃu:z]	chose [tʃəʊz]	chosen ['tʃəʊzn]	auswählen
come [kʌm]	came [keɪm]	come [kʌm]	kommen
cost [kɒst]	cost [kɒst]	cost [kɒst]	kosten
cut [kʌt]	cut [kʌt]	cut [kʌt]	schneiden
do [du:]	did [dɪd]	done [dʌn]	machen, tun
draw [drɔ:]	drew [dru:]	drawn [drɔ:n]	zeichnen
drink [drɪŋk]	drank [dræŋk]	drunk [drʌŋk]	trinken
drive [draɪv]	drove [drəʊv]	driven ['drɪvn]	fahren
eat [i:t]	ate [et]	eaten ['i:tn]	essen
fall [fɔ:l]	fell [fel]	fallen ['fɔ:ln]	fallen
feed [fi:d]	fed [fed]	fed [fed]	füttern
feel [fi:l]	felt [felt]	felt [felt]	fühlen
find [faɪnd]	found [faʊnd]	found [faʊnd]	finden
fly [flai]	flew [flu:]	flown [fləʊn]	fliegen
forget [fə'get]	forgot [fə'gɒt]	forgotten [fə'gɒtn]	vergessen
get [get]	got [gɒt]	got [gɒt]	holen, bekommen
give [gɪv]	gave [geɪv]	given ['gɪvn]	geben
go [gəʊ]	went [went]	gone [gɒn]	gehen
grow [grəʊ]	grew [gru:]	grown [grəʊn]	(an)pflanzen, wachsen
have [hæv]	had [hæd]	had [hæd]	haben
hear [hɪə]	heard [hɜ:d]	heard [hɜ:d]	hören
hide [haɪd]	hid [hɪd]	hidden ['hɪdn]	(sich) verstecken
hit [hɪt]	hit [hɪt]	hit [hɪt]	schlagen
hold [həʊld]	held [held]	held [held]	halten
hurt [hɜ:t]	hurt [hɜ:t]	hurt [hɜ:t]	verletzen, weh tun
keep [ki:p]	kept [kept]	kept [kept]	(be)halten
know [nəʊ]	knew [nju:]	known [nəʊn]	wissen, kennen
lay [leɪ]	laid [leɪd]	laid [leɪd]	legen
learn [lɜ:n]	learned [lɜ:nt], learnt [lɜ:nt]	learned [lɜ:nt], learnt [lɜ:nt]	lernen
leave [li:v]	left [left]	left [left]	(ver)lassen
lend [lend]	lent [lent]	lent [lent]	(ver)leihen

infinitive	simple past	past participle	German
let [let]	let [let]	let [let]	lassen
lie [laɪ]	lay [leɪ]	lain [leɪn]	liegen
make [meɪk]	made [meɪd]	made [meɪd]	machen
mean [mi:n]	meant [ment]	meant [ment]	bedeuten
meet [mi:t]	met [met]	met [met]	treffen, begegnen
pay [peɪ]	paid [peɪd]	paid [peɪd]	zahlen, bezahlen
put [pʊt]	put [pʊt]	put [pʊt]	setzen, stellen, legen
read [ri:d]	read [red]	read [red]	lesen
ring [rɪŋ]	rang [ræŋ]	rung [rʌŋ]	klingeln, anrufen
ride [raɪd]	rode [rəʊd]	ridden ['rɪdn]	reiten, fahren
run [rʌn]	ran [ræn]	run [rʌn]	laufen, rennen
say [seɪ]	said [sed]	said [sed]	sagen
see [si:]	saw [sɔ:]	seen [si:n]	sehen
sell [sel]	sold [səʊld]	sold [səʊld]	verkaufen
send [send]	sent [sent]	sent [sent]	schicken, senden
shoot [ʃu:t]	shot [ʃɒt]	shot [ʃɒt]	schießen
show [ʃəʊ]	showed [ʃəʊd]	shown [ʃəʊn]	zeigen
sing [sɪŋ]	sang [sæŋ]	sung [sʌŋ]	singen
sit [sɪt]	sat [sæt]	sat [sæt]	sitzen
sleep [sli:p]	slept [slept]	slept [slept]	schlafen
speak [spi:k]	spoke [spəʊk]	spoken ['spəʊkn]	sprechen
spell [spel]	spelled [spelt], spelt [spelt]	spelled [spelt], spelt [spelt]	buchstabieren
spend [spend]	spent [spent]	spent [spent]	ausgeben, verbringen
stand [stænd]	stood [stʊd]	stood [stʊd]	stehen
swim [swɪm]	swam [swæm]	swum [swʌm]	schwimmen
take [teɪk]	took [tʊk]	taken ['teɪkn]	nehmen, bringen
tell [tel]	told [təʊld]	told [təʊld]	erzählen, sagen
think [θɪnk]	thought [θɔ:t]	thought [θɔ:t]	denken
throw [θrəʊ]	threw [θru:]	thrown [θrəʊn]	werfen
understand [ˌʌndə'stænd]	understood [ˌʌndə'stʊd]	understood [ˌʌndə'stʊd]	verstehen
wake [weɪk]	woke [wəʊk]	woken ['wəʊkn]	wecken, aufwachen
wear [weə]	wore [wɔ:]	worn [wɔ:n]	tragen (Kleidung)
win [wɪn]	won [wʌn]	won [wʌn]	gewinnen
write [raɪt]	wrote [rəʊt]	written ['rɪtn]	schreiben

⟨In the classroom⟩

What you can say to your friends or to the teacher

Hi (there)! Hello everybody/you two/… Good morning.	**Begrüßen**	Hallo, ihr da (alle)! Guten Morgen.
Can I open the window? Can I go out for a moment? Can we act this story? Can't we do something else?	**Bitten**	Darf ich das Fenster öffnen? Kann ich kurz mal hinausgehen? Können wir diese Geschichte spielen? Können wir nicht etwas anderes machen?
Can I/we/he/… do this/that? Let's write/read/sing/act/…? Can we play/make/sing/clap/…? Can I start/go on/ …? Can we do that in pairs/in groups/ together/…?	**Arbeits-vorschläge**	Kann ich/er … können wir das/dieses hier machen? Wir möchten gern … Kann ich anfangen/weitermachen …? Können wir das zu zweit/in Gruppen … machen?
I'm/We're against it. That's not the same at all. How do you know? I don't agree with you.	**Dagegen**	Ich bin/Wir sind dagegen. Das ist überhaupt nicht dasselbe. Woher willst du/wollt ihr das wissen? Ich stimme nicht zu.
Thank you (very much). Thanks. Thanks a lot.	**Danken**	Danke schön/sehr. Vielen Dank.
I'm sorry! Sorry! I'm so/very sorry. I'm sorry I'm late.	**Ent-schuldigen**	Entschuldigung. Es tut mir (sehr) leid. Tut mir leid, dass ich zu spät komme.
What's the matter with you? Are you feeling ill? What's wrong with you? Are you better now?	**Erkun-digen**	Was ist mit dir? Fühlst du dich krank? Stimmt etwas nicht? Geht es dir jetzt besser?
That's wrong, I'm afraid. Sorry, that's not right. I think you're wrong there. I think he/she's got it all wrong.	**Falsch**	Das ist leider falsch. Tut mir leid, aber das ist nicht richtig. Ich glaube, da irrst du. Ich glaube, er/sie hat das alles nicht richtig mitgekriegt.
Finished! I've done it already. I've finished.	**Fertig**	Fertig! Ich habe das schon gemacht. Ich bin fertig.
What's that in English/German? What does that mean? Can I ask a question, please? What's next? Who's next?	**Fragen**	Wie heißt das auf Englisch/Deutsch? Was heißt/bedeutet das? Kann ich bitte etwas fragen? Was ist als Nächstes dran? Wer kommt als Nächste(r)?
(Very) Good! That's good! Well done! Fantastic!	**Gut**	(Sehr) gut. Das ist gut. Gut gemacht. Phantastisch!

What must we do for homework? What's for homework? Have you done your homework?	**Hausaufgaben**	Was sollen wir zu Hause machen? Was sind die Hausaufgaben? Hast du/Habt ihr deine/eure Hausaufgaben gemacht?
Can/Could you help me, please? Can I have your …? How do you do this exercise? How do you pronounce this word? Could you spell this word? Could you write it down for me?	**Hilfe**	Kannst du/Könnten Sie mir bitte helfen? Kann ich dein(e)/euer/eure/Ihre … haben? Wie geht diese Übung? Wie spricht man dieses Wort aus? Könntest du/Könnten Sie diese Wort buchstabieren? Könntest du das für mich aufschreiben?
Sorry, I can't hear/see that! It's so/too loud in here. Sorry, that's too fast. That's very/too difficult.	**Klagen, Ablehnen**	Tut mir leid. Ich kann das nicht hören/sehen/… Das ist so laut hier drinnen. Tut mir leid. Das ist zu schnell. Das ist sehr/zu schwierig.
Can I get the OHP ready? Can I get the cassette recorder/CD player/video …? Can I play/rewind/ … the tape? Can I operate the video recorder?	**Lerngeräte**	Kann ich den OHP fertig machen? Kann ich den Recorder/…/ holen? Kann ich das Band/…/ abspielen/zurückspulen …? Kann ich den Videorecorder bedienen?
I'm not feeling well. I've got a headache. Can I go to the toilet, please?	**Mir geht's nicht gut**	Ich fühle mich nicht gut. Ich habe Kopfschmerzen. Kann ich mal zur Toilette gehen?
Could you repeat that, please? I'm sorry, I don't understand this! Pardon! Could you explain that again?	**Nicht verstanden**	Könntest du/Könnten Sie das wiederholen, bitte? Tut mir leid. Ich hab's nicht verstanden. Wie bitte? Könntest du/Könnten Sie das noch einmal erklären?
Correct! That's right. You're right.	**Richtig**	Korrekt. Das ist richtig. Du hast recht.
Quiet, please. Silence, please. Be quiet.	**Ruhe**	Ruhig, bitte! Ruhe, bitte! Sei(d) ruhig!
Where's my … I can't find my … Has anyone seen/taken my …? I must look for my …	**Suchen**	Wo ist mein(e) …? Ich kann mein(e) … nicht finden. Hat jemand mein(e) … gesehen/genommen? Ich muss mein(e) … suchen.
I'm not sure. Is that right?	**Unsicher**	Ich bin mir nicht sicher. Ist das richtig?
Bye. Goodbye. See you.	**Verabschieden**	Tschüs. Wiedersehen. Bis bald.
Sorry, I've forgotten it. I'm afraid I've forgotten my … Sorry I can't/don't remember …	**Vergessen**	Tut mir leid. Ich hab's vergessen. Ich fürchte, ich hab mein(e) … vergessen. Tut mir leid. Es fällt mir nicht ein.
Sorry, I don't know. Sorry, no idea.	**Weiß nicht**	Das weiß ich leider nicht. Tut mir leid. Keine Ahnung.
I think he's/she's/you're right. I agree. I thinks so, too.	**Zustimmung**	Ich glaube er/sie hat/ihr habt/Sie haben recht! Ich stimme zu. Das glaube ich auch!

Bildquellen

S. 10: Liverpool City Council (o.li., o.re., u.re.), Topham Picturepoint, Edenbridge (u.re.); S. 12: *I hate school* Cartoon from The Crazy World of School © Bill Stott 1991. Reprinted with permission of Exley Publications; S. 25: The World of Robin Hood, Retford, Notts (re.o.); S. 31: Melanie Smith, Peabody's Communication Group, Nottingham (li.o.); Topham Picturepoint, Edenbridge (li.mi.); Geophotos/Tony Waltham, Nottingham (re.u.); S. 35: *Somewhere with no irregular verbs,* Punch; S. 47: J. Allan Cash Ltd., London (re.mi., li.u.); Jörn Sackermann/Das Fotoarchiv, Essen (li.mi.); Melania Smith, Peabody's Communication Group: (li.o., re.o.); S. 62: Greenhill, London (li.o.); Topham Picturepoint, Edenbridge (re.o., li.u.); Rudi Meisel/Visum, Hamburg (re.u.); S. 77: Melanie Smith, Peabody's Communications Group, Nottingham (mi.re.); J. Allan Cash Ltd, London (u.); S. 90 *Have you eaten?* © Oxford University Press. Reprinted by permission of Oxford University Press; S. 95: J. Allan Cash Ltd, London (re.o.); Topham Picturepoint, Edenbridge (li.o., li.u., re.u.); S. 106: J. Allan Cash Ltd, London (re.o., re.u.); Harding, London: (li.o., li.u.); S. 109 Bildagentur Mauritius, Mittenwald: (u.li.); S. 111: Topham Picturepoint, Edenbridge (re.o.); S. 113: J. Allan Cash Ltd, London (re.o.); S. 117: J. Allan Cash Ltd, London; S. 123 *First tooth* © Oxford University Press. Reprinted by permission of Oxford University Press; S. 130: J. Allan Cash Ltd, London (re.o.); Harding, London (li.u.); S. 139 *Car wash* Drawing by W. Miller; © 1979 The New Yorker Magazine, Inc.; S. 143: Greenhill, London (li.o.); Topham Picturepoint, Edenbridge (re.o.) Nottingham Evening Post, Nottingham (mi); Adam Butler/dpa/PA, Frankfurt (re.u.); S. 152: *Even boys who don't like school* Cartoon from The Fanatic's Guide to Dads © Roland Fiddy 1990. Reprinted with permission of Exley Publications; S. 156: 3. Ullstein Bilderdienst, Berlin; 4. Thelen, dpa, Frankfurt; S. 157: 2. Hanns Hubmann, Bildarchiv Preußischer Kulturbesitz, Berlin; 3. Gerd Schütz, Archiv für Kunst und Geschichte, Berlin; 4. Archiv für Kunst und Geschichte, Berlin; 6. dpa, Frankfurt

Textquellen

S. 9: *What a wonderful world* Text und Musik Sam Cooke, Herb Alpert, Lou Adler. © by Abkco Music Inc. Für D/A/CH: Abkco Music Publ. GmbH, Hamburg; S. 29 *This old man:* Traditional; S. 35 A sailor went to sea: Public domain; S. 49 *The Hokey Pokey* Text and music: Jimmy Kennedy, © by arrangement with Conelly Musikverlag für D/A Dr. Hans Sikorski KG, Hamburg; S. 63: *500 miles* © von Hedy West, © 1961 by Friendship Music Corp. N.Y. Für S/A/CH Musik Ed. Europaton P. Schaeffers/ Ebony Musikverlag; S. 78: *You'll never get to heaven:* Traditional; S. 78 *The Nothing Doings* © 1984 by Jack Prelutsky; S. 82: *The Return of Heroic Failures* by Stephen Pile, published by Martin Secker & Warburg Ltd; S. 88 *The ice cream rhyme*: Davenport; S. 92 *Humpty Dumpty:* Traditional; S. 94: *There was an old lady who swallowed a fly:* Traditional; S. 101: *Mr Alligator:* Traditional; S. 107 *Row, row, row your boat:* Traditional; S. 131 *One finger, one thumb:* Traditional S. 147 *A rope rhyme:* Public domain; S. 148 *Thirteen* From A cup of giggles compiled by Annette Kosseris, (Macdonald) Futura Publications; S. 158: *Jeans on* Text und Musik David Dundas/Greenway © by Air Music London Ltd. Für D/A/CH/Osteur. Länder. EMI Music Publishing Germany GmbH, Hamburg; S. 160 *Boots* by Tony Bradman © Tony Bradman S. 161 *Skip to my Lou:* Traditional; S. 176-178 *Jesus' Christmas Party* by Nicholas Allan © Nicholas Allan 1991. First published by Hutchinson 1991.